BOOTS ON THE GROUND

STORIES OF AMERICAN SOLDIERS FROM IRAQ AND AFGHANISTAN

BOOTS ON THE GROUND

STORIES OF AMERICAN SOLDIERS FROM IRAQ AND AFGHANISTAN

EDITED BY CLINT WILLIS

Thunder's Mouth Press
New York

BOOTS ON THE GROUND: Stories of American Soldiers from Iraq and Afghanistan

Compilation copyright © 2004 by Clint Willis
Introductions copyright © 2004 by Clint Willis

Published by
Thunder's Mouth Press
An Imprint of Avalon Publishing Group Incorporated
245 West 17th St., 11th floor
New York, NY 10011

Library of Congress Cataloging-in-Publication Data is available.

ISBN 1-56025-587-0

Book design: Sue Canavan

Printed in the United States of America

Distributed by Publishers Group West

For the peacemakers

c o n t e n t s

ix   Introduction

1   *The Marine*
by Mike Sager

25   *The Green Berets Up Close*
by Donatella Lorch

33   *The Legend of Heavy D and the Boys*
by Robert Young Pelton

57   *The U.S. Bomb That Nearly Killed Karzai*
by John Hendren and Maura Reynolds

65   *Fragile Alliances in a Hostile Land*
by John Hendren and Richard T. Cooper

81   *Anaconda*
by John Sack

109   *The Make-Believe War*
by Evan Wright

121   *Not Much War, but Plenty of Hell*
by Evan Wright

139   from *McCoy's Marines: Darkside Toward Baghdad*
by John Koopman

175   *All Kinds of Metal Was Flying Through the Air*
by Phillip Robertson

183   *With the Invaders*
by James Meek

207   *Beyond Baghdad*
by Paul William Roberts

221   *My Two Wars*
       by James Harris

229   *Survivor: Iraq*
       by Lawrence F. Kaplan

235   *Memories Don't Die So Easily*
       by Geoffrey Mohan

241   *Where the Enemy Is Everywhere and Nowhere*
       by Daniel Bergner

255   *Stretched Thin, Lied to & Mistreated*
       by Christian Parenti

265   *Night Raid in Baghdad*
       by Jen Banbury

273   *Making Enemies*
       by Nir Rosen

279   *Dispatch from Iraq*
       by John Hendren

283   *War Wounds*
       by Yaroslav Trofimov

289   *A Soldier's Life*
       by Nancy Gibbs with Mark Thompson

299   Acknowledgments
300   Permissions
303   Bibliography

Introduction

These pages include 22 attempts to describe the experiences of American soldiers in Afghanistan and Iraq during recent years. Those experiences are not easy to uncover, in part because few soldiers are yet in a position to write or to speak openly about their life in these wars. That will come later; it always does. Meanwhile, most of the work at hand is written by journalists and other camp followers.

That said, many of these witnesses share at least some of the risks and indignities these wars inflict upon the soldiers who fight them. Journalists have suffered casualties in Afghanistan and Iraq, and the work featured in these pages suggests that some writers who survive their exposure to these wars are permanently marked by what they have seen.

Some of these writers have taken up the task of trying to understand and describe the experiences of the mostly young Americans who must fight these new wars. That experience is more interesting than the romanticized and sentimental reports that dominate some popular media outlets. Such reporting distorts and exploits the experience of the young soldiers it pretends to honor.

The reports in this book offer a more complex mosaic. The mosaic isn't a pretty one: American soldiers are competent by some standards; they also make terrible mistakes, sometimes killing each other or harmless civilians. Some American soldiers are compassionate and open-minded; others are narrow and cruel. Many American soldiers badly want to believe that they are doing the right thing, and some do believe it; others are angry or skeptical about their mission. Some American soldiers are brave and selfless; others are not. Their sentiments include some that you won't hear on the Fox network: *I'm scared. Get me out of this place. Why are we here?*

Similar sentiments echo down the halls of our recent history, from other American wars. Each war has had its critics—no exceptions—and so do American incursions into Afghanistan and Iraq. Some writers who have contributed work to this collection are strong critics of our recent wars; most keep their distance from such questions. All of these writers offer valuable and often moving glimpses of what life is like for the men and women who must try to implement our country's military policies at the beginning of the 21st century.

Bumper stickers and editorialists urge us to support our troops. We can't begin to do so without trying to understand and acknowledge the complex and grueling nature of their experience.

—*Clint Willis*

The Marine
by Mike Sager

Mike Sager's piece about Lieutenant Colonel Robert Sinclair and his Marines appeared in Esquire *(December 2001).*

D ragon Six is Oscar Mike, on the move to link up with Bandit. Foot mobile along Axis Kim, he is leading a detachment of ten U.S. Marines across a stretch of desert scrub in the notional, oil-rich nation of Blueland. He walks at a steady rate of three klicks per hour, three kilometers, muscle memory after twenty-three years of similar forced humps through the toolies, his small powerful body canted slightly forward, his ankles and knees a little sore, his dusty black Danner combat boots, size 8, crunching over branches and rocks and coarse sand.

His pale-blue eyes are bloodshot from lack of sleep. His face is camouflaged with stripes and splotches of greasepaint—green, brown, and black to match his woodland-style utilities, fifty-six dollars a set, worn in the field without skivvies underneath, a personal wardrobe preference known as going commando. Atop his Kevlar helmet rides a pair of goggles sheathed in an old sock. Around his neck hangs a heavy pair of rubberized binoculars. From his left hip dangles an olive-drab pouch. With every step, the pouch swings and hits his thigh, adding another faint, percussive thunk to the quiet symphony of his gear, the total weight of which is not taught and seldom discussed. Inside the pouch is a gas mask for NBC attacks—nuclear, biological, or chemical weapons. Following an attack, when field gauges show the air to be safe once again for breathing, regulations call for the senior marine to choose one man to remove his mask and hood. After ten minutes, if the man shows no ill effects, the rest of the marines can begin removing theirs.

The temperature is 82 degrees. The air is thick and humid. Sounds of distant fire travel on the wan breeze: the boom and rumble of artillery, the pop and crackle of small arms. He is leading his men in a northwesterly direction, headed for an unimproved road designated Phase Line Rich. There, he will rendezvous with Bravo Company, radio call sign Bandit, one of five companies under his command, nearly nine hundred men, armed with weapons ranging from M16A2 rifles to Humvee-mounted TOW missile launchers. In his gloved right hand he carries a map case fashioned from cardboard and duct tape—the cardboard scavenged from a box of MREs, meals ready-to-eat, high-tech field rations that cook themselves when water is added. Clipped to the map case is a rainbow assortment of felt-tip pens, the colors oddly garish against the setting. His 9mm Beretta side arm is worn just beneath his right chest, high on his abdomen. The holster is secured onto his H harness, a pair of mesh suspenders anchored to the war belt around his waist—which itself holds magazine pouches with spare ammo and twin canteens. Altogether, this load-bearing apparatus is known as deuce gear, as in U.S. Government Form No. 782, the receipt a marine was once required to sign upon issuance. These days, the corps is computerized.

Near his left clavicle, also secured to his H harness—which is worn atop his flak vest—is another small pouch. Inside he keeps his

Leatherman utility tool, his government-issue New Testament, a bag of Skittles left over from an MRE, and a tin of Copenhagen snuff, a medium-sized dip of which is evident at this moment in the bulge of his bottom lip, oddly pink in contrast to his thick camo makeup, and in the bottom lips of most of the men in his detachment, a forward-command element known as the Jump. They march slue-footed in a double-file formation through California sage and coyote bush and fennel, the smell pungent and spicy, like something roasting in a gourmet oven, each man silent and serious, deliberate in movement, eyes tracking left and right, as trained, each man taking a moment now and then, without breaking stride, to purse his lips and spit a stream of brownish liquid onto the ground, the varied styles of their expectorations somehow befitting, a metaphor for each personality, a metaphor, seemingly, for the Marine Corps itself: a tribe of like minds in different bodies, a range of shapes and sizes and colors, all wearing the same haircut and uniform, all hewing to the same standards and customs, yet still a collection of individuals, each with his own particular style of spitting tobacco juice, each with his own particular life to give for his country.

In the center of his flak vest—hot and heavy, designed to stop shrapnel but not bullets or knives—is a metal pin about the size of a dime, his insignia of rank, a silver oak leaf. Ever since he was young, growing up on the outskirts of Seattle, the second of four sons born to a department-store manager and a missionary's daughter, Robert O. Sinclair always wanted to be a marine. Now, at age forty, he has reached the rank of lieutenant colonel. He has what many consider to be the ultimate job for an infantry officer in the corps, the command of his own battalion, in this case BN One-Four—the 1st Battalion, 4th Marine Regiment. A proud unit with a distinguished history, the One-Four saw its first action in 1916, during the Banana Wars in the Dominican Republic. In the late twenties, the 4th Marines became known as the China Regiment when it was sent to Shanghai to protect American interests. During World War II, the One-Four was part of a larger force that surrendered to the Japanese at Corregidor. Its colors were burned; the survivors became POWs, forced to endure the infamous Bataan Death March. Re-formed two years later, the unit avenged itself in the first wave of landings on Guam. It has since fought in Vietnam, Desert Storm, and Somalia.

Come January, Sinclair and the One-Four—expanded to include tanks, artillery, amphibious and light armored vehicles, engineers, and 350 additional troops—will ship out on three Navy amphibious assault vessels as the 13th MEU (SOC), Marine Expeditionary Unit (Special Operations Capable), bound for the western Pacific and the Persian Gulf, ready for immediate action, fully equipped to wage combat for fifteen days without resupply or reinforcement, a unit precisely suited to a war against terrorism. "We specialize in conducting raids," says Sinclair. "We're tailor-made for special ops. We're trained to get in, hit a target, kill the enemy, and friggin' pull back to our ships again. We can go by helo. We can infiltrate by land. We can go ashore conventionally. We can put together anything. We're ready to do whatever it takes."

At the moment, in marine lingo, it is twenty-four sixteen thirty uniform May zero one, 4:30 in the afternoon on May 24, 2001, well before the prospect of going to war suddenly became real and imminent this fall. It is the fourth day of something called the Battalion FEX—a field exercise, on-the-job training for Sinclair and his marines. Truth be told, this is the first chance Sinclair has ever had to take his entire battalion out for a spin. Eight months ago, he had a lower rank and a different job in another unit somewhere else. Eight months ago, 90 percent of the men in his battalion were somewhere else; a good percentage of them had only recently graduated from high school.

All told, between the time he took the flag of the One-Four—a dragon wrapped around a dagger on a blue diamond; the motto: Whatever It Takes—and the day this January or sooner when he and his men and all their equipment steam out of San Diego Harbor— wives and families and a brass band left behind on the dock—Sinclair will have had only eighteen months to build from scratch a crack fighting force, trained for every contingency from humanitarian aid to police action to strategic guerrilla raids to full-scale invasion. He has seven more months to get the bugs out. There is much to be done.

And so it is that Bob Sinclair is Oscar Mike across a stretch of desert scrub in the notional country of Blueland, which is actually in the state of California at Camp Pendleton, the largest amphibious training base in the world, spread across 125,000 rugged and breathtaking acres along the Pacific coastline. In ten mikes or so, ten minutes, over the next rise, Sinclair will link up with Bandit, the main effort in this five-phase operation. From there, Sinclair will lead his marines into the mountains, toward a BP, a battle position, high atop a steep, no-name hill. At zero four hundred hours, with the pop and arc of a white double-star-burst flare, the battle will commence: a non-supported, nonilluminated night attack against the invading enemy forces of Orangeland, dug in at a critical crossroads, eyes on the Jesara oil fields.

Or that is the plan, anyway. Like the bubbas say: A plan is only good until the first shot is fired. Sometimes not even until then.

At Phase Line Rich, Sinclair and his men take cover in a stand of high weeds. The four young grunts who form his security element—a corporal and three privates, pimples showing through camo paint—employ along a tight circular perimeter. They assume prone positions on the deck, in the rocky sand, cheeks resting against the stocks of their weapons, three M16A2 rifles and an M249 SAW, Squad Automatic Weapon, a 5.56mm light machine gun with a removable bipod.

The ground is riddled with gopher mounds, busy with ants, bugs, and small lizards. Three types of rattlesnakes inhabit the area, along with scorpions, coyotes, roadrunners, and mountain lions. Overhead, against a backdrop of rugged mountains and gray sky, a red-tailed hawk backpedals its wings, suspended in flight, talons flexed, fixing a target far below.

Sinclair sits with his legs crossed Indian-style. A fly buzzes around his head; bees alight upon the intricate yellow flowers of the black mustard weeds. Filled to capacity, his assault pack and his ass pack form a backrest, a comfortable pillow on which to lounge. Inside the packs, among other items, he keeps a roll of toilet paper; extra socks; reserve tins of Copenhagen; map templates; his NVGs, night-vision goggles; his CamelBak, a one-gallon water reservoir with a long drinking tube attached; and his MOPP suit and booties, Mission Oriented Protective Posture, marine lingo for the overclothes worn with the gas mask in case of NBC attack.

Five feet six inches tall, Sinclair has a quick, high-pitched giggle and bulging biceps, a Marine Corps tattoo on each shoulder. He is, in the words of one of his officers, "a good human being who's able to be a taskmaster." He has a pretty wife, his second, and a baby son and partial custody of his eleven-year-old stepson. They live among civilians on a cul-de-sac in a cookie-cutter subdivision about thirty minutes from the base, a black Isuzu Trooper and a black Volvo station wagon parked side by side in the driveway. He loves fishing, prays before eating his MREs in the field.

Though Sinclair was once lampooned in a skit as the Angry Little Man, he is known to his marines as a teacher and a father figure. Above all, he is known as a bubba, a fellow grunt. Unlike most marine officers, Sinclair joined the corps right out of high school. He spent the summer in boot camp in San Diego, then went off to Western Washington University. Following graduation (he majored in political science), upon completion of his basic officers' training, Sinclair was asked to list three career choices. He wrote infantry three times. He was chewed out by his CO for disobeying orders—if the Marine Corps says three choices, it damn well means three—but it was worth it to him to make the point.

At twenty-two, as a lieutenant, Sinclair became a rifle platoon commander. At twenty-nine, as a captain, he was a company commander in an infantry battalion similar to the One-Four and saw action in Somalia and Rwanda. In his early thirties, as a major, he served time as both a key member of a general's staff and as the director of the Infantry Officer Course in Quantico, Virginia. Today, as CO of the One-Four, he is known for his attention to detail, his almost wonkish expertise in battlefield tactics and techniques. Important also is his reputation for pushing down power to the NCOs, for delegating authority to the noncommissioned officers, the sergeants and the corporals, an essential managerial concept in this bottom-heavy organization. The smallest of all the services—about 170,000 compared with the Army's 480,000 (800,000 including reserves)—the Marines also have the lowest officer-to-enlisted ratio, one-to-nine, compared with the Army's one-to-five. More than half of the corps is composed of the three lowest pay grades—lance corporals, Pfc.'s, and privates. Every year, more than 30 percent of the enlisted ranks muster out and return to civilian life. Discounting career officers and NCOs, that means a complete recycling of bodies about every three years.

Now, as Sinclair sits in the weeds near Phase Line Rich, dark clouds gather ominously over the mountains. "Guess we're in for a nice little hike," he says, flashing his trademark smile, toothy and overlarge.

"Yes, sir!" sings out Sergeant Major, sitting to his right. John Hamby, forty, is the ranking noncommissioned officer in the One-Four, the most senior of all the enlisted, though still junior to the greenest second lieutenant. A good ol' boy from Georgia with a booming gravel voice, he is always at Sinclair's side, offering advice and support, implementing orders, watchdogging the interests of his men. Asked about his favorite marine memories, he thinks a moment, names three: the day, at age twenty-nine, that he received his high school diploma, the 4.0 valedictorian of his class; the day his father pinned his sergeant major chevrons to his collar; the day, when he was stationed in Vienna as an embassy guard, that his son was born by emergency C-section.

"Those peaks behind Basilone Road are gonna be a ball buster," Sinclair says. "Holy Moses!"

"Been there many times," Sergeant Major says. He spits a stream of brownish liquid into the weeds. "Character builder, sir."

"It won't be as steep as yesterday, but it's a lot friggin' higher," Sinclair says, his flat northwestern accent flavored with a bit of southern drawl, affected to a greater or lesser extent by most marine officers, no matter what their regional origins—homage, perhaps, to the antebellum notion of the southern gentleman, upon whom the patriotic ideal of a young American military leader was modeled. He spits a stream of juice, then kicks some dirt over the wet spot on the ground, covering it up.

"You would think there'd be a limit as to how much character you can build, sir. But I ain't reached it yet."

"Oo-rah, Sergeant Major."

"Ain't that right, Colon?" Sergeant Major cuffs the shoulder of the nervous young radio operator sitting behind Sinclair, nearly knocking him over. Pfc. Mike Colon is twenty years old, a slight youth just this side of pretty: five feet four with long curly lashes. The twelve-pound radio he's carrying—a one nineteen foxtrot SINCGARS, a single-channel ground-and-airborne radio system—fits with some difficulty into his assault pack. The ten-foot whip-style antenna makes balance difficult. Thirty minutes into the hump, he has already slapped Sinclair on the helmet several times with the thick rod of rubber-coated steel.

Born in Puerto Rico, raised in the ghetto of Holyoke, Massachusetts, Colon speaks English with the singsong rhythms of his home island. Both of his earlobes are pierced, a remnant of his days with the Latin Kings. Six months ago, Colon was breaking rocks with a ten-pound sledge in the CCU, the Correctional Custody Unit at Camp Pendleton, busted down to private for drinking in the barracks. It was his third offense; the Old Man could have run him out of the corps. But Sinclair prides himself on being able to judge his marines, to see into their souls. As he likes to say: "You can't friggin' command from behind a damn desk." In battle, you have to know what to expect from your men. That's the whole reason they practice everything so many times. That's the whole reason he's out here on the Jump rather than back in the rear, commanding from a camp chair in the relative comfort of the COC, the Combat Operations Center, a big black tent with a generator, lights, computers, and a banquet-sized coffee urn.

Sinclair saw something in Colon, and Colon responded: He was down but he never dropped his pack, as the bubbas say. Now he has found himself assigned as the Old Man's radio operator. He darts a look at Sergeant Major. Privilege in the Marine Corps is often a two-edged sword. Had he not been so honored by this assignment, he'd be back at the COC himself, pulling radio watch. He aims a stream of brownish juice toward the ground. A little bit dribbles down his chin, onto his flak vest. "A definite character builder, Sergeant Major."

Sinclair twists around, flashes Colon his smile. "There ya go, stud," he sings encouragingly.

"Here comes Bandit right now," announces the OpsO, the operations officer, indicating the lead element of Bravo Company, coming around a bend double file.

Major Minter Bailey Ralston IV—Uncle Minty to his friends—is Dragon Three to Sinclair's Dragon Six. He plans and coordinates all battalion movements in the field. Thirty-two years old, a strapping six feet two, he's a graduate of the Virginia Military Institute. Since 1856, every Minter Bailey Ralston before him had been a pharmacist. Growing up in the tiny town of Westin, West Virginia, the only boy of four children, he set his sights early on the Marines. "John Wayne and comic books took me to the dark side at a very early age," he says.

Blond and blue-eyed, with circles under his eyes, Ralston was up all last night on the laptop computer in the COC, pecking out Battalion Frag Order zero one tach four, the detailed, six-page battle plan for tonight's movement. Grimacing, he pops two large pills without water. Three weeks ago, he underwent surgery on his right calf muscle. He is not yet cleared for exercise of any kind.

Sitting next to Major Ralston is the FSC, the fire-support coordinator, Major Randy Page. Six feet four with green eyes, thirty-four years old, Page hails from Wagon Wheel, New Mexico, population fifty. His job is coordinating artillery and other weapons fire to support the grunts on the ground. Married with no kids, a foreign-film buff, a self-professed computer geek, Page loves being in the field. His favorite marine moment is a snapshot: "You're in the rain, you're on a knee, and everyone's just miserable. And you just kinda look around and it feels like—you feel like crap because you're cold or hot or wet or whatever—but it just feels good."

Now Page hoists himself off the deck. He scans the horizon, taking a deep draft of the spicy air. "Looks like that fog is comin' in a little early, sir."

"Roger that, Major Page," Sinclair says, grunting a bit as he rises, as men of a certain age begin to do.

"On your feet, marines," growls Sergeant Major. He kicks playfully at the boot of Lance Corporal Joseph Gray, the other radio operator on the Jump. Gray has been dragging lately. He's newly married to a very young Cuban girl. There are troubles at home, a baby on the way. Sergeant Major reaches down and offers Gray a helping hand. "Move it, Devil Dog," he barks.

After a long, steep climb—the last bit a 70-degree slope through sharp thistles—Dragon Jump and Bandit are in place on the summit of No Name Hill, looking down upon Battalion Objectives Four and Five. Huddled together in the pitch-dark, Sinclair and his men are totally assed out. They sit in rocky sand, on a firebreak cut across the topographical crest of the hill. A cloud bank has settled over them. Visibility is nil; their NVGs, which use ambient light, are inoperable. It is cold and wet and quiet, the silence broken only by the beep and crackle of the SINCGARS radios.

The time is zero one thirty hours. According to intelligence, there is a company-minus, about 150 men, of Orangeland forces dug in around the two key crossroads in the valley below, just to the northeast of No Name Hill, fifteen hundred meters away as the crow flies. Scout/sniper reports have the enemy armed with AK-47 rifles, light and medium machine guns, and 82mm mortars. Based upon documents taken from the body of a notionally dead officer (members of the One-Four's H&S company, headquarters and service, are playing the role of the enemy), there is reason to believe that the Orangeland forces, members of the dictator's elite Revolutionary Guard, will attempt to hold their positions at all costs.

Though the original frag order tasked Bravo Company as the main effort of the attack, it has become clear that the plan is no longer viable. Not apparent on the contour map was the fact that the north-east face of No Name Hill is a sheer cliff. There is no way Sinclair is going to order a company of green marines down the side without rap-pelling systems. Likewise, the firebreak is useless as an avenue of approach; cut by giant bulldozers, one hundred feet wide, that piece of terrain is completely exposed—the face sloping down gradually onto the objective like a ski run.

Because they're here to learn how to think on the fly, Sinclair has ordered Ralston to recast the attack, a laborious process that began with Ralston—owing to the blackout conditions in effect—lying for a time beneath his rain poncho, his red-lensed flashlight in one hand, a pen in the other, writing up formal orders for the new attack, composing sentences such as: o/o ATK TO DESTROY EN VIC BN OBJ 4. Once com-pleted, the orders were disseminated via radio down the chain of com-mand. Upon receiving his orders, each marine made a few notes for himself in his olive-drab journal, part of his required gear.

The new play goes like this: Charlie Company, down in the valley, formerly the supporting effort, becomes the main effort in the attack. It will move across the desert floor, around the bottom of No Name Hill, then turn left in a bent-L formation. Upon seeing the signal flare—a green double star burst—it will attack the enemy's flank. Bravo Company will remain on No Name Hill in a support-by-fire position. In addition, Sinclair has called up the CAAT platoon, the Combined Anti-Armor Team, a motorized unit comprising Humvee-mounted .50-caliber machine guns and wire-guided TOW missile launchers.

While Charlie Company moves into its new position—difficult in the dark without NVGs, foot mobile at the excruciatingly slow rate of five hundred meters an hour through the difficult terrain—Sinclair and his men hunker down on the firebreak atop No Name Hill, a dark circle of faceless shadows enveloped in a fine, cold mist.

Lounging against his assault pack, Sinclair's camies beneath his flak vest are sopping with sweat. He's cold and tired, and his knees ache. He's "dawggone friggin' miserable"; he's happy as he can be. This is what he signed up for. He's glad he chose to go out on the Jump tonight, down and dirty with the men, the more miserable the better, commanding with his eyes instead of a radio handset. There's a purity to being in the field. It helps you keep your edge. It helps you keep your sense of perspective. You learn not to take your lifestyle and your freedoms for granted. You learn not to care so much about what year the wine was bottled, what brand of clothing you wear, all that horse-shit that people think is oh-so-civilized. Being out here, you learn to appreciate the simple things, like just how great it is to sit on a toilet to take a dump.

Over the years, Sinclair has endured conditions much worse than these. He's been in the desert in Kuwait, 130 degrees. He's looked into the eyes of starving infants in Somalia. He's rescued civilians from the American embassy in Rwanda. And he's seen men die; he's written impotent letters home to inconsolable mothers after a firefight with Somali thugs in pickup trucks. It's bad out here tonight on No Name Hill, but it's not so bad. In real-world time, he's a thirty-minute drive from home. Come tomorrow evening, he'll be in his living room with Jessie for their fifth wedding anniversary—the first such celebration he's ever been able to attend.

"I read the other day that gas prices have gone up 149 percent in the last year," Sinclair says, trying to pass the time.

"The cost of living here has gotten to be more expensive than Hawaii," says Page, seated to Sinclair's left. His words come out a little slurry. He chides himself for not sleeping last night. He shakes his head, trying to rid the cobwebs.

"Guess there's no chance we're gettin' a raise anytime soon," Ralston says. Though no one can see it, he has his boot off, an instant ice pack on his badly swollen calf. He missed the last big exercise because of his surgery—if you can't do your job, the Marines will replace you. Someday Ralston would like to be in Sinclair's boots; this is too good a billet to let go because of a little pain. Or that's what he thought. Now the calf is throbbing. Could I be happy as a civilian? he asks him-self, only half kidding.

"The president has already submitted his supplemental budget this year, so we're looking at zero three at the earliest for any kind of COLA," Sinclair says, meaning cost-of-living adjustment, his wonkish side still apparent through his own physical exhaustion. Oddly missing from his encyclopedia of knowledge is the exact amount of his salary. For that information, you must see Jessie. He draws $72,000 a year, plus an additional $1,700 a month for food and housing.

"That's just peachy," Sergeant Major says. He pulls down about $45,000 a year, plus $1,500 a month for food and housing. "Maybe I'll trade in my car and get a beat-up old Volkswagen. Put the wife on the street corner."

"We won't quote you on that, Sergeant Major," Sinclair says.

"Definitely not," says Page.

"Even I don't go that far," Sergeant Major says. His voice softens, grows sentimental, like a guy talking to the bartender late at night. "There ain't none like her. She's mine. We have our times, but it wouldn't be no fun if there wasn't a little challenge."

"Damn," says Ralston. "The wind's kickin' up."

"I'm kinda hoping that stink is you and not me," Sergeant Major drawls. "You know it's time to take a shower when you can smell your own ass."

"Jeez-Louise, Sergeant Major!" Sinclair says. "Thanks for sharin'."

At zero three fifty atop No Name Hill, the rain has subsided; the clouds remain.

Sinclair and his men are on their feet now, helmeted shadows milling between two Humvees. Parked on the firebreak, on the crest of the hill, each of the four-wheel-drive vehicles is fitted with a TOW missile launcher and an infrared sight. In a few minutes, when the liquid nitrogen in the mechanism reaches a temperature of −318 degrees, Sinclair will be able to look through a rubber-capped eyepiece and see the heat signatures of his otherwise-invisible foes, tiny red human forms in the valley far below. Mounted to turrets atop the roofs of the vehicles, the TOW sights emit a loudish ticking noise, a strangely familiar sound, like the timer on a heat lamp in a hotel bathroom.

"Spare a dip, Sergeant Major?"

"Sorry, Major Page, I'm plum out."

"What about you, OpsO?"

"I was just gonna ask you."

"Well, isn't this a fine damn thing," Sergeant Major says. He pauses a beat, thinking. A few days ago, back at Camp Horno—the One-Four's compound at Pendleton—Sergeant Major needed a sleeping bag for a reporter to take on the FEX. Informed by supply that the battalion was fresh out of sleeping bags, Sergeant Major ordered the lance corporal on the other end of the line to shit a sleeping bag posthaste. The bag was delivered in ten minutes.

Now, five days into the FEX, twelve hours into this movement, what Sergeant Major needs—what they all need—is a good whack of nicotine. He turns to Sinclair. "What about you, sir?"

Sinclair pulls off his right glove with his teeth, reaches into the pouch secured over the left side of his chest. He takes out his tin of Copenhagen, opens it. "A few dregs," he says, disappointed. Then he brightens. "Criminy! Check my assault pack!"

Sinclair turns his back and Sergeant Major unzips him, rummages carefully through his gear. Though entirely offhand, it is an intimate act. He comes out with a fresh tin. "You ain't been holdin' out on us now, sir, have you?"

"Pass it around, by all means!"

"An officer and a gentleman," Sergeant Major declares.

"Anything for my marines," Sinclair says. He looks around the loose circle of his men, the faceless shadowy figures so distinctly recognizable, even in the murky gloom. In boot camp there are no walls between the shitters in the latrine—that's how close you get to the other guys. And when you have to lead them, when your word is literally their command, well . . . it's hard to find a way to express it. Eight months into his tenure as the CO of the One-Four, Sinclair finds himself stepping back every now and then and thinking, Dawggone, I still can't believe I have this authority! You go through the years, gaining experience, working hard, moving up. And then one day you're the

Old Man. But you still feel like you; you're the same as always—a little bit afraid of fucking up. It makes you want to be careful. Not cautious, just more careful to consider things from every imaginable side. Bottom line is a most awesome fact: He has lives in his hands.

When he looks at one of his marines, Sinclair doesn't care what age or color he is, what MOS or billet he occupies. He doesn't care if he's a wrench turner down in the motor pool or one of his company commanders. If he didn't need that man in the One-Four, the Marine Corps wouldn't have assigned him. Every truck driver hauling water and chow to the grunts in the field; the comm guys running wire and maintaining the nets; the eighteen-year-old rifleman toting a 60mm mortar launcher over his shoulders, sucking on his water tube like a pacifier as he humps up a hill—they're all important to him as a commander. They all need to know that Sinclair's thinking, Hey, stud, I know that job may not seem fun or exciting, but I need your skills to make this whole thing work.

"So what do we do now?" asks Sergeant Major. He takes a pinch and passes it on. He's feeling better already.

"We could fight this little battle," says Ralston.

"I make it zero three fifty-nine," says Page, taking the tin from Ralston.

"I know," Sinclair says. He rubs his hands together greedily. "Who can we meritoriously promote?"

"Excellent idea, sir!" Sergeant Major says.

"How about Rivers?" suggests Page.

"He's ready?" asks Sinclair.

"Definitely, sir."

"What do you think, Colon?"

"Definitely, sir," says the radio operator, taking a dip, passing the tin.

"All right, good to go," Sinclair says, inserting his own pinch of dip between lip and gum. He steps up onto the fat tire of the Humvee, swings himself into the turret. "We'll just take care of business here," he calls down from his perch, "and then—"

Now there comes the distinct explosive pop of a flare, and everyone turns to see. A green double star burst, lovely and bright and sparkling, it floats down toward earth on its invisible parachute, as languid as an autumn leaf falling from a tree, illuminating the target below in surreal shades of magnesium green.

Down in the valley, Charlie Company opens fire. There is the crackle of small arms shooting blank rounds, clusters of bright muzzle flashes against the dark, the loud cacophony of voices that accompanies a firefight—men on both sides shouting orders and epithets as the battle is waged at close quarters.

Atop No Name Hill, fore and aft of the vehicles, platoons from Bravo Company are set along different elevations of the firebreak. As this is only an exercise, the budget for the FEX is limited. The men of Bravo Company have been told not to expend their blank rounds. They have humped ten difficult miles in the last twelve hours to get into position for this attack, through fields of cactus and thistles, up steep slopes and through ravines, weighted with myriad weapon systems and gear. They have shivered in their own sweat in the fine, cold rain, faces in the sand with the insects and the weeds, fighting boredom, dehydration, fatigue. They have done everything the Old Man has asked, and they have done it without question or excuse or complaint. On order, they open fire.

"Bang bang bang bang BANG!" they shout into the darkness, two hundred strong, every shape and color, all wearing the same haircuts and uniforms, their voices echoing across the valley, a shit-storm of simulated plunging fire raining down death upon Orangeland's elite Revolutionary Guard: "Bang bang bang bang BANG!"

By zero seven thirty, the enemy has been vanquished.

Dragon Jump and Bandit have humped down the firebreak, consolidated with Charlie Company. Together, they occupy Battalion Objectives Four and Five.

It is cool and overcast. The two key crossroads are little more than dirt trails etched through the valley. Sinclair and his men mill about. No

Name Hill looms above them, impossibly high from this vantage point, a scrubby, humpbacked ridge stippled with boulders, the firebreak running like a raw scar over the crest. Colon and Gray and the other enlisted are circled up, passing a rumpled menthol cigarette that Colon has found in his pack. Sinclair and Sergeant Major lean against a Humvee, shooting the shit with the battalion XO, the executive officer, Major Rich Weede. Thirty-seven years old, a graduate of VMI, Weede is Dragon Five to Sinclair's Dragon Six, responsible for many of the nuts-and-bolts issues of command. Since 1935, there has continuously been a Weede on active duty in the Marine Corps. His grandfather retired as a lieutenant general. His father retired as a colonel. His brother is a captain.

Sinclair has logged only about six hours of sleep over the last five days. His eyelids are sprung like window shades. His smile seems plastered onto his face. His knees feel disjointed, as if he's walking on eggshells. He feels thready and insubstantial, oddly gelatinous, a little queasy, as if he's treading water in a vitreous sea of adrenaline and dopamine, nicotine, and excess stomach acid. Now the drifting conversation has turned toward a mutual friend of Weede and Sinclair's, a retired officer.

"So he's got a beer distributorship?" Sinclair asks, his voice tight and forced.

"Every day he's gettin' invitations to fuckin' golf tournaments," Weede says, breaking out a couple of cheroot cigars.

"That's like the time I met this guy through my father-in-law," says Sergeant Major, accepting a cheroot, taking a bite. "He flies me down to Texas to play golf at his country club, and we played a round, and then he takes me over to his warehouse. He tells me how he's having problems with his employees, how he can't get them motivated. And then he says, 'Your father-in-law seems to think you're pretty good at that shit. You want a job? I'll make it well worth your while.'"

"I'd a friggin' asked how well," Sinclair says, taking a bite of his cheroot, working it down to his gum.

"That's like Gunner Montoya," Weede says, blowing a smoke ring. "He said he told the guy, 'I'm a marine gunner, I don't know a friggin' thing about this business.' And the guy tells him, 'You're a marine, you can manage this shit, trust me.' "

"The salary kicks up to a hundred grand after a year," Sergeant Major says. "He put in his papers this month."

"I can't even fathom that kinda money," Sinclair says. He looks off toward No Name Hill, shaking his head.

OpsO Ralston limps over, and Weede offers him a cheroot. "Time to head back to the barn, sir," Ralston says to Sinclair. It's a three-hour hump back to Camp Horno.

"We goin' up Sheepshit Hill, sir?" asks Sergeant Major.

"Only the best for my Devil Dogs!" Sinclair sings.

"They'll be back by this afternoon and too tired to bitch," drawls Sergeant Major. "Then they'll get up tomorrow all sore and thinking, Fuuuuuuuck! But come Sunday, their tune'll change. It'll be: That wasn't shit!"

"Twenty-four hours from now they'll be bragging about how tough it was," Sinclair says. He spits a stream, kicks some dirt over the wet spot.

"You know," Sergeant Major says, "I didn't sign up for infantry. I was gonna be a mechanic."

"Well, I did. All I ever wanted to be was a grunt."

"Then I guess all your dreams have come true, sir."

"Oo-rah, Sergeant Major."

On a sunny Sunday afternoon a few weeks later, Sinclair is sitting beneath a striped umbrella on the patio behind his house. He is barefoot, dressed in a tank top and surfer shorts. His face and neck are deeply tanned; his shoulders and legs are milky white. Even on his day off, he sports a fresh shave. In his mind, he's never off duty; he's a marine every hour of every day. He doesn't even go to Home Depot without shaving first. He has his whitewall-style haircut trimmed weekly, seven dollars a pop.

Sinclair was up early today, ripping out the roots of a tree in the front yard that had begun to encroach upon the sidewalk. For a tool he used an old bolo knife he bought in the Philippines when he was a second lieutenant. A short machete made from dense steel, the thing hasn't been sharpened in twenty years and it's still the best dawggone piece of cuttin' gear he's got. Now that the tree roots have been vanquished, Sinclair needs to repipe the irrigation in that area. Not to mention all the other chores. His tidy two-story house, decorated in earth tones, is filled with projects not yet completed: a partially painted wall, a set of dining-room chairs only half reupholstered. An epic list maker, he has yellow Post-its everywhere at home and at work. He's got a lot to do before January.

At home, Jessie is the idea guy; the Old Man is the grunt. When he comes through the front door, he always says, "Just tell me what to do. I don't want to make any decisions." Jessie and Bob met on a blind date eight years ago. He was a captain then, a company commander; her sister was dating his radio operator. They went to a Japanese restaurant. When he returned home that night, Bob looked in the mirror and told himself he had found the woman he was going to marry. Two days after their date, Jessie came down with the flu. Bob drove an hour to bring her some medicine. "I could tell right then he was a keeper," she says.

Jessie sees Bob as being tough in his professional life, yet very tender in his personal life. He is honest and sincere, a mature man with a lot of integrity, very different from other men, a grownup in every way. When she was laid up in the hospital before their son, Seth, was born, he took off work and camped out in the room with her for an entire week. Five years into their marriage, he still refers to her as "my bride."

Soon after they began dating, Bob went off on a six-month deployment. Jessie sent him care packages filled with Gummi Bears and pistachio nuts. They wrote letters every day. She didn't know where he was, exactly. Somewhere out on a ship. Bob is an awesome letter writer. He would write about what he did that day and how he was feeling about stuff. And then there were the romantic parts. Those were her favorite.

One night when he was on the float, Jessie's phone rang. It was Bob. "I just wanted to tell you I love you," he said casually, and Jessie thought, Uh-oh, I don't like the sound of this. Before he hung up, he mentioned that she should watch CNN the next day. Sure enough, there were the Marines, evacuating civilians from the embassy in Rwanda.

Following his deployment, Bob was transferred to Quantico, Virginia, for three years. The couple maintained a long-distance relationship, getting married along the way, holding their reception at the Japanese restaurant where they'd had their first date. Though she doesn't want to say it in so many words, Jessie is not looking forward to this deployment. Bob's been home now for a long stretch. She's used to having him around. He's funny, he's good company, he has sexy arms and a nice smile. He doesn't mind doing the vacuuming. He thinks everything she cooks is delicious. And though he's not much into television—not even sports—he's happy to sit with her and watch her shows: *Friends, Ed, The West Wing, ER, Malcolm in the Middle*. When he goes away, it's always hardest in the beginning. Then she bucks up and gets in the groove; she just kind of goes about her business. In time, she even starts to enjoy being on her own—pretty much, anyway. It's funny, but having Bob gone so much has taught her just how secure a person she really is. In that way, the Marine Corps has been good for her as well.

This time the float will be a little different for the Sinclairs. They'll have e-mail. And because he's the battalion commander and she's the Key Volunteer Adviser—informally in charge of overseeing all the dependents—he'll be calling her by telephone weekly.

The biggest difference, of course, is Seth, eighteen months old, a towhead like his mom. The first time Bob left for two weeks in the field, he came home and Seth wouldn't go to him. You could see it really crushed Bob. And now he'll be gone six months. He's seen kids hide from their dads when they return from a float; he's seen kids cower in fear. And Luke, her son by her first marriage, has grown close to Bob as well. Luke likes to tell the story of how Bob took him fishing for the first time. Luke caught a catfish that was this long. Actually, Bob helped. "But he told everyone I caught it myself," Luke says proudly.

With everyone out of the house for a while, Sinclair is taking some time to reflect, a little reluctantly, on his career. He rocks back and forth gently in his chair. "This is probably going to sound like propaganda," he says, taking the opportunity, in his family's absence, to indulge himself in a dip, "but my primary motivation for being a marine is that I love this country. I feel that being born in this country is a privilege. Right, wrong, or indifferent, this is still the greatest country in the world. All you have to do is travel to figure that one out. I thank the good Lord that we have a lot of great men and women in this country who feel the same way as I feel, who are willing to make that ultimate sacrifice for what they believe in. None of us wants to die. But we know if we have to, it's for the greatest reasons.

"I have to admit that becoming a dad, especially this late in life, has completely changed me. When you're younger, it was like, Okay, if you die, you can leave your parents behind, or your brothers. That would be sad, but you know, you can kind of accept that. Once you get married, you're kinda like, Hmmm. But you can justify that, too. The wife's an adult, she's intelligent, she's beautiful, she can get on with life. But then all of a sudden you've got that child. I never understood it until Seth was born and lying there in the hospital weighing two pounds, not knowing whether he was going to live or die. And I just looked at him and said, 'This is a life that we've created and that I'm responsible for.' His entire hand could grab around the knuckle of my little finger when he squeezed."

He rocks in his chair; he is a man who is seldom at rest, who wakes up at full speed and doesn't stop until he shuts his eyes, whereupon he falls instantly into a deep, untroubled sleep, as he did on the couch after the FEX, on the night of his anniversary. At least he made it through dinner.

Birds sing in the trees. A lawn mower drones, echoing through the cul-de-sac. The grass in his backyard is lush and green; the fence line is planted with riotous bougainvillea, rich shades of red and purple and pink. An old dog naps at his feet. A small fountain gurgles at the back corner of the lot. "I know this float is going to be tough," Sinclair says.

"But it's like anything else. We'll get on that ship, we'll do what we have to do, and then we'll come back, and life will continue to move on. That'll be six months you can never make up, but what we do as marines is that important. Nobody wrenches your arm to sign that contract. These men do this on their own. They all know the risks. That's why leading them is just an honor beyond belief.

"I am loyal to the corps, but my family is more important to me. If you take it in order, I'd say it's God, country, family, and then way down at number four on the list is the Marine Corps. That's not insulting the corps; it's just that the bottom line is that someday the corps is gonna kick every one of us out. Even the commandant of the Marine Corps is gonna retire, and they're gonna say, 'Thank you very much for all your years of service, General, but it's time to move on.' They're gonna do the same to me. They always say we're here to train our own replacements. There will always be plenty of great people to take my place. But my family will always be there for me. I mean, I'll probably be up for colonel soon. But with our family situation—the fact that, you know, Jessie can't leave the state to share custody of Luke . . ." His voice trails off. "I'd hate to leave the corps, but I can't leave my family and become a geographical bachelor again."

He spits a stream of brownish juice onto the lawn. "The bottom line comes down to this: It's hard to put into words. It's more like a feeling. You feel it, and you know it's right. It's like trying to explain morals or religion or love. The Marine Corps exists to fight and win America's battles, to help keep our country free. It sounds corny, I suppose. But like they say, somebody's got to do it. I guess one of those somebodies is me."

September 2001: Sinclair is at his desk at Camp Horno. There is a heightened security aboard the base, but training continues as normal. Sinclair's deuce gear and his flak vest and his helmet lie in a heap in the corner of the small room. His M9 side arm, holstered, is atop his desk.

On September 11, upon waking to the horrific news from the East Coast, Sinclair called his XO, Major Weede, and told him he was going to stay put for a while and watch the events unfold on television. He felt a need to be home with his family. He also knew he didn't have to hurry to the base; it takes a long time to plan military action, Sinclair points out. The Japanese bombed Pearl Harbor on December 7,1941. The first ground offensive by U.S. forces against the Japanese didn't occur until August 7,1942, when the 1st Marine Division—the division that includes Sinclair's One-Four—invaded Guadalcanal.

Come January, however, or whenever Sinclair and his 13th MEU (SOC) steam out into the WestPac, things will probably be much different. The kind of campaign they're talking about is the kind the One-Four has been trained to undertake. With the threat of war, perhaps a sustained one, Bob and Jessie Sinclair must put their worries about career and future and geographical bachelorhood aside. There is no doubt about the order of his priorities at a time like this.

"It's one of those things where you train your whole life for something you hope you never actually have to execute. But I think there's something primal about each one of us marines. If we're at war, you want to be in the operating forces. You don't want to be sitting on the sidelines. This is what we do. This is what we're trained for.

"The initial thing I felt, seeing that plane fly into the tower, seeing the pictures of the Pentagon, was absolute anger. You realize that your country has been attacked. That is a deep, deep wound, a sharp slap to the face. You wanna strike back. But at the same time you have to keep your head. You know that you've got this whole system in place. There are politicians and diplomats. In a way, you're angry deep down inside your gut, but you're also in realization that, okay, there are people who are much smarter than me, and they are in charge, and I completely trust their leadership. As a member of the military, I'm here to support and implement whatever decision they make.

"Like the president said, 'Get ready.' Well, we are ready. This battalion is ready right now. We'll do what needs to be done."

The Green Berets Up Close
by Donatella Lorch

Special Forces played an important role in the early stages of the war in Afghanistan. This report ran in Newsweek *(January 14, 2002).*

They landed in darkness on an early November night, deep in the mountains of northern Afghanistan. For six hours, they'd hunkered down in the freezing hold of the transport helicopter, tossed by heavy winds, before setting down 6,000 feet above sea level. Shouldering 200-pound packs stuffed with weapons, ammunition and communications gear, the U.S. Army's First Battalion, Fifth Special Forces A-team piled out of the chopper and onto the snowy turf. The helicopter retreated, a roar of rotor wash kicking dirt and ice into the men's faces. Then silence. For weeks, the 13-man Green Beret team had trained and studied and obsessed about their mission. They were a tight-knit group, each man trusting the others with his life. Yet it wasn't until the chopper faded from view and the vastness of the landscape came into focus that they realized how far from home they were, and how alone: 90 miles behind enemy lines, in the heart of Taliban territory.

To the men, standing in the blackness that night, the mission ahead seemed almost impossible. The team was to find and win the trust of an elusive Northern Alliance commander they knew virtually nothing about and whose language they didn't speak, supply his ragtag team of fighters and then, with his help, storm a key Taliban stronghold, the northern city of Mazar-e Sharif. After wresting control from the enemy, they were to restore order and help local leaders begin rebuilding the ravaged city. Along the way, they were to sneak up on armed Taliban camps and caves, helping to laser-guide U.S. bombers to the targets.

In the harrowing, heroic days that followed, they did just that. The fall of Mazar-e Sharif turned out to be a critical moment in the Afghan war, setting off a domino effect that quickly led to the fall of the major cities of Kabul and Kandahar, and the collapse of Taliban rule. It also provided a dramatic victory for the elite Special Forces, whose daring missions in the past had sometimes gone disastrously wrong.

Though sustained fighting in much of the country has subsided, at least for now, the U.S. servicemen who remain in Afghanistan are still at risk. Last Friday a Green Beret, Sgt. 1/c Nathan Ross Chapman, was shot and killed when he was ambushed by enemy fighters near the Pakistan border in the east. A CIA agent was also wounded in the attack. U.S. soldiers continue to comb through southern cave complexes looking for Taliban and Qaeda fighters—frustrated that they still have no clue where Mullah Mohammed Omar and Osama bin Laden might be. At the same time, Special Forces teams remain on hair-trigger alert in Mazar-e Sharif, keeping violence at bay.

Secretive and publicity averse, Special Forces units usually shun outsiders, refusing to divulge details of their missions even years after the shooting stops. But over the past week, a *Newsweek* reporter was granted round-the-clock access to the Special Forces soldiers who helped capture Mazar-e Sharif, providing an unprecedented, real-time glimpse at an ongoing Green Beret mission—and a look at how foreign wars will likely be fought in the future. In this exclusive report, the soldiers recount how they fought their way to the city, and detail the difficult second phase of their mission: trying to keep peace in a country that for so long has known nothing but war.

Gathering up their gear that first night, the team spotted a campfire in the distance. It was their guides, a shabby group of Afghan fighters dressed in blankets and plastic shoes, trying to get warm over the low flames. In preparation for the mission, the American soldiers had grown their hair long and sported bushy beards. But one look at their underfed, ragged allies made it clear that no one would ever mistake them for locals.

The Afghans would take them to meet Atta Mohammed, a Northern Alliance commander who was waiting for them in a hamlet miles away. The A-team knew little about him. Preparing for the mission, they'd asked for any information the Army had about Atta Mohammed. They were instead given files on Mohamed Atta, the lead September 11 hijacker.

For the next two days, the men did not sleep as they made their way across the countryside. They were used to working through extreme fatigue and hunger. In training, they routinely performed complex tasks after days or weeks with little food or rest. They followed their guides through the night, down narrow icy trails and across steep drop-offs. Bobby, the team's communications sergeant, looked at the Afghans' skimpy clothing as a way of convincing himself that he wasn't freezing.

At daybreak, they came to the hamlet, a collection of mud huts sheltered by the mountains. Atta, a bearded, 38-year-old former schoolteacher, came out to greet them. One problem quickly became apparent: Atta spoke no English, and none of the A-team members knew Dari, Atta's language. Accomplished linguists, everyone on the team spoke Arabic and at least two other languages. One spoke French, another Chinese. No luck. At last Dean, the team commander, tried Russian, and one of Atta's men answered him. They'd found their translator.

The men had expected to encounter bumps like this, and much

worse, along the way. The A-team had been together for more than two years, training all over the Middle East and Central Asia for just such a mission. Though almost none had seen combat, they had been taught to thrive in the worst of conditions. Unlike infantry soldiers, who rigidly follow the commands of their superiors, the small Special Forces teams are expected to operate as a self-sustained unit, completely on their own, without continual direction from above. If a problem arises, they've got to solve it themselves; if their plan falls apart midmission, they have to come up with a new one; if they don't know the local language, they quickly learn it. More cerebral than their Airborne or Ranger colleagues, Green Berets like to say that their training—physically brutal as it is—favors brains over brawn. Team leader Dean quotes Shakespeare from memory. Mike, the weapons expert, keeps Teddy Roosevelt's passage about men who fight "in the arena" in his diary. The young and the mindlessly gung-ho rarely make the cut. In an Army of fresh-out-of-high-school infantrymen, Special Forces are typically in their mid-30s and have college degrees.

After lengthy Afghan pleasantries, Atta got down to business. He told the Americans that he had 2,000 troops in the Darya Balkh Valley, south of Mazar-e Sharif. On the narrow, winding mountain trails, the trip would take more than a day. The team split in two, one group staying with Atta, the other circling around the mountains. Special Forces A-teams are designed to break in half. Each team of 12 has two experts in each specialty, from weaponry to communications—allowing the team to become a mirror of itself, carrying out its mission from two different locations. (In Afghanistan, the team had a 13th man, an elite Air Force Special Operations airman who helped direct airstrikes from the ground.)

The men slowly made their way down the narrow road, flanked by hidden land mines on both sides. The Afghans provided horses, but saddled them with so much gear that four of the animals collapsed from exhaustion. Two others broke their legs on the badly rutted terrain. The thousands of Northern Alliance soldiers who met the team at the other end were a sorry-looking lot. The Americans got on the radio and called in for an airdrop of uniforms, shoes, blankets, food and ammo.

Clothed and fed, the Afghans quickly warmed to the U.S. soldiers, who began drawing up a list of targets they needed to hit on their way to Mazar-e Sharif. First up: Aq Kopruk, a Taliban town a few miles away. The aim was to catch the enemy utterly by surprise in a massive air-bombing raid that would break the Taliban's hold over the region. Split up on two mountainsides, one part of the team called in the airstrikes while the other "painted" the targets with lasers, guiding the bombs to their marks.

The bloody accuracy of the attacks instantly lifted the spirits of Atta and his troops. During one bombing raid, Stan, the A-team's warrant officer, was showing Atta how the lasers worked. Just as Atta put his eye up to the viewfinder, an American bomb obliterated a distant target. Atta could see the bodies of Taliban soldiers blown into the air. "We wanted to show him we could help him beyond boots and clothes," says Dean. "From that point on, all Atta wanted was more laser." In a matter of days, Aq Kopruk fell.

The A-team won more trust by treating dozens of wounded Northern Alliance soldiers. The team was among the first American soldiers to deal with serious land-mine injuries in the country. On the night before the attacks on Aq Kopruk, as they tried to get a few hours of sleep on the floor of a cramped mud hut, wounded fighters started streaming in. One Afghan soldier had stepped on a land mine, blowing off most of his leg, leaving just a mangled bone protruding beneath his knee. His fellow soldiers had heard there were American doctors nearby, and lugged the man up the hillside for five hours on top of an old door. Jason, one of the team's two medics, had ordered an amputation saw before he left the United States, but it hadn't arrived in time. Improvising, he stretched the man out on a blanket in the mud courtyard and used his Leatherman pocket tool to saw through the bone. All the while Mike, the team's senior weapons man, kept an eye out for a mangy stray dog who tried to jump out and gnaw at the bone.

The team spent just one night in Aq Kopruk. They didn't want to lose the momentum of their first attack, or give the fleeing Taliban forces time to regroup. Stealing two Taliban trucks and one car, they ditched their horses and continued north toward Mazar-e Sharif with Atta and his men. Along the way, they called in more airstrikes. After guiding the bombs to their targets, the men moved through a gorge dotted with caves, the road littered with bodies of Taliban soldiers and the charred carcasses of bombed-out trucks.

Meanwhile another U.S. Special Forces team was also heading to Mazar from a different direction. It accompanied Gen. Abdul Rashid Dostum, a Northern Alliance commander and Atta's rival for control of the city. A third Northern Alliance commander, Mohaqqeq Mohammed, was on the way as well.

On Nov. 9, Atta's men met up with Dostum and his troops, about an hour's drive south of Mazar-e Sharif. As Taliban soldiers, demoralized and outgunned, fled Mazar, Atta pressed on to the city. He arrived in Mazar the next day with the A-team, to cheering crowds. Screaming and crying, men, women and children rushed over to thank the American soldiers, greeting them like a rescuing army. "It was surreal," recalls Mike, the weapons man. "We didn't know what to expect. We were locked and loaded, and didn't know whether there were any more Taliban. I wondered whether it was the same feeling the Allies had when they liberated Paris." The men were astonished to have captured the city so quickly. They had expected to spend a long, miserable winter camped out in the mountains. None thought they would defeat the Taliban until at least the spring.

In the months since the fall of Mazar, something resembling normal life has slowly returned. People watch TV, take photographs and listen to music. Children fly kites, a favorite pastime. Most women still wear burqas, but now with high-heeled sandals and painted toenails. The A-team has shifted its focus from fighting to diplomacy—a key component of Special Forces training. The men cheerfully endure the seemingly endless rounds of greetings and tea drinking that precede any meeting with local leaders. "First it's 15 minutes of I love you and you love me," says one team member. "Then drink tea, then eat fruit, then eat some more nuts and eat candy and talk a bit." By now, the soldiers all have basic Dari down.

Yet the men know better than to let their guard down. Tensions between Atta, Dostum and Mohaqqeq, the three competing Northern Alliance commanders, persist. The interim government named Dostum deputy Defense minister and Atta commander of Northern Forces. Each appointed a mayor to govern Mazar, leaving the city with two competing administrations. Heavily armed fighters loyal to all three commanders patrol the city, keeping an uneasy balance of power. A-team members never move out of their secure compound without their weapons, and keep four-wheel-drive vehicles loaded with ammunition, water, food and fuel. As one team member put it, they don't like it when people on the street come up behind them.

The caution may have saved their lives. Last Friday night, as the A-team drove through the city, they suddenly found themselves confronted by men with guns. Instantly, the diplomats once again became soldiers and drew their automatic rifles. Dean, the team leader, told each of his men which attacker to shoot if necessary. Wisely, the Afghans lowered their weapons and moved on. As it turned out, the men weren't Taliban but Northern Alliance fighters loyal to Dostum, flexing their powers and ready to shoot. For Dean and his men, it was a chilling reminder that in Afghanistan, "peace" may just be another word for war. For now, at least, it is a different kind of war than the one a few brave men helped to turn around.

The Legend of
Heavy D and the Boys

by Robert Young Pelton

Robert Young Pelton went to Afghanistan in November 2001 to report on the U.S. war against the Taliban. This article appeared in National Geographic Adventure *(March 2002).*

The regulators flew in from Uzbekistan at night on a blacked-out Chinook helicopter and landed near a mud-walled compound in a remote valley in northern Afghanistan. As they began unloading their gear, they were met by Afghans in turbans, their faces wrapped. "It was like that scene in *Close Encounters* where the aliens meet humans for the first time," one soldier says later. "Or maybe that scene in *Star Wars*: These sand people started jabbering in a language we had never heard." The Americans shouldered their hundred-pound rucksacks while the Afghans hefted the rest of the equipment. The gear seemed to float from the landing site under a procession of brown blankets and turbans.

The next morning, about 60 Afghan cavalry came thundering into the compound. Ten minutes later, another 40 riders galloped up. General Abdul Rashid Dostum had arrived.

"Our mission was simple," another soldier says. "Support Dostum.

They told us, 'If Dostum wants to go to Kabul, you are going with him. If he wants to take over the whole country, do it. If he goes off the deep end and starts whacking people, advise higher up and maybe pull out.' This was the most incredibly open mission we have ever done."

Before heading in-country, the soldiers had been briefed only vaguely about Dostum. They'd heard rumors that he was 80 years old, that he didn't have use of his right arm. And they'd been told that he was the most powerful anti-Taliban leader in northern Afghanistan. "I thought the guy was this ruthless warlord," one soldier says. "I assumed he was fricking mean, hard. You know: You better not show any weakness. Then he rides up on horseback with one pant leg untucked, looking like Bluto."

Dostum dismounted and shook everyone's hand, then sat on a mound covered with carpets. He talked for half an hour. Dostum's strategy was now their strategy: to ride roughshod over Taliban positions up the Darra-e Suf Valley, roll over the Tingi Pass in the Alborz Range, then sweep north across the plains and liberate Mazar-e Sharif, Afghanistan's second largest city. When the council broke up, Dostum stood and motioned toward the horses. America's finest were about to fight their first war on horseback in more than a hundred years.

The rocket howls over the roof of General Dostum's house in Khoda Barq at about 10 p.m. It's November 26, my second day in Afghanistan, and already I'm in the middle of a hellacious firefight. Although nighttime gunfire is normal in Afghanistan, there is an urgency to the sound of the deep explosions that come from the 19th-century fortress of Qala Jangi, just over a mile east from Khoda Barq, a Soviet-era apartment complex west of Mazar. The heavy shooting, the worried soldiers, the rapid radio chatter—all signal that something ugly is going on over there.

Meanwhile, I'm hunkered down, waiting for Dostum. I've arranged through intermediaries to spend a month with the general, but for the past week, he has been a hundred miles east, trying to subdue Taliban forces that control the city of Kunduz. General Abdul Rashid Dostum is a man who has rarely been interviewed but has often been typecast as a brutal warlord—usually because of his reputation for winning. He is a man who is said by some journalists to define violence and treachery. (In *Taliban*, author Ahmed Rashid reports a tale he heard that Dostum once ordered his men to drag a thief behind a tank until all that was left was a bloody pulp of gore.) Beyond that, all I know is that Dostum, born a poor peasant, grew up to be a brilliant commander, a general, and a warlord—one of the many regional leaders across Afghanistan whose power derives both from ethnic loyalties and from military strength. That he is known to be a deft alliance maker—and breaker. And that he became the first Afghan commander to take over a major city when he entered Mazar-e Sharif on November 10. It's an irresistible story, made all the more so by a convincing rumor I've been hearing since my arrival: that Dostum triumphed with a little help from his friends—specifically, the Green Berets.

As I wait for Dostum to return, though, the constant chatter of machine guns and the *badoom badoom* of cannons from an American gunship bombarding the fort—Dostum's military headquarters—suggest that I might be a bit premature in offering any congratulations on winning the war. I soon learn that yesterday some 400 foreign Taliban prisoners overpowered their guards, broke into arsenals, and took over part of the fortress.

At 3:30 a.m., I go to bed. Three hours later, I am awakened by a massive explosion a few yards from the house—another near miss by a rocket fired from inside the fort. The sound of bombing continues without a break but at a slower pace. Villagers come out in the crisp, golden light of morning, shivering and tired. Some huddle together to watch the gray pillars of smoke from the bombing runs. Others begin the work of the day without even paying attention to the nearby fighting.

In the afternoon, when I visit Qala Jangi, bullets sing over my head. Up on the parapets, Dostum's troops stream toward a gap in the ramparts created yesterday by what I've heard was an errant American bomb. Soldiers run up to the bite in the wall, shoot into the fort, and then scurry back down. I watch a fighter go up to the top, then crumple into a black pile of rags. Astoundingly, after two days of bombardment, the prisoners still control the fort.

Late in the afternoon, a convoy of mud-spattered off-road vehicles pulls up, and a dozen dusty Americans in tan camo climb out. They have Beretta pistols strapped to their thighs like gunslingers and short M-4 rifles slung across their chests. They're polite but wary about having their pictures taken as they set up their night-vision scopes. After a final check of their gear, they head into the fortress. Later, I find out that they've come hoping to retrieve the body of Central Intelligence Agency officer Johnny Micheal Spann, who was killed by Taliban prisoners—the first American combat casualty in Afghanistan.

Dostum arrives that night, ducking to avoid banging his head as he strides through the guest-house door. He takes my hand in a meaty grip and apologizes for being dirty and tired; he has just driven eight hours on a shattered road from Kunduz. He has two weeks of beard, beetling eyebrows, and a graying brush cut. When Dostum frowns, his features gather into a dark, Stalin-like scowl—his usual expression for formal portraits. But when he smiles, he looks like a naughty 12-year-old.

He sits and makes small talk, then excuses himself to take a shower. When he returns, the dark weariness has lifted. Over *chai* (tea), he announces good news. He has ended the bloody battle for Kunduz by negotiating with Mullah Faizal and Mullah Nuri, the two most senior Taliban leaders in the north. It seems that the "brutal warlord" has engineered the biggest peaceful surrender in recent Afghan history— more than 5,000 Afghan Taliban fighters and foreign volunteers laid down their arms. He waves the accomplishment aside with a shy smile even as he promises to introduce me to his new trophies—the mullahs. It turns out they're staying next door, guests in Dostum's house.

Dostum proves to be significantly more expansive in conversation than his scant press clippings would suggest, and he's happy to fill me in on his background. (Over the next few weeks, as these conversations work to humanize the warlord, I privately coin for him a nickname: Heavy D, after the 1980s rapper.) He was born Abdul Rashid in 1954 in the desolate village of Khvajeh Do Kuh, about 90 miles west of Mazar. The most significant tidbit I glean about his childhood is that he was adept at the game of *buzkashi*, in which teams of horsemen attempt to toss the headless carcass of a calf into a circle. Dating at least to the days of Genghis Khan, the violent game is not so much about scoring as it is about using every dirty trick possible—beating, whipping, kicking—to prevent the opposing team from scoring. Buzkashi is the way Afghan boys learn to ride—and it's the way Afghan politics is played: The toughest, meanest, and most brutal player takes the prize.

After the seventh grade, Dostum left school to help his father on the family farm. At 16, he started working as a laborer in the government-owned gas refinery in nearby Sheberghan, where he dabbled in union politics. When a Marxist government came to power in a bloody coup in 1978, the new regime's radical reforms ignited a guerrilla war with the *mujahidin* who based themselves in the country's remote mountain ranges. Dostum enlisted in the Afghan military—one of the few ways for poor men to escape lives of labor and hardship in rural Afghanistan.

The people of Dostum's village were so impressed with his leadership that they recruited 600 men for him to command. It was about this time that Abdul Rashid became "Dostum." In Uzbek, *dost* means "friend"; *dostum* means "my friend." It was a nickname that the young soldier was given for his habitual way of addressing people. When a local singer wrote a song about "Dostum," the name stuck.

In the bewildering matrix of Afghan politics, Dostum has frequently—and nimbly—switched allegiances. In the 1980s, as a young army officer in the Soviet-backed government, he fought against the mujahidin. When the regime fell in 1992, three years after the Soviets departed, Dostum fought alongside the mujahidin and helped the Northern Alliance's legendary Ahmad Shah Massoud battle the fundamentalist Pashtun forces of Gulbuddin Hekmatyar and gain control of the capital. The shelling, raping, pillaging, looting, and house-to-house fighting that then befell Kabul stained the name of every mujahidin commander, including Dostum's, and fueled his reputation for brutality. I show Dostum the chapter in Rashid's book that includes the account of the gruesome execution of the thief. Dostum chuckles and denies the allegation. He freely admits that in two decades of war, abuses have been committed by the troops of every commander. "What else do you expect my enemies to say?" he asks. "That I am kind and gentle? I will let what you see be the truth."

In 1996, when the Taliban rolled into Kabul, Dostum was forced to retreat to his stronghold in Mazar as the mullahs instituted their version of a pure Islamic state. "At first I thought, Why not let them rule?" he says. "Power is not given to anyone forever. If the Taliban can rule successfully, let them." A year later, betrayed by his second in command, who had defected to the Taliban, Dostum fled to Turkey.

Those among Dostum's men who had remained in Afghanistan now became guerrilla fighters, holed up in the mountains, attacking the troops of the latest regime. Dostum's lieutenants would call him in Turkey and tell him how difficult life had become. They had to kill their horses for food. They didn't have enough cloth for shrouds, so they had to bury dead comrades in burqas. "People demanded that I do something," says Dostum. "Commanders, clergymen, women—they would all tell me very bitter stories. I was full of emotions. My friends were struggling against the Taliban, and I was sitting there."

Dostum says that to help him get back into the fray, the former president of Afghanistan, Burhanuddin Rabbani, raised about $40,000. The Turks, long staunch enemies of Islamic extremism, contributed a small sum as well, and, on April 22, 2001, General Dostum and 30 men were ferried into northern Afghanistan on Massoud's aging Soviet helicopters. "That," says Dostum, "was when the war against terror began."

Living in caves and raiding Taliban positions, Dostum's men slowly began to harass the well-entrenched Taliban along the Darra-e Suf. They moved and attacked mostly at night, riding small, wiry Afghan horses that are well suited to steep slopes and long desert walks. "The money was hardly enough for feeding my horses," Dostum says. "They had tanks, air force, and artillery. We fought with nothing but hope."

Then came September 11. Using a United Nations envoy as an intermediary, Dostum suggested that the United States might want to give him some help.

The morning after Heavy D's return from Kundus, he greets me with a deep, booming "Howareyou?" Today, he tells me, he is eager for me to meet his trophy mullahs.

Next door, in Dostum's pink house, Mullah Faizal and Mullah Nuri sit on pillows in a small room. These are two of the Taliban who chased Dostum out of Mazar in May 1997, but still he treats them more like honored guests than prisoners of war. Faizal has his prosthetic leg off. He is a thick man with a pug nose, bad skin, tiny teeth, and a cruel stare. Nuri has the black look of a Pashtun who has endured a lifetime of war. Wrapped in blankets, members of the mullahs' entourage fix me with soulless stares. Nuri is chatty, although he often looks to the silent Faizal before answering my questions. During the Taliban's reign, thousands of Hazara Shias were murdered in northern Afghanistan; the mullahs are unrepentant. "We fought for an idea," says Nuri. "We did all that we could. Now we hope that America will not be cruel to the Afghan people."

That afternoon, Dostum and I set off for the fort, where the uprising has been all but quelled. He brings the mullahs along, to show them the havoc incited by their foreign volunteers. Perhaps they'll convince any surviving prisoners to surrender.

After four days of bombardment, the interior of the fort is a scene of utter devastation. Blackened, twisted vehicles are perforated with thousands of jagged holes. The crumpled bodies of prisoners, frozen in agony, are scattered everywhere. Most of the fallen look as if they were killed instantly. Some are in pieces; others have been flattened by tank treads. More than 400 prisoners are said to have died; I count only about 50 bodies in the courtyard. The estimated 30 Alliance soldiers who died have already been taken away by their friends. When an American team finally recovered Spann's body, they discovered it had been booby-trapped with a live grenade (which they removed without incident).

It is also rumored that there are many dead and at least two live prisoners holed up in the subterranean bomb shelter. The entrance to the bunker was pierced by cannon shots and is blackened from explosions. Dostum's men have been throwing down grenades and pouring in gasoline and lighting it, but the foreign Taliban refuse to come up. Dostum implores the mullahs to call down to the bunker and tell the remaining men to surrender. Mullah Faizal and Mullah Nuri refuse: They claim they don't know these people.

The trapped Taliban volunteers, it seems, remain hungry for martyrdom. A day later—Thursday, five days since the uprising broke out—they are still firing sporadically at soldiers removing bodies from the courtyard of the fortress. At least two Red Cross workers who descend into the bunker are shot and wounded.

Later that week, Dostum casually mentions that 3,000 other foreign fighters from the surrender at Kunduz are in a Soviet-era prison in the city of Sheberghan, 80 miles west. Anticipating more fireworks, I head there with him and move into another of his residences, a huge, high-walled compound that includes a mosque and, improbably, an unfinished health-club complex.

Some American soldiers are billeted upstairs in the guest houses; men in camo pants run up and down the stairs. Their rooms are filled with green Army cots, dirty brown packs, and green flight bags. Rifles, night-vision gear, and boots are strewn everywhere. I head downstairs and discover a group of soldiers bantering cheerfully, mostly in southern accents. They've just finished installing a satellite TV. When the television begins to blare, the men stare at the screen. "We haven't seen a TV or news in two months," one soldier says apologetically. Transfixed, they watch the Christmas tree being lit in Rockefeller Center.

These are the soldiers I saw back at Qala Jangi preparing to go in and retrieve the body of the dead CIA agent, Mike Spann. "Don't I know you?" one of them says. "Aren't you the guy who goes to all those dangerous places?"

It feels more than a bit odd to be recognized for my books and TV show—as someone who specializes in traveling to the world's hot spots—while poking around a war in Afghanistan. It feels even more odd when I discover that these are Green Berets—soldiers who truly specialize in the world's hot spots. But I never travel without a few "Mr. DP" hats, so I dig them out of my bag and pass them around.

Over the ensuing days, I take every opportunity to spend time in these makeshift barracks, particularly once I discover that this is the very unit of Green Berets that I'd been hearing rumors about—this is Dostum's covert support team. At night we sit around talking over stainless steel cups of coffee. Some details of their mission they can't discuss. Some are provided by Dostum and others. But the story gradually emerges.

There are twelve Green Berets here and two Air Force forward air controllers. Green Berets work in secrecy, so only their first names can be used: There's Andy, the slow-talking weapons expert who is never without his grenade launcher; back home, he keeps the guns in his collections loaded "so they are ready when I am." Both he and Paul, a quiet, bespectacled warrant officer, have been in the unit 11 years. Then there's Steve, a well-mannered southern medic; Pete, the burly chaw spitter; Mark, their blond, midwestern captain; and so on. It's like a casting call for *The Dirty Dozen*. Their motto is "To Free the Oppressed"—something they have done so far in this war with no civilian casualties, no blowback, and no regrets.

These soldiers, I soon realize, come from much the same background as Dostum's: sons of miners, farmers, and factory workers; men whose only way out of poverty is the military. They range in age from mid-20s to late 30s. They are men with wives, children, mortgages, bills. Men who are the Army's elite, who are college educated and fluent in several languages, yet who are paid little more than a manager at McDonald's. They spend every day training for war, teaching other armies about war, and waiting for the call to fight in the next war.

They are direct military descendants of the Devil's Brigade, a joint Canadian-American unit that fought in Italy during the Second World

War. That group was disbanded and then re-formed in the early 1950s as Special Forces, which John F. Kennedy later nicknamed the Green Berets. The men I'm staying with have dubbed their unit the Regulators, after the 19th-century cowboys who were hired by cattle barons to guard their herds from rustlers. The Regulators have served in the gulf war, Somalia, Saudi Arabia, the United Arab Emirates, and in other places they can't talk about. Their home base is Fort Campbell, Kentucky, but they spend only a few months of the year there. The rest of the time they travel.

On the morning of September 11, the team was returning to base after an all-night training exercise. "The post was in an uproar," says Paul. No one knew just when or where the team would be sent. They cleaned and stowed their gear and awaited the order. And waited. There was talk that the team might be split up—rumors of differences with a commanding officer who didn't appreciate the traditional independence of the Green Berets. But toward the end of September, the word came down: "Pack your shit."

Fifteen days later, the team boarded a C-5 Galaxy with a secret flight plan. The Regulators' final destination turned out to be Uzbekistan, where they spent a week building a tent city and waiting for a mission. "We were at the right place at the right time," says Steve. "Fifty tents later, they told us to pack our shit again."

"We had two days to plan," another Regulator says. "The CIA gave us a briefing." Although the Regulators were among the first, other small teams of U.S. forces would soon be airlifted in for similar missions, a response to Dostum's request for American assistance to be sent to other Northern Alliance commanders. Atta Mohammed, for example, would get his own Green Beret escort several weeks later as he raced Dostum to claim Mazar. Once they hit the ground, the Regulators would be writing their own game plan. "Our commanders said they didn't know what to expect, but at least they were honest enough to admit it," the Green Beret continues. "They said, 'You guys will be on the ground; you figure it out.' "

• • •

Within half an hour of meeting Dostum at the mud-walled compound in the Darra-e Suf, the Regulators swung into action. Some stayed behind to handle logistics and supplies. The rest mounted up and rode north. "It was pretty painful," Paul says. "They use simple wooden saddles covered with a piece of carpet, and short stirrups that put our knees up by our heads. The first words I wanted to learn in Dari were, 'How do you make him stop?' "

Their most important immediate order of business was to establish themselves in Dostum's eyes. "The first thing we wanted to do was to say to Dostum, 'The Americans are here,' " Paul explains, "and to make it a fearsome prospect to mess with us." The Americans set up their gear at Dostum's command post—which overlooked Taliban positions about six miles away—and immediately began the process of calling in close air support, or CAS. "You see the village; you see the bunkers," says a second Steve, one of the two Air Force men attached to the team to help coordinate air strikes. "You call in an airplane; you say, 'Can you see that place? There are tanks. You see this grid? Drop a bomb on that grid.' Pretty straightforward stuff."

It took a few hours for bombers to arrive from their carriers. At first, the planes wouldn't fly below 15,000 feet—the brass was worried about surface-to-air missiles—so targeting was sketchy. But coordination soon improved, and the improbable allies fell into a rhythm: The Americans would bomb; Dostum's men would attack.

A crude videotape made by one of Dostum's men shows a battle in the rolling hills of the Darra-e Suf, where the yellow grass contrasts with the deep blue sky. The Americans, up on the ridge, are using GPS units to finalize coordinates. Down below, small Afghan horses are nipping the dry grass on the safe side of the hill, their riders chatting while awaiting the order to charge. The horses cast long shadows in the late afternoon. The only sign that something is about to happen is a white contrail high in the sky. The radio crackles with call signs and traffic broadcast between bombardiers and the American soldiers. First, a soft gray cloud of smoke rises in a lazy ring. Then the concussion: *ka-RUMPH!*

The tape now shows Dostum, leaning against a mud wall, watching through large binoculars. The dirty gray mushroom cloud slowly bends in the wind. Dostum stays in contact with the Americans by radio, working to help focus the bombing: a man with a seventh-grade education directing the fire of the world's most powerful military.

Ka-RUMPH! More hits: Tall, fat smoke plumes cast moving shadows on the grass. The riders mount their horses, check their weapons, and begin the one-kilometer sprint to the Taliban front lines. There's the erratic chatter of AK-47s and the deep *dut dut dut dut* of Taliban machine guns. Then the radios are jammed with Dostum's men shouting and celebrating. The Taliban are running.

The videotape cuts to the next morning. Dostum's men are touring the battle scene. The twisted rag doll bodies of dead Taliban fighters lie heads back, fingers clutched, legs sprawled as if they fell running. Dostum's men kick the corpses into the trenches and cover them with the tan dirt, not bothering to count the dead.

The Regulators were joined by at least three CIA officers kitted in full combat gear, including a 32-year-old ex-Marine named Mike Spann. "We were surprised at how good they were," says Captain Mark. "What we are doing now has not occurred since Vietnam. Up until now the CIA has been hog-tied. Now the CIA and spec ops have been let loose."

Each night, Dostum would sit down with the Americans and lay out the battle plan for the next day. "He would say he is going to attack at about 2 p.m.," says Air Force Steve. "So we would put in for priority for the planes." The team's primary weapons were not pistols or rifles; they were the most fearsome tools in the American arsenal: F-18s, F-16s, F-14s, and B-52s. They chose not bullets or grenades but ordnance that ranged from Maverick missiles to laser-guided bombs.

In contrast to the Americans' high-tech warfare, some of Dostum's tactics would have seemed familiar to the British troops who tried and failed to pacify this region in the 19th century. Before the arrival of the Americans, Dostum fought mostly at night. "He couldn't expose his small force to Taliban missile strikes," explains Captain Mark, "so they would hit and retreat. He never sacrificed his men. He would take a village by getting the mounted guys up close. When it looked like they would break the back of the position, he would ride through as fast as he could and keep the Taliban on the run."

With their knowledge of military history, the Regulators appreciated the ironies of this strange war: "The Taliban had gone from the 'muj' style of fighting—in the mountains, on horseback—to working in mechanized columns," says Will, another Green Beret. That heavy reliance on tanks and trucks meant the Taliban wound up fighting a defensive, Russian-style war. "Then, here is Dostum," says Will, "a guy trained in tanks who's using tactics developed in Genghis Khan's time."

The Regulators' job was to invent a new form of warfare: coordinating lightly armed horseback attacks with massive applications of American air power—all without hitting civilians or friendly forces.

"In an air attack," says Air Force Steve, "you do one of two things. You can bomb it until there is no resistance, or you bomb and, as soon as the bomb goes off, you charge. By the time they come up and look, you are on them." The latter approach was well suited to Dostum's style of attack. "A cavalry charge is an amazing thing," Will says. "At a full gallop, it's a smooth ride. The Afghans shoot from horseback, but there is no aiming in this country. It's more like, 'I am coming to get you—whether I hit you is another story.' It's Old World combat at its finest.

"There's one time I'll never forget," he says. "The Taliban had dug-in, trench-line bunkers shooting machine guns, heavy machine guns, and RPGs [rocket-propelled grenades]. We had an entire 250-man cavalry ready to charge." The Regulators wanted Dostum's right-hand man, Commander Lahl Mohammed, to hold off while they got their aircraft in position, but Lahl had already given the order. In seconds, 250 men on horseback were thundering toward the Taliban position a mere 1,500 meters away.

"We only had the time it takes 250 horses to travel 1,500 meters, so I told the pilot to step on it," Will says. "I looked at Lahl and said,

'Bombs away.' We had 30 seconds till impact; meanwhile, the Afghan horde is screaming down this ridgeline. It was right at dark. You could see machine gun fire from both positions. You could see horses falling." An outcrop obscured views of the last 250 meters to the target. The lead horsemen disappeared behind the rocks, and the Regulators all held their breath, praying the bombs would reach the bunkers before the cavalry did. "Three or four bombs hit right in the middle of the enemy position," says Will. "Almost immediately after the bombs exploded, the horses swept across the objective—the enemy was so shell-shocked. I could see the horses blasting out the other side. It was the finest sight I ever saw. The men were thrilled; they were so happy. It wasn't done perfectly, but it will never be forgotten."

Around eight o'clock on Saturday night, while I'm talking with the Green Berets, one of Dostum's men comes into the house and asks us to follow him outside. Beyond the high steel gates is a confusion of trucks, headlights, and guns, and the sound of men moaning in pain. Lined up against a wall is the most pathetic display of humanity I have ever seen: the survivors of the bunker at Qala Jangi fortress. Dostum's men had finally flooded them out by sluicing frigid water into the sub-terranean room. Instead of the expected handful of holdouts, no fewer than 86 foreign Taliban emerged after a week in the agonizing dark and cold—starved, deaf, hypothermic, wounded, and exhausted. Their captors brought them here en route to the Sheberghan prison.

They send off steam in the cold night, their brown skin white with dust. Some hide their faces, others convulse and shiver. I talk to an Iraqi, as well as to Pakistanis and Saudis—all of whom speak English. On another truck are the seriously wounded. Some cry out in pain, some are weeping, and others lie still, their faces frozen in deathly grimaces.

They put the prisoners back on the truck. A few minutes later, one of Dostum's men runs up breathlessly, saying there is an American in the hospital. I grab my cameras and ask Bill, a pensive Green Beret medic, to come with me.

The scene at the hospital is ugly. The warm smell of gangrene and human waste hits me as I open the door to the triage room. Shattered, bearded men lie everywhere on stretchers, covered by thin blue sheets. The doctors huddle around a steel-drum stove, smiling and talking, oblivious to the pain and suffering around them. In the back, a doctor leans over a man with a smoke-blackened face, wild black hair, and an unkempt beard. He lies staring at the ceiling. The doctor yells in halting English, "What your name?" He jabs at the half-conscious man's face. "Open your eyes! What your name? Where you from?" The man finally answers. "John," he says. "Washington, D.C."

The man is terribly thin and severely hypothermic. At first he is hostile, like a kitten baring its claws. He won't tell me who to contact, or provide any information that would get him out of the crudely equipped hospital. I convince the staff to move him to an upstairs bed, where Bill inserts an IV of Hespan into the man's dehydrated body to increase blood circulation. As Bill checks for wounds, he talks to the young man briefly in Arabic. I tell the prisoner where he is and who he's talking to. Bill finds a shrapnel wound in the emaciated man's right upper thigh and wounds from grenade shrapnel in his back; he also finds that part of the second toe on his left foot has been shot away.

As the Hespan drips into his veins, I fire up the video camera, and the man begins to tell his story. His name, he says, is John Walker. He studied Arabic in Yemen and then enrolled in a *madrasah*, or religious school, in northern Pakistan. He says it was an area sympathetic to the Taliban and that his heart went out to them.

Six months ago, he traveled to Kabul with some Pakistanis to join the Taliban. Since he can't speak Urdu, he was assigned to the Arab-speaking branch of Ansar ("the helpers"), a faction that Walker claims is sponsored by Osama bin Laden—whom Walker says he saw many times in the training camps and on the front lines.

He ended up in the Takhar Province, in the northeastern part of the country. Then the war began. After the American bombing campaign decimated their forces, Walker and members of his unit fled on foot nearly a hundred miles west to Kunduz—all for nothing, as it turned out. Mullah Faizal and Mullah Nuri soon surrendered Kunduz to

Dostum, and Walker was imprisoned with the other foreign volunteers in the bunker at Qala Jangi.

When I look at the terrible conditions and the predicament that Walker is in, I have to ask him if this is what he expected.

"Definitely."

Was his goal to become martyred?

"It is the goal of every Muslim."

Then the morphine begins to kick in. I suggest to Bill that we remove Walker from the hospital, where he might be killed by other patients, many of whom were fighting against him at the fortress. We transfer him to Dostum's house, and the next day he's spirited away at the same time that his story is being broadcast around the world.

When the videotape of my interview with Walker hits the airwaves back in the U.S., the country focuses its white-hot anger on him, and some of that anger spills over onto me. In the conservative press I am criticized for being too gentle in my questioning of an obvious traitor, on the left for cold-bloodedly tricking a helpless boy into incriminating himself.

If you drive west from Mazar, past Qala Jangi, past Khoda Barq, past the ancient, crumbling city of Balkh, and head south toward a ridge of snow-dusted mountains called the Alborz Range, you will see a gap— the Tingi Pass. This is where the Taliban made their last stand. The Green Berets call it the Gap of Doom.

Two of the Green Berets I've been chatting with—Andy and Paul, the pair with the longest tenure in the company—have decided that I need to see this place for myself, or maybe simply that they need to go see it again one last time. We jump in an off-road vehicle and set off. Soon we're winding past an ancient brick bridge that crosses a roaring gorge; on the west side are large caves that shepherds have scooped out of the soft rock over the centuries.

As we drive, Paul tells me that, back in the U.S., even the Regulators are subject to a military culture of rules and red tape. Planning a one-day live-ammo training exercise can require six months of paperwork.

"If there is no enemy, then bureaucracy is the enemy," he says. But on the ground in Afghanistan, they're on their own. The greatest restrictions they face have been placed on them by Dostum himself. "Dostum was very concerned about us getting too close to the battlefield," Captain Mark had told me back at the barracks. "In the last two semi-wars we have been in, every time American soldiers get killed we pull out. That is one of the premises Osama bin Laden operates under." Dostum wasn't about to let an American casualty put a premature end to his battle plan.

Their closest call came toward the end of the campaign, before they'd reached the Tingi Pass; I'd gotten an account of it last night from Mike, a big, bearded, soft-spoken soldier. The conflict began with several hundred Taliban troops moving into positions on an adjacent hill. Outmanned, the Green Berets decided to move out on horseback. They had gone only about 600 meters when they started taking fire. "I figured I could whip my horse and run across an open area," Mike said. "I whip my horse, it takes three steps, and stops. The rounds are zinging over my head. Somehow I make it across the open area. I get off the horse and say, 'Screw this; I'm walking.'

"We set up in a bomb crater and used it as our bunker. We were receiving more fire. It was somewhere between harassing and accurate—enough to keep our heads down. We called in a couple of bomb strikes. We could see a bunch of Taliban come out of another bunker complex off to the south and disappear behind a hill. It took about an hour to get the aircraft. All the while, we could see troops moving and disappearing. I'm looking through the optics while rounds are zinging all around us." At this point in the tale, Mike nodded toward Paul, who was sitting next to him on the couch at Dostum's guest house. "Paul here is busy shooting at guys. What we didn't realize was that the Taliban who we saw coming out of the bunker had gone into the low ground and were sprinting up the hills at us in a flanking maneuver.

"Our Afghans are running out of ammo. Their subcommander has told us at least six times over the radio to get out of there. You have to understand: Dostum had told them, 'If an American gets hurt . . . you die.' We were focused on calling in an air strike to take out this truck that had rumbled into view, and now RPG rounds are flying over our heads. We're not about to stand up and watch what's going on. The pilot asked us, 'What's the effect [of the bomb attack on the truck]?' We yell over the radio, 'We don't know! We're not lifting our heads up!'

"When we turn around and notice what's going on, we see our Afghans have split."

The team decided to call in a B-52 strike practically on their own position—a drastic move considering the planes were flying above 15,000 feet. The enemy was 700 meters out and moving quickly. "Matt yelled, 'Duck your head and get down!' And that pilot dropped a shit-load of bombs," Mike said. "You felt the air leave. After the bombs hit, I peeked over the side of the bunker; our horses were gone. We grabbed our stuff and ran."

Paul, Andy, and I drive past villages of round, domed huts, past a checkpoint manned by Dostum's men, and up along the winding road to the Tingi Pass. Three years of drought have broken: A cold rain pours down in gray sheets. We pass the twisted, stripped wrecks of trucks. Afghans in a blue truck are scavenging for parts. The two Green Berets are solemn; they insist on driving through the gap so they can tell their story from the right perspective.

We wind through the tight pass alongside a swollen mountain river, go over the pass, then head a kilometer down the south side of the divide and stop at a freshly mudded house. We get out of the jeep and stand in the rain and slick mud. Paul picks up the story, raindrops dotting his gold-rimmed, government-issue glasses.

"We kept moving north on horseback, but at that point, no one could tell where the front line was anymore. Once we hit Keshendeh-ye Bala, we picked up a road and followed it north in a truck Dostum's men had captured from the Taliban. At eight that night, we pulled into Shulgareh, which is the biggest town in the valley. We were ready to throw down the mattress and settle in for the night when one of the security guards came up with a radio and said that Dostum needed someone to go up to the front to call in aircraft. We jumped in the back of a truck and drove up to Dostum's HQ here in this house."

In the courtyard, a soft-eyed cow tries to eat spilled oats just beyond its reach. A hundred yards away, villagers stand against a long compound. They huddle in brown blankets, trying to avoid the soaking rain. Paul points to a misty, triangular peak that forms one side of the gap. It served as Paul's command post.

"When we climbed up to the top of that hill, we could see the Taliban on the other side, regrouping for the final attempt to stop us. They were setting up fixed positions—bunkers with Y-shaped fighting trenches—on the northern side of the gap. It works against tanks, but it's plain stupid in this terrain. We had unrestricted movement into the gap, which gave us the high ground."

Andy chimes in. "Whoever gets the high ground first wins the wars here." From their perch on the east side of the gorge, the Green Berets could shoot directly into the trenches of the Taliban.

"Once the plane got there, it circled about six times," Paul says. "Every time the plane would circle, the Taliban would run behind their bunker. After four times or so, they didn't get bombed, so they just stayed there. I targeted a spot right next to this guy's head. I was sick of this guy running back and forth getting ammo. Then the bombs are dropped, and I look through the scope and see body parts flying everywhere. We moved our targeting up along the ridgeline to the second bunker. Same thing: We identity it and *boom!* No more Taliban. I target the third bunker. They just can't figure it out. The bomb lands and hits and *bam!* After that hit, all of them took off on foot to Mazar. And that ended the resistance." As the three of us climb back into our vehicle, I glance at the battlefield. All I see is grass growing beside abandoned trenches. Only Paul and Andy are able to appreciate what happened here.

Early in the afternoon on November 10, Dostum reached Mazar. His men rounded up vehicles that the Taliban had left behind, and Heavy D entered the city as a conquering hero, standing through the sunroof of a 4x4. The crowds quickly grew; people threw money in the air for good luck. Dostum's first stop was the blue mosque at the tomb of Hazrat Ali, the revered son-in-law of the Prophet. Men wept as the imam prayed and thanked Dostum for deliverance.

The joy was short-lived. It turned out that 900 Pakistani Taliban had been left behind in a madrasah in the center of a compound about the size of a city block, and they were ready to fight to the death. Dostum and his commanders wanted to negotiate, but the foreign Taliban shot and killed their peace envoys, which left Alliance leaders with little choice. "We had hardened fighters holed up in the middle of an urban area who wanted to die," says Will. "And we were going to oblige them."

The team set up on the roof of a building about 400 meters from the madrasah and called in a strike. When the two aircraft were on location, the Green Berets radioed Alliance commanders to evacuate civilians from the area. The pilots, however, could not lock in on the laser-sighting device that the team was using to identify the target. The madrasah was surrounded for about a mile on each side by identical buildings, which made it difficult for the pilots to pick out the school. "Finally, the pilot says he has the target in sight. I asked him to describe it, just to be sure," says Will. "He described the building we were sitting on to a T." Finally, Air Force Steve guided the pilot to the correct building, and he dropped the ordnance: direct hit.

The team cleared him for immediate re-attack, but the pilot radioed back that he had "hung a bomb"—a bomb had not released. When the pilot radioed that he needed to return to base, the other pilot swung into action. On the next pass, three more bombs went through the hole in the roof made by the first bomb, killing most of the holdouts inside.

Under intense pressure, the Regulators had called in a perfect surgical strike—a bomb drop in a crowded urban area without a single civilian casualty. "This is the first close-air-support strike in years in an urban area," says Air Force Steve. "It was old-fashioned professionalism. The whole team jelled."

• • •

The steel gate to the guest house opens, and Dostum strolls out, hands in pockets, and is ushered into a black sedan with tinted windows. Dozens of dark-eyed men in turbans scramble into battered pickup trucks and assorted four-wheel-drive vehicles. Armored personnel carriers jerk to life in clouds of black diesel exhaust. It's three weeks after the madrasah bombing, and word has come down that 3,000 Taliban are still occupying the city and environs of Balkh, Alexander the Great's old walled capital, a few miles west of Mazar. Dostum has decided to clean up the region's last remaining pocket of Taliban himself.

I ride in the warlord's white communications truck. The Regulators rush to catch up in two mud-covered cars. We roll past weathered villages unchanged in two millennia. Abandoned Soviet-era tanks are scattered about the flat countryside like dinosaur skeletons.

This part of Afghanistan is ancient, arid, windblown—and is the real cradle of its history and wealth. This is where Alexander ruled, where Zoroaster was born, where Buddhists came on pilgrimages, a center of art, poetry, and study where lions were hunted and where Genghis Khan came to conquer. Now, in a scene that has been repeated over and over for the past 2,000 years, a warlord is arriving.

In a village on the outskirts of Balkh, the convoy rumbles to a halt near an ancient castle that is now a rounded mound of tan mud. The truck-mounted ZU antiaircraft guns are cranked down to eye level. Twenty Urgan missiles point toward the village. Dostum's men load RPGs and check their ammo drums. About 200 men have taken up positions around the village, eyeing ragged locals, who stare back from a careful distance. It feels like a scene out of a bad Mexican movie.

After a cinematic pause to allow the implications of his arrival to sink in, Dostum phones the village leadership from the car: Send out your weapons and any fighters or we're going in. The deadline is noon.

The general climbs out of the tiny black car and tucks his hands into his belt. He rolls in a John Wayne walk to Commander Lahl, who's in charge of the standoff. The two Afghan leaders study a map with Captain Mark, just in case air strikes are needed. When noon comes and goes, I expect the order to fire. I am surprised, then, to see Dostum wrap his blue turban around his head and chin and stride into the village . . . to talk.

Ironically, it was this sort of diplomatic triumph—the surrender at Kunduz just before my arrival—and not a battle that gave the Regulators their most bitter experience of the war. "We thought Kunduz was [going to be] a full-scale attack," says Captain Mark. "When we got there, we were sitting on our asses." It was while they watched the drawn-out surrender that Mike Spann was attacked at Qala Jangi and the uprising began. "This was a guy we considered part of our unit," says Mark. "If we had been there, Mike's death would not have happened."

When they got word of the incident, the unit desperately wanted to get back to the prison. "The info I had was that he was MIA," Mark says. "We thought he was wounded. The old creed is that we never leave a guy behind." The Regulators wanted to find the prisoners who had killed Spann and attacked a second CIA man who was questioning the Taliban. "We begged," Mark says, "but we were told to stay away." (In the end, the Regulators wouldn't get clearance to enter Qala Jangi until the uprising was over.)

Commander Abdul Karim Fakir, who was in charge of the fortress while Dostum was in Kunduz, had worked with the Green Berets since they landed in Afghanistan. "I saw this look in Fakir's eyes," says Mark, "like, Why didn't you help?"

Dostum has not been home in five years to the village of Khvajeh Do Kuh. His father is old. Two weeks after Dostum descended on Balkh, things have calmed down, so the warlord climbs into the front passenger seat of a sedan, and we head across a sandstorm-blasted desert. This time there is no convoy; just a son paying his respects to his father. As we drive through a drought-ravaged wasteland, he points out battlefields and the sites of ambushes and skirmishes. Dostum tells me that he has fought on every inch of Afghan soil and can recite the names of his men who have died, describe each battle in detail, and tell you what he has learned from every encounter. He says it sadly.

A few yards before the turnoff to Khvajeh Do Kuh, he gestures to a place where 180 of his men died fighting the Taliban. All I see is brown dirt and men on donkeys leading camels along the road. Nothing of the war, death, exile, and victory that have shaped the man sitting in the front seat. There is an emotional landscape here I cannot see.

As we approach the village, the men and boys are lined up in a perfect row a hundred yards long, waiting to greet Dostum. The general gets out of the car and goes down the line, trying to embrace and talk to each person, but it is getting dark. The crowd of men follows Dostum into his father's compound.

In a tiny, sparse room are his father, Dostum's former teacher, and a village elder. The old men are frail, with deeply lined faces. The teacher giggles, his white beard shaking with joy. Dostum's father talks to his son as though he were a child, telling him that he and the teacher have been praying for his success. They reach out to shake his hand, to embrace him. The men in the room try to act formally, but as Dostum starts to leave, some begin to cry. An old man yells, "God bless you. We are alive thanks to you." As Dostum stands on the porch, looking at the place of his birth, he chokes up.

He takes me to the hilltop above the village. It's a high, lonely place. When war first came to Afghanistan, two decades ago, he built his first stronghold here to guard the village. Dostum points to the fresh dirt of new graves in the cemetery. "The men who first defended this post with me are all dead now. The new graves belong to those who were fighting terrorists." He is silhouetted against the slate-blue sky, the long tails of his silver turban whipping in the wind.

For a brief moment, the general stands triumphant, the conquering hero, the bringer of peace, the warlord who has ended war in the north—and, therefore, perhaps eliminated his own reason for being. As he leans into the Afghan wind, the light falls, and a moment in history fades.

Dostum must now change his focus from fighting to rebuilding his country. (Within a week, he will be named deputy minister of defense for the new interim government of Afghanistan.) Now, on most mornings,

Dostum emerges from his house, squinting into a crowd of turbaned men waiting for an audience. They sit patiently for hours, clutching tiny pieces of paper, seeking his aid. Dostum's meetings do not end until well after midnight.

Not long before I'm to leave, Dostum asks for help with a letter of condolence to the widow of Mike Spann. The task inspires him to try to express his feelings about the past two months. He confesses that he had worried at first how the Americans would handle Afghan warfare: "It was cold; the food was bad. The bread we ate was half-mixed with dirt. I wondered if they could adapt to these circumstances. I have been to America and know the quality of life they enjoy. To my surprise, these men felt at home."

And more than that: The Afghan warlord and his tiny band of American soldiers had clearly formed a bond that only men who have been through combat can understand. "I now have a friend named Mark," Dostum says, referring to the Green Beret captain. "I feel he is my brother. He is so sincere; whenever I see him, I feel joy." He pauses for a moment, lost in reflection. "I asked for a few Americans," he says finally. "They brought with them the courage of a whole army."

Down the road at the Regulators' makeshift barracks, a call comes over the Motorola: "Pack your shit." The men quickly gather their gear, as they have so many times before. Within hours, they are gone.

The U.S. Bomb That Nearly Killed Karzai

by John Hendren and Maura Reynolds

This story appeared in The Los Angeles Times *in March 2002.*

S HOWALI KOWT, AFGHANISTAN—The blast rocked the hilltop, scattering American and Afghan dead and wounded in a morning haze of blood and smoke. Some of the men thought the ground beneath them had been raked by Taliban mortar fire.

Yet only one thing in the Afghanistan war could convulse the earth with such force.

"As I was flying in the air, I knew," Green Beret Capt. Jason Amerine recalled. "We were hit by our own bomb."

One of the most celebrated bombs in the U.S. arsenal, a satellite-guided 2,000-pound explosive, had detonated on a huddle of Green Berets and allied Afghans. The "friendly fire" incident became one of the most publicized in the Afghan war and almost killed the man the Green Berets were assigned to protect: Hamid Karzai, who later that day was named the country's interim prime minister.

Defense Department officials, speaking on condition of anonymity, say that a U.S. target finder on the ground mistakenly gave his own coordinates to a B-52 bomber pilot overhead. The bomb plunged unerringly along its deadly trajectory.

The U.S. military is still studying the Dec. 5 event. But interviews with local Afghan officials and U.S. military sources strongly suggest that the number of casualties was far greater than the Pentagon disclosed at the time. The explosion killed three Green Berets and about 25 of their Afghan allies, four times as many Afghans as initially reported. Local fighters counted nearly 80 casualties. Even today, questions linger about the total number of dead and wounded. Afghan fighters insist that some Americans were unaccounted for the next day and that a CIA agent might have been killed. CIA officials deny the report.

Today, the bomb's crater remains in the dirt and rock, about 6 feet in diameter and 3 feet deep, on the crest of the hill where the Americans and Afghans had been meeting, as the battle waned, to plan their next mission.

"That's the blood of the Americans," Dr. Syed Mir Ahmad Shah, the manager of a nearby clinic, said recently as he climbed the barren hill where the massive bomb struck. He pointed out dark patches among the rocks. "That's another one. That's another one."

Battle at Village Commenced Dec. 3

The battle of Showali Kowt began Dec. 3. The northern two-thirds of the country had already been wrested from Taliban control, and Amerine and the 11 other men in his team were escorting Karzai and his band of fighters southward.

Karzai was eager to take Showali Kowt, 10 miles from the Taliban's final stronghold of Kandahar.

After a series of firefights, the coalition forces seized the village, sending the Taliban fleeing south across a bridge over a small river.

The Taliban retook the village in a raid that night. But the Americans marked the enemy's location with infrared pointers, visible only to an AC-130 gunship pilot in night-vision goggles overhead. The aircraft's 105-millimeter cannons and artillery fire strafed the ground, driving the Taliban back across the bridge.

On Dec. 4, the coalition decided to take the bridge to isolate the enemy. As Amerine moved toward it with about 60 men, a second contingent gave covering fire. A hundred yards short of a hilltop Taliban observation post, Amerine's men took machine gun fire from Taliban troops entrenched in orchards near the riverbank.

"We were pinned down pretty well," Amerine recalled last week in an interview at the 5th Special Forces Group headquarters in Ft. Campbell, Ky. "You poke your head up, get down and dirt would kick up around you."

When fire raked the trench line that protected them, one Green Beret stood and raised a finger in a universal rebuke, drawing laughs from his Afghan allies. Then he declared, "Let's go," and led a charge that captured the observation post.

Some of the Taliban began to retreat in four-wheel-drive trucks. The Americans called in airstrikes that destroyed about 25 vehicles. The coalition forces inflicted dozens of casualties, while taking almost none.

As the fighting waned that night, the atmosphere among the Americans in Showali Kowt grew festive. They had fought for 48 hours with little food and no sleep, but now a second 12-member team of Green Berets had arrived, and a supply drop had brought care packages.

The Americans had made the clinic their headquarters. "It really was kind of like Christmas," Amerine said. "So everybody was reading letters, sharing food with one another. Sharing it with the [Afghans]."

They congratulated Karzai on the advance word that he would be the nation's new interim leader, a decision that would be announced in Germany the next day. Taliban surrender overtures had begun in Kandahar. It meant that Karzai would be headed for Kabul, the Afghan capital, and with the Taliban's demise apparent, the Americans' mission was all but over. They got their first night's sleep in three days.

By morning, the number of Americans at the clinic had reached about 45, recalled Shah, the village doctor. Others say the number was smaller. Local Afghans and U.S. military sources said the American contingent included CIA operatives.

With Taliban still huddled in ridges across the river, a commander in the second team of Green Berets called for airstrikes to wipe out the enemy. One of two Air Force TAC-Ps, tactical air control parties whose training puts them a level below more seasoned combat controllers, calculated the distance to the enemy. He radioed in the coordinates.

Defense officials would later conclude that he relayed the wrong numbers—giving his own position instead of the enemy's. The airman failed to reenter the target's coordinates after changing the batteries on his global positioning system unit. After a battery change, the unit automatically displays its own location.

About 9:30 a.m. came the rumble of a Vietnam-era B-52.

At that moment, a group of soldiers who belonged to Karzai's Pushtun ethnic group were gathered about 100 feet from the clinic. With them was Amerine's No. 2, Master Sgt. Jefferson Donald Davis, 39, an unflappable Tennessean who two weeks earlier had helped snatch four pickups from wary Afghan fighters and headed his men toward a fight with the Taliban, yelling, "Ride 'em like you stole 'em!"

He was joined by Sgt. 1st Class Daniel Henry Petithory, 32, of Massachusetts, whose childhood friends knew him as "Ninja Dan." Standing nearby was Staff Sgt. Brian Cody Prosser, 28, of Frazier Park, Calif.

Amerine sat cross-legged about 50 feet away, talking to a staff officer. Karzai sat next door to the clinic in a four-room schoolhouse, meeting with advisors.

The satellite-guided explosive landed directly at the feet of the Pushtun fighters. Davis and Petithory were killed instantly, along with about 25 Afghans. Prosser died of his wounds later that day.

The explosion knocked Amerine into the air and blew out both his eardrums, and a bolt of shrapnel tore into his leg. Rock and shrapnel shot through the clinic, where a bloodstained doorjamb records the spot where another Green Beret was standing, the doctor said. In the schoolhouse, Karzai was bloodied by flying glass that penetrated his face and head, said the doctor, who bandaged the wounds.

"A bunch of us had to keep everybody calm and say, 'Deal with the casualties. We're not under attack,' " Amerine said.

Anyone who could walk helped the medics tend to the wounded. Open chest wounds had to be packed, limbs amputated, arteries clamped, burns wrapped. One medic rushed from one patient to the next, ignoring a serious wound to his own head. Their work saved the lives of at least five Americans and numerous Afghans, Amerine said.

Recalled Shah, the local doctor: "We collected some body parts, but they could not be identified. Sometimes we could only find a head or a hand."

The Air Force target finder survived. There is no record of him being wounded.

At its base in Pakistan, three hours away by helicopter, a team of Air Force rescue specialists was alerted by urgent radio calls.

Among them was a 32-year-old helicopter captain named Steve who had led the first Air Force choppers to the World Trade Center after the Sept. 11 terrorist attacks. He was thinking of the crumbled buildings as he suited up.

"It was surreal," said Steve, who like other special operations soldiers asked that his last name be withheld. "To have those visions in your mind and then to be part of taking action to help ensure that America is safe from that again really gives you a sense of purpose."

When his crew members asked for a casualty count, the response took them by surprise: "We'll give you as many as you can take."

Two doctors and a crew of Air Force pararescuers, or PJs, climbed into the back of two MH-53 J/M choppers, a long-range aircraft with a history of rescue missions. They left without knowing whether they were headed into a secure area or into Taliban territory.

Navy fighters escorted the choppers as they flew over Afghan airspace. The choppers skimmed the ground at 200 to 300 feet, low enough to make out individual Taliban soldiers on the ground without giving them time to launch their Soviet-era surface-to-air missiles.

The casualty numbers coming in over the radio kept rising. The extra bodies meant extra weight. The copters wouldn't have enough fuel to make it back. Steve's helicopter crew jettisoned equipment to save fuel.

After they descended to Showali Kowt, the PJs were taken aback. Rolling toward them was a convoy of at least half a dozen Toyota pickup trucks riddled with shrapnel, their windows blown out, one with the roof ripped off. Each carried at least two wounded men on litters.

The PJs and survivors piled one slain Green Beret and 31 of the most severely wounded men into Steve's helicopter. Someone had draped an American flag over the Beret.

"That guy must have been carrying that flag around for weeks," said Steve, the pilot.

The second chopper loaded up with injured, and the two aircraft lifted off for Camp Rhino, the U.S. Marine encampment near Kandahar. The PJs and doctors worked on up to three men at a time in the severely crowded aircraft, on a floor wet with the mingled blood of Afghan and American fighters. The engines drowned out the noise of the PJs amputating limbs.

In short order, both helicopters needed fuel. On the outskirts of Taliban-held Kandahar, a KC-130 air-refueling tanker answered their call and joined the formation.

Air Force rules forbid midair refueling for pilots who have been on duty more than 16 hours. Steve was in hour 23. As fuel flowed into the chopper's nosecone, the front rotor blades missed the refueling craft by mere feet.

The helicopters reached Camp Rhino, deep in the war zone, more than an hour later and then delivered the more critically wounded to another hospital that military officials declined to name.

When they reached the hospital, the casualties included the copters themselves. A C-130 cargo plane had been dispatched with a team of mechanics to get the choppers in shape for the flight back to Pakistan.

As the mechanics peered into the back of Steve's chopper, it looked as if someone had spray-painted the cargo space red.

"Everything was covered in blood—the walls, the litters, the cargo straps, all the equipment inside," said Jan, a 38-year-old master sergeant and maintenance supervisor. "It looked like hell in there."

Within three hours, the mechanics repaired the hydraulics and other problems on the aircraft and sent the crews on their way.

"A lot of lives were saved that day," said Jan, now back at his base at Hurlburt Field, Fla. "It makes a lot of lonely times, away from the family and everything, worthwhile."

Locals Insist That Death Toll Was Higher

Hours afterward, Pentagon spokeswoman Victoria Clarke told reporters that the errant bomb killed three U.S. service members and six allied Afghan fighters, wounding an additional 20 Americans and an untold number of Afghans.

But local commanders and villagers, including the doctor who managed the clinic that Americans used as their headquarters, insist that the death toll was much higher.

Ali Mohammed, a 25-year-old Karzai bodyguard who spent a month aboard a U.S. aircraft carrier being treated for wounds from the attack, said he and his comrades believe that the number of anti-Taliban Afghan dead is closer to 25. Precise figures remain elusive because the extent of the wounds obliterated the distinctions of nationality, and, where Afghans are concerned, there is no official tally.

"The Americans and Afghans were mixed up, so we didn't really know who was who," recalled Mohammed, who suffered broken arms and shrapnel wounds to his chest, abdomen and leg. Thirty more wounded Afghans were on the U.S. vessel with him, he said.

His estimate is confirmed by Karzai's brother, Ahmed, who is now on the local governing council in Kandahar. Ahmed Karzai said his brother lost 25 men.

"It was hard to count because there were lots of body parts and they loaded them so fast into the helicopter," Ahmed Karzai said in an interview.

Pentagon officials have declined to comment on the incident, citing

an ongoing investigation. Asked about the account offered by Ahmed
Karzai and Mohammed, Rear Adm. Craig Quigley, chief spokesman for
the U.S. Central Command, which is directing the war, said he had no
reason to challenge it.

"I would simply defer to those Afghans in a position to know,"
Quigley said. "We do not have good numbers."

Afghan fighters and villagers dispute even the official account of
American casualties. Though military casualties would be especially
difficult to hide because officials must notify families, there is another
government employer, the Central Intelligence Agency, that reserves
the right to withhold such information.

By local accounts, there were far more Americans at Showali Kowt
than the Green Berets described by the Pentagon.

Asked about the discrepancy between the Pentagon figures on Americans at the battle and those of witnesses at the scene, one military official said the Pentagon numbers did not account for CIA officers
accompanying Karzai. Pentagon officials simply omit information on
officials from "OGAs"—other government agencies—such as the CIA.

"We have been forthcoming on every American—well, certainly
every [Department of Defense] death in the war," Quigley said. Asked
if that meant the Pentagon would not report the activities of
employees of other agencies, such as the CIA, he said, "That's correct."

A U.S. intelligence official confirmed that CIA officers were in the
area, although not necessarily in the battle. The official said he knew
of no CIA operative injured in the battle.

The CIA official attributed the dispute over the number of dead to
"the fog of war."

Fragile Alliances in a Hostile Land
by John Hendren and
Richard T. Cooper

This report ran in The Los Angeles Times (May 5, 2002).

K ANDAHAR, AFGHANISTAN—Protected by darkness, the 574th Team of the U.S. Army's 5th Special Forces Group had ridden "right into the lion's mouth," landing deep inside Afghanistan's Oruzgan province—the cradle of the Taliban. A rocket-propelled grenade had whizzed past the descending MH-60 helicopters.

As the Green Berets unloaded their gear and the helicopters clattered away, Capt. Jason Amerine heard a cheery voice calling to him through the lingering dust cloud, in an incongruous British accent: "Hello, hello, hello! Welcome."

The Oxbridge–New Delhi accent belonged to Hamid Karzai, the anti-Taliban resistance leader. Karzai was supposed to be raising an army of 200 or more seasoned fighters, a force capable of driving the Taliban out of the all-important southern region of Afghanistan.

Yet barely a dozen ragged Afghans were waiting at the edge of the landing zone, along with a handful of pathetic-looking pack mules. And one of the Afghans, a teenager, confessed it was he who had fired the grenade at the helicopters—in a fit of exuberance.

This did not look like a promising start.

From the earliest days of the Afghan war, small teams like Amerine's—Green Berets and other Special Forces troops—lived and fought alongside anti-Taliban commanders and fighters, playing a unique and largely unseen role: part soldier, part diplomat, part psychologist.

Some GIs were embraced as trusted partners by their warlords. Others were not. Some worked with hundreds or thousands of hardened Afghan fighters; others found only inexperienced sometime-soldiers quick to flee danger.

These intimate, on-the-ground dealings with the Afghans proved vital in directing warplanes to their targets. And not incidentally, they nurtured the rise of Karzai to the post of interim prime minister, where he represents a fragile hope for his country's future. The Green Berets and their fellow Special Forces troops were arguably the decisive single factor in the success of the war.

They ate goat meat. They slept in crude huts. They drank green tea laced with gingery cardamom seeds and swapped family stories with bearded warlords.

Then, when it came time to fight, they "brought the magic"—calling down fire from the sky to destroy Taliban and Al Qaeda forces.

"More laser, more laser!" one Afghan commander cried as he peered through a Special Forces laser sight and watched smart bombs destroy enemy positions.

Some see this teamwork between Special Forces and local fighters, combined with air power and other advanced U.S. technology, as a model for future conflicts, a prescription for confronting adversaries who are beyond the reach of conventional forces.

Others warn that the tactics that succeeded in Afghanistan, where an entrenched opposition stood ready to accept U.S. help, may not work as well in other trouble spots.

In Afghanistan, there were failures, cases where plans went awry or good advice was ignored with painful results—including the death and injury of Americans in a November prison revolt near the northern city of Mazar-i-Sharif.

And there were frequent reminders of how vulnerable the Green Beret teams were, of the thin margin between survival and catastrophe.

When the system worked, the results were spectacular—and were toasted in Afghan style.

A skeptical anti-Taliban leader was gnawing on a huge piece of roast goat as he waited impatiently for a promised airstrike. When it came, with devastating effect, he got so excited he tore off a chunk of meat and stuffed it into the mouth of an astonished Green Beret.

The A-Team arrives with a plan and meets up with a band of ragtag fighters. Almost too quickly, things go their way.

The Karzai–Green Beret contingent began operations in Oruzgan province near midnight on Nov. 14.

Loading the mules, which one American said "looked more like dogs," they set out through the mountains on a narrow trail with a sheer drop of several hundred feet on one side. They tried to move quietly, but the men swore aloud as they twisted their ankles on the rough ground.

Out ahead walked Afghan guides with flashlights. "If the Taliban were planning an ambush," Amerine confessed, "I'd hoped they would first hit my Afghans with the flashlights. Then we could take care of the threat."

Hours later, after climbing down a cliff and crowding into a waiting van and a small truck, they reached a farming community. Its 30 families risked their lives to feed and shelter the exhausted party.

Amerine's unit was the standard Special Forces detachment of a dozen men, counting the captain:

- A team sergeant, the veteran executive officer who served as "team daddy," since the captains who headed the teams rotated through so quickly that some called them "Kelly girls."

• Two weapons sergeants trained to operate and maintain an array of foreign and domestic arms.

• Two engineers who could handle chores ranging from demolishing bridges to fortifying them.

• Two communications experts, the team's lifelines to the outside.

• An intelligence specialist who majored in maps, enemy tactics and local mores.

• Two medics.

Often, as in this case, the A-Team included an Air Force combat air controller who took the lead in arranging for close air support.

Together, they carried a lot of firepower—M-4 assault rifles with especially sophisticated sights; sniper guns; M-203 grenade launchers; the M-249 squad automatic weapon; explosives and more. And they had air support almost constantly on call.

Their mission would reflect what is possible when a Special Forces team establishes an exceptional level of trust with a foreign counterpart who gives it free rein to manage the military side of things.

Unlike most other Afghan leaders, who considered themselves accomplished field marshals, Hamid Karzai left most of the warmaking to his American advisors. War, after all, was their specialty.

"The mission that we in theory are always training for is this very mission," Amerine said. "Infiltrating deep behind enemy lines and linking up with a totally disorganized force that has no logistics capability at all and making things happen."

With Karzai, the Americans had their chance. The man who in a few short weeks would become Afghanistan's interim prime minister had deep family roots in the southern province of Oruzgan. He devoted himself to politics—dickering with village elders, inducing local commanders to switch sides, establishing himself as the go-to man who might pull a divided country together.

Not long before Amerine's A-Team arrived, Karzai had been hunted down and almost killed by the Taliban, as other prominent opposition leaders were. A CIA-Special Forces rescue unit had airlifted him to a temporary haven in Pakistan.

Now he was back, and the Green Berets had a long-range plan for bringing down the Taliban.

One element, Amerine recalled, was "to feed all the impoverished villages in the area ... and in so doing, we would both increase Karzai's credibility and also they'd be saying that they weren't getting anything from the Taliban—only starvation and tyranny."

They had a military strategy as well: to demonstrate American power and deliver weapons and even cash to win over local Afghan leaders whose commitment to the Taliban was pragmatic rather than ideological. Gradually, they would develop a fighting force capable of seizing Oruzgan province and the city of Kandahar, the seat of Taliban power, to the south.

"We expected to be there for six months to a year at least," Amerine said. The Green Berets brought blankets and food for farmers and villagers, as well as weapons and ammunition for local fighters.

That was the plan as Karzai rushed out onto the landing zone. It barely survived the night.

The next day, Nov. 15, as the Green Berets were bringing in more supplies, they learned that the regional capital of Tarin Kowt had revolted. With no Taliban garrison nearby, local leaders achieved the coup with a single act of violence—hanging the Taliban mayor from a lamppost.

Karzai saw an opportunity; the Americans had no choice but to help him seize it.

"Tarin Kowt represents the Taliban's heart," he said. "Crush that heart and we kill the Taliban."

As they prepared to leave the village for Tarin Kowt, word spread that the Americans were handing out weapons and food. Hundreds of potential fighters streamed in. But this apparent windfall of troops quickly vanished.

"We first thought this would be the army, and were kind of happy with the numbers," Amerine recalled. "But once we armed them, they returned to their own villages."

Only 60 ragtag fighters accompanied Karzai and the Americans as they set out.

What they didn't know was that the Taliban was raising an army, one that dwarfed the 574th Special Forces team and Karzai's irregulars. A convoy of about 100 vehicles was moving toward Tarin Kowt, carrying as many as 1,000 men.

With Karzai translating, local fighters explained that the most likely Taliban approach would be along a road that led over the mountains and into the valley where Tarin Kowt sits.

At dawn, the Americans and two dozen local fighters loaded weapons and communications gear into six pickup trucks and drove out to find an observation site with a good view of the road.

They chose a ridgeline that offered a perfect vantage point. Some of the Americans positioned the irregulars. "You're gonna be here. And you're gonna be here," they told the Afghans.

Meanwhile, the communications specialists and the combat controller established contact with F/A-18s and other warplanes overhead. It promised to be a turkey shoot.

As the vanguard of the Taliban convoy came into sight, a half-dozen bombs ripped it up. But the Americans had not reckoned with the impact such a blitz might have on their allies.

Terrified by the thunderous explosions barely a mile away, and by the sight of so many Taliban vehicles still moving toward them, the local fighters jumped into the trucks and bolted for town.

With much of their ammunition and other gear still in those pickups, the Green Berets had no choice but to jump aboard too.

The rush back to Tarin Kowt was like an episode of the Keystone Cops. The Americans in one truck would persuade a driver to stop, only to have panic overtake him at the sight of another local fighter speeding past.

By the time they reached Karzai's headquarters, the Americans were livid. They forced the Afghan drivers out of the vehicles and headed back alone.

Too late. The observation post had been overrun by the Taliban.

The Green Berets, facing an overwhelming enemy, seized the highest ground still available and went to work. By now, the sky was stacked with American aircraft.

"I think the pilots knew how dire a situation it was, because we told them our position. It amounted to 11 guys on a small piece of ground, and here comes this giant convoy," Amerine said. "They'd get on the radio, calling to us, wanting a piece of the action."

As quickly as the A-Team could call in coordinates, the pilots unloaded their bombs, then dropped down through volleys of Taliban rocket-propelled grenades to hose down the convoy with machine-gun fire.

Despite the huge holes torn in their line, the Taliban forces kept coming.

Word of the fighting attracted a mob of now-emboldened towns-people to the Special Forces' position. The Green Berets found themselves surrounded by a milling crowd of children and elderly men. War, Afghan-style.

The Green Berets pleaded with the elders to take the children away as the battle surged back and forth.

A small group of Taliban fighters on foot managed to slip onto the Green Berets' flank. They got within 400 yards of the Americans before they were spotted by a crowd of townsmen, who somehow drove them off.

Gradually, the airstrikes broke the Taliban assault. About half the attacking force was destroyed, radio intercepts indicated. Some Taliban vehicles made it back to Kandahar. Others tried to hide and were ferreted out by American pilots.

By the skin of their teeth, the Special Forces had survived and, with the help of their air power, prevailed.

Word of the victory spread through the region. Almost overnight, the campaign entered a strikingly different but equally important phase for the Special Forces, and for Karzai.

First, a group of religious leaders came to express their thanks for the food and blankets, and for the defense of Tarin Kowt. Without the Green Berets, the leaders of the uprising would have been slaughtered, they said.

Then, it seemed, every leader in the area wanted to talk to Karzai. He sent runners to surrounding areas to invite leaders in, and continually worked his satellite phone.

As the Americans arranged for air drops of more supplies, all but the hard-core Talibs could see the wind was shifting. Through long afternoons and longer nights, large groups would arrive at Karzai's mud-and-brick headquarters in Tarin Kowt to discuss switching sides. Karzai, often with Amerine sitting beside him, would tip the scales with offers of food or cash.

One night, Amerine noticed an unfamiliar Afghan with Karzai. The man was staring at the American and grinning broadly.

"Oh, he's Taliban," Karzai explained. Amerine and the Taliban mullah, who was negotiating his own surrender, locked eyes and burst out laughing.

With his dual status as a native Pushtun, Afghanistan's largest ethnic group, and bringer of American bounty, Karzai also received urgent petitions on more mundane issues, including one from a man who wanted money for a new bull. His old one had died.

"I'd sit down with Karzai at these meetings, and all of these tribal leaders are yelling at each other, and he'd look over in amusement and tell me what they were fighting about. We'd kind of be laughing at some of the silliness that went on," Amerine said.

"He'd let it go and let it go, and then he'd make whatever decision he had to make and everybody would abide by it."

In the meantime, the medics, weapons specialists and other members of the A-Team were doing their part to cement relations with the local tribes. They not only handled battle wounds but also brought in medicine for a common local stomach malady and treated the locals' other minor ailments.

Karzai responded by going out of his way to chat with the soldiers about their wives and girlfriends and their lives back home.

There would be one more battle on the march to Kandahar—at Showali Kowt, 10 miles from the Taliban's last stronghold. Three Green Berets, including two from Amerine's team, died in a "friendly fire" bombing there, and Karzai himself was slightly injured. Kandahar fell two days later, Dec. 7.

But it was the cooperation begun at Tarin Kowt that set the dominoes falling.

If Hamid Karzai was a Special Forces dream, Gen. Mohammed Qassim Fahim was something of a nightmare.

Chief Warrant Officer David Diaz, 39, leader of the 555th Green Berets, had seen a lot in 18 years of soldiering, including Iraq, Somalia and a previous stint in Afghanistan when the U.S.-backed moujahedeen were fighting the Red Army. But he hadn't encountered Fahim.

Just getting to Fahim almost got Diaz killed twice. The first time, navigating on a moonless night with poor maps, the heavily laden U.S. helicopter almost flew into a mountain before turning back. The next time, the crew aborted its mission after a Taliban antiaircraft battery "locked on."

And when they finally made it through, on Oct. 17, the welcome was not especially cordial.

At least there were no mules. Two CIA agents greeted them at the landing site north of Kabul, the Afghan capital. Also on hand were some Northern Alliance soldiers with old Soviet jeeps to haul Diaz's team to Fahim's foothold at Bagram air base, some 40 miles away.

Fahim served up the obligatory huge introductory meal, but he did not hide his anger at the United States for abandoning Afghanistan after Soviet forces ended their 10-year occupation in 1989.

Heavyset, bald and clean-shaven, Fahim had served as intelligence chief and right-hand man for the legendary Ahmed Shah Masoud, who founded the Northern Alliance, fought the Soviets in the 1980s and the Taliban in the 1990s—only to be killed by Al Qaeda suicide bombers just before Sept. 11.

Fahim had received his initial training from the Soviet KGB, before joining the resistance.

Now, at least in American eyes, he was a secretive, ambitious schemer who meant to use— but not serve—the Green Berets.

"I don't trust Americans," Fahim said. "I know why you're here. If it wasn't for Sept. 11, you wouldn't be here."

Diaz, of modest size by Green Beret standards, was dwarfed by the massive Fahim. The American, known as "the chief" and admired by his men for his experience and what they considered an outsize command presence, told the warlord that he had a point but that they could still help each other.

The first task was to capture Bagram, a former Soviet air base with great strategic potential.

The situation at Bagram was a stalemate out of World War I. From trenches, Northern Alliance and Taliban fighters faced one another across a no man's land that sometimes narrowed to 100 yards.

Fahim was irritated that, for several weeks, U.S. agents had promised air support that did not come.

Worse, other anti-Taliban commanders were getting air support. Why were the Americans shunning him?

The day after the strained meeting with Fahim, Diaz and his Air Force controller—wearing Northern Alliance garb, complete with sabers, vests, scarves and caps—surveyed the situation from the airfield's control tower, which stood on ground occupied by Fahim's troops.

From that aerie, targets were etched by sunlight.

"That's 'me' over there," a smiling, potbellied general named Babashan told Diaz, pointing to an enemy hut a mile away that was occupied by his Taliban equivalent. The Taliban commanders' huts could be identified by the large number of radio antennas bristling, porcupine-like, on their roofs.

Diaz nodded to his controller, an Air Force sergeant named Calvin.

Quietly, Calvin radioed a bomber and gave a thumbs-up.

"OK, sir," Diaz told Babashan. "At that target you pointed out, where their general is, in exactly 30 seconds there will be a 2,000-pound bomb on it."

For a moment, Babashan's face was a picture of doubt.

Then, Diaz recalled later, "All of a sudden this thing just disintegrated."

For 24 straight days, Diaz's men and U.S. warplanes laid waste to enemy positions that had stood impregnable for three years.

The carnage was all the greater because it claimed enemy leaders from Kabul who often spent the night in the supposedly secure Bagram bunkers. Accustomed to the Soviets' "dumb" bombs, they assumed U.S. planes could not hit them without risking injury to their own troops nearby.

Sometimes, Northern Alliance soldiers used the radio to trick Taliban commanders into revealing their positions, which the Americans then bombed.

Fahim's manner changed, suggesting the ice had broken. The Afghans began placing their right hands over their hearts to express their gratitude. Some insisted on walking hand in hand with their American counterparts.

To bolster morale among allied soldiers, the Berets would order many times the number of bombs needed to destroy some targets, especially those housing the fearsome "martyr units"—Al Qaeda fighters who painted their faces to look more intimidating and fought with abandon because, it was said, their families expected them to die in battle.

"It was a lot of overkill," Diaz said. "We dropped numerous bombs on a small area just for the psychological effect for our guys. And we did it in daylight instead of at night so they could see it all.

"It was good for the generals to see that they were eliminated. I think sometimes for us too."

The fall of Bagram would open the way to capturing Kabul, and Diaz soon learned just how limited the rapport with Fahim really was.

Never as accessible as Karzai, he became steadily more remote and seemingly paranoid. Meetings with Diaz scheduled for 3 p.m. would be held at 2 a.m.; locations changed without notice.

"I never knew when we were meeting. He would just send a driver for me. When I did meet him, I was frisked," Diaz said.

For a country as ethnically fragmented as Afghanistan, the question of which commander's soldiers entered the capital first was an explosive one. Fahim, as an ethnic Tajik, could inflame ancient tensions and complicate the U.S.-Afghan relationship after the war. The issue was so important that Washington insisted that Fahim sign an agreement with the U.S. commander, Gen. Tommy Franks, pledging not to enter the city.

In a candid moment, however, Fahim warned Diaz what was to come.

"Gen. Fahim had told me once he gave the thumbs-up for the ground offensive, there would be some ground commanders he could control, some he couldn't," Diaz said. It would be essentially a race to Kabul.

"He wanted to be the first in Kabul. He had no intention of stopping."

As the final push got underway, Taliban armor evaporated under assaults by Special Forces and U.S. air power. Wholesale side-switching followed.

"I could literally see them, the same guys that were just shooting at us an hour or so ago, were now on our side," Diaz said. "And they, in turn, would point out who were Al Qaeda, if they didn't in fact kill them themselves."

Fahim split his army—now grown to nearly 8,000 men—as he approached Kabul, and the Berets split too. Diaz decided that if Fahim was going to roll in, they had no choice.

As Fahim led the first convoy into Kabul, surrounded by huge crowds, the Green Berets were screened by the tinted glass of the commanders' vehicles, and by their native garb, long hair and beards.

"So we went into the city," Diaz said. "We came rolling along, and I'm thinking, 'OK, we'll roll in low-key, like we do in Special Forces, kind of melt our way into the city and we'll find a place to hole up.'"

But as Fahim's efforts to establish sole control over Kabul became more aggressive, Diaz separated his troops from him once and for all. Fahim's bid to exclude other factions from Kabul, and thus ensure for himself a place in the post-Taliban government, violated U.S. policy—which the Special Forces were supposed to advance.

Fahim's gambit succeeded: He became defense minister in the interim government.

"We should have stayed together," Diaz said, "but there were things that he was starting to do, attempted to do . . . that we just needed to separate ourselves from. It was a lot of tribal fighting. He was going to do whatever he needed to do to prevent anyone else, any other ethnic Afghan unit or tribe, from getting into Kabul."

Bonds formed over meals and on horseback melt away when the bullets start flying. Ancient honor codes trump reason and caution.

In a land less chaotic than Afghanistan, Americans would have considered a man like Gen. Abdul Rashid Dostum part of the problem, not the solution.

A burly, ethnic Uzbek originally trained by the Soviets, Dostum was a maverick in the Northern Alliance, with a record of human rights abuses and a history of betrayal and side-switching fit for a Mafia don.

But in the earliest days of the Afghan war, U.S. Army and Air Force special operations personnel found themselves on horseback with the fearsome Dostum and his troops for more than a week, on mountain trails that were seldom more than 3 feet wide, along 1,000-foot drops into the valleys below.

It was cold and wet. The undisciplined horses, rebellious over moving single file, looked for opportunities to push past one another.

Under such conditions, a skilled rider would have been tested. Most of the Americans had little experience on horseback. All struggled to stay upright in wooden saddles that inflicted pain with every step.

Out in front like a feudal baron rode Dostum, whose goal—backed by American air support—was to capture Mazar-i-Sharif. A strategic highway junction near the country's northern border, Mazar was considered the necessary first step to toppling the Taliban.

During the first days, things went well.

The trails Dostum and the Green Berets traveled passed above valleys dotted with towns held by the Taliban. From the heights, the Americans would "bring down a rain of bombs," as one combat controller described it later. Then Dostum would order his men, accompanied by Green Berets, to attack the dazed and fleeing enemy.

The Afghans' delight at what air power could do was clear. "I remember one instance, we hit a target directly and the Northern Alliance commander happened to be eating a piece of goat at that time," an air combat controller named Matt recalled. "He ripped off a big chunk of meat and shoved it in a Special Forces guy's mouth because he was so happy."

Between raids, Dostum was on the radio talking to his forces and negotiating with opposition leaders. Air controllers, including a 26-year-old California native with long sideburns named Mike, were coordinating airdrops of food, Gore-Tex gloves and warm jackets.

Drinking water was delivered by young boys riding donkeys and wearing boots with pointy rubber toes that reminded Mike of Aladdin's footwear.

At night, they slept in caves, out of the wind. When the horses moved in the dark, sparks flew as their iron shoes struck the rocks.

One night, bored with American field rations, Mike joined the Afghan soldiers eating a mixture of meat, rice, grapes and carrots called palau. He was sick for three days.

But when Dostum and the Special Forces got into position to assault Mazar-i-Sharif, such personal relationships seemed to melt away.

The Special Forces team and its assigned Afghan fighters established a forward observation post on a hilltop and began calling in airstrikes. But Taliban units spotted the post, and more than three dozen enemy troops armed with machine guns, AK-47s and grenade launchers came at it like angry bees.

The Afghans bolted. Alone with his Special Forces teammates, Matt remembered firing his M-4 with one hand and vectoring in more bombs with the other.

Only after they had escaped to a sheltering ravine did the Americans find Dostum's men, waiting safely out of range.

But Mazár-i-Sharif fell faster than anyone expected, and afterward a nearby fortress became a prison for hundreds of captured enemy fighters. Guns and grenades were clearly visible beneath their clothing, but Northern Alliance fighters brushed aside the Americans' requests that the prisoners be carefully searched.

The prickly alliance between the Americans and Dostum was no match for an Afghan honor code that held that respect for a vanquished foe precluded searching him.

Or for the religious and ethnic politics that led the Afghans to keep some of the most dangerous prisoners out of American hands.

The result was predictable. When the well-armed prisoners revolted, CIA officer Johnny "Mike" Spann became the first U.S. combat casualty of the war.

Anaconda

by John Sack

United States forces attacked Taliban and al-Qaeda forces in the mountains of Eastern Afghanistan in March 2002. The operation led to some of the bloodiest fighting of the war. This account ran in Esquire (August, 2002).

I. Company C (March 2 to March 3)

Imagine this. Imagine you're a country doctor up in the Adirondacks, and your first patient today is your brother. "I have this cough," he reports, and the X ray reveals he has lung cancer, clearly terminal. Bad enough, but your second patient today is your sister, and the Pap smear shows terminal cervical cancer. And knock, knock, knock on your door come your beloved brothers, sisters, close cousins, come all morning, afternoon, evening, come in the throes of some dreadful disease—imagine it, I ask you. Imagination aside, no doctor in the Adirondacks (or anywhere else in America) has had the unbearable heartache such a cortege would occasion, but in the American infantry lots of medics have had it. In combat, when they hear a cry of "Medic!" "Corpsman!" or "Doc!"—a hysterical cry that like "Help!" "Man overboard!" or "Fire!" pounces on everyone's senses like a

Doberman pinscher, generating adrenaline, dilating carotid arteries, pounding on everyone's heart like the kettledrums in *Day of Wrath*, by Berlioz—when they hear a cry of "Medic!" "Corpsman!" or "Doc!" it comes from one of their buddies, someone they've lived with, trained with, partied with, someone they love as they love their blood brothers.

Near the Adirondacks stands the 10th Mountain Division. In one platoon of one company of one battalion of one brigade, the one and only medic is a twenty-one-year-old from Ellenville, New York, near the Catskills: Specialist Eddie Rivera. One day in September, two airplanes hit the World Trade Center, and Rivera watches the TV incredulously, his fingers against his forehead, *my head's still here, my head's still here, no, I'm not dreaming this,* as the two towers collapse, as two towers of ashes supplant them, as ash-plastered people run from the great catastrophe. "An attack on America," the TV announcer calls it, and Rivera at once phones the girl he fell deeply in love with in medic (not medical) school and tells her, "I may have to go somewhere."

Unpromising. That's what Rivera was until three years ago. His parents both Puerto Rican, his skin olive-colored, his hair curly black, his brows black, too, his mustache a thin black streak that at one end broke up into shapeless bristles, he usually was a no-show at Ellenville High. At six every day, his mother went to work making knives, and Rivera (an hour later) called up his friends and said, "I ain' goin' to school today. You shouldn' either, come over here." If the truant officer didn't come too, Rivera and a half dozen friends would party, drink Bacardi, listen to rappers, and on TV play video games as their cheerless peers sat in accounting, studying double entries. The parties sometimes continued past three, past Rivera's mother's return, Rivera's mother saying, *"No tienes tiempo para esto,"* "You don't have time for this!"

But one day Rivera was partied out and, still hung over, showed up at Ellenville High. "You're late," the accounting teacher said.

"So what? I'm *always* late."

"We're taking a test today."

"Oh, no." The test being handed him, the very first question stumped him. Rivera took out his textbook, raised his hand, and said, "What page is it on?"

The whole class laughed, but the teacher didn't. "You can't ask me! You can't look it up!" the teacher cried. "Ten points off!" and the class laughed again. Went *hahaha*, its teeth almost biting at Rivera.

Now, Rivera liked being laughed *with*, not *at*. He liked being class clown but not class knucklehead, and he stopped playing hooky, made up his classes, graduated, and joined the American Army.

At medic school in Texas he smelled a few aromas absent from basic in Georgia, aromas like Bath & Body Works. They came from the women soldiers—*women soldiers*—who barracked upstairs of him and did their exercises beside him, the panty lines pressing against their shorts. He soon went so steady with one, the sergeants discovered her field blanket in his rucksack and his RIVERA camouflage shirt upon *her*. The sergeants called them Mr. and Mrs. Rivera and said, "You two like being together? All right, go down together," meaning drop to the ground and do twenty push-ups together. A runner-up for Miss San Francisco, Krystal was black, round-faced, long-haired, a girl whose smile melted artillery pieces, and Rivera yearned to spend every day of his life with her. From medic school, Rivera went to the camp near the Adirondacks and Krystal (an army reservist) went to a college nearby, and it's she who on Tuesday, September 11, Rivera tells presciently, "I may have to go somewhere."

"I'll wait for you, I promise," Krystal says.

He and his whole platoon, company, battalion don't go to Afghanistan, not yet. A country to its immediate north is where they're deployed, a country known as Uzbekistan. As rich as it is in Asian relics, golden temples, marble mosaics, intricate filigrees, turquoise cupolas, towers, all the marvels of Xanadu, the soldiers immured in their secret camp are of necessity bored, bored, bored. All there's to do is play spades, crazy eights, and Scrabble and eat Combos from the PX. Never did they salute officers back in the Adirondacks, but they must crisply salute them here in Uzbekistan. So despondent is one lonely soldier that he shoots his brains out and ("Medic!") becomes Rivera's first case. "Breathe, breathe," incants Rivera. "You're all right, buddy, breathe," he conjures, his Ringer's solution dripping into the soldier's corpse.

Rivera becomes despondent, too. He walks around like an abandoned dog, his head hanging down. He broods that Krystal will slough him off, and either to precipitate this or forestall it, he phones her and says, "I know you miss me—" "I do. I miss hanging out with you. I miss cooking dinner for you. I miss kissing you, and I miss laying with you."

"But Krystal. I know you're crying. I know you're going through heartache. If you're unhappy, then I'm unhappy, too. I don't know when I'm coming home. Just leave me, Krystal. Do what you want to, and have a good time doing it."

"Stop talking crazy," says Krystal, and Rivera can see her right index finger shaking at him from the Adirondacks. "I want many things, you're right. But for them all, I want you."

And hanging up, Rivera thinks, *As soon as I'm home, I'll put a ring on her finger.* But home isn't where the sergeant says that Rivera's assigned. "We got another mission," the sergeant says as Rivera's hands curtain his eyes, *No, I don't want to believe it.* He flies by cargo plane to a camp in Afghanistan, then by Chinook (a long green helicopter, one rotor fore, one rotor aft) to what's about to be America's bloodiest battle since Somalia a decade ago. His "aid bag" between his shoulders, he flies by this giant helicopter to Operation Anaconda.

His aid bag. As big as an ottoman, inside it are scissors, needles, catheters, syringes, bags of Ringer's solution, vials of Nubain—a synthetic narcotic—vials of EpiPen, ketorolac, Rocephin, and Xylocaine, bandages, dressings, cravats, and a few hundred yards of Kerlix gauzes and Ace wraps. As if this weren't enough, on the previous evening the chief medic stuffed it with many more needles, catheters, et cetera, until the bag weighed forty pounds and Rivera, carrying it, his rucksack, his sleeping bag, his helmet, his bulletproof jacket—his aptly named Interceptor—and his shotgun, needed help to stand up. At two in the morning, sitting on a steel runway waiting for the Chinooks, he griped to his fellow soldiers, "Who do I look like? Hulk Hogan?" He flexed his miniature biceps and said, "Do I look like I work out at Gold's? Look at this monster aid bag. I feel there's a child inside it."

At five in the morning came the Chinooks, and with someone's heave-ho he stood up and got on. By now it's six and his helicopter still isn't at Anaconda's locale, seventy-five miles south of Kabul. The helicopter's at ten thousand feet, and Rivera stares out a rare window at snow-sided mountains and at—well, what? camels? gazelles? oryxes? yaks? at animals running down them and, in the valleys, at Afghan people outside their adobe homes. *A real nice place*, thinks Rivera. *It's sad what'll happen here. Hey Eddie*, he corrects himself as his eardrums detect the Chinooks coming down. *Snap out of it! You're not a tourist today!* In one corrugated valley the helicopters land, the sergeants cry, *"Get out, get out!"* and after saying, "Help me up," Rivera jumps onto the red-colored, snow-covered mud.

It's chilly outside. The helicopters take off. The plan is, up in the mountains are hundreds of Qaedas who our Afghan allies should rout and who the Americans should subsequently ambush. But the first casualty of any war is the Plan. In seconds, a boy in Rivera's platoon cries, "I see somebody." He then cries, "He's wearing black," and Rivera, using binoculars, says, "Oh, I see somebody, too," a Qaeda, a scared civilian, an anthropomorphic oryx—*what?* running from left to right forty meters away. Shoot him, is that what these soldiers should do? No one has answered when the black-wearing apparition drops into a little hollow and *ffft! ffft!* starts shooting at the soldiers themselves. *Let's light his ass up*, Rivera thinks, but as soon as the whole platoon and (*"Hooah!"* the jubilant soldiers cry) two Apache helicopters, two cannon-shooting, rocket-shooting, missile-shooting helicopters, try to light it, *boom*, near the platoon there falls a rocket-propelled grenade. One, two, three kilometers away, high on a snow-sided mountain, unpurged by our Afghan allies, a Qaeda (a man who's invisible but by inference is Qaeda) has shouldered something like a bazooka, and the foot-long grenade inside it has fallen close to Rivera's wards. And within minutes from the same unassailable mountain there comes a mortar round, *boom*, and Rivera hears someone cry, "Doc! Doc! Doc!"

No, not this soon, Rivera thinks, but he runs toward the "Doc!" while the boy who's shouting it runs to Rivera. In all this platoon, there's no one who's less of a brother to Rivera than this Private Horn. Just after training, he joined the platoon in Afghanistan, and Rivera's only encounter with him was "Hey, I'm your medic. If anything's wrong with you, tell me." Today there's nothing terminal wrong with Horn. A piece of the mortar round grazed him, his shin started bleeding, his pants became bloody. Off comes Rivera's aid bag. Swiftly, Rivera cuts open the red-stained pants, looks at Horn's minor wound, and says, "You're all right." He swathes it in Kerlix and says, "How you feelin'?"

"I'm good."

"You're lucky."

"I'm ready to go."

"Then go," says Rivera with a big-brotherly slap on Horn's other leg, and Horn returns to the uninterrupted battle.

A battle it is. To the platoon, from the distant mountain, the bullets, grenades, and mortar rounds come. The dirt kicks up as if underneath is a new volcano announcing itself. A bullet bounces off a boy's rifle barrel, sending sparks like a children's sizzler, and the boy bitches, "My fuckin' weapon got hit!" A boy who's a Muslim but even more an American prays, "Hey, Man Upstairs? If it's my time to go, I want to go fightin'!" At what, they don't know, but the boys fire guns, machine guns, and, in time, mortars ("Adjust! Two hundred meters left! Adjust! Go back fifty meters!") in the mountain's direction. Also firing are the Apaches, but no one in this platoon is now shouting "Hooah." On everyone's face, Rivera's included, is an it's-game-time mien. Anaconda! We aren't playing soldier! We can get hurt, very hurt!

And three soldiers are. No soldiers in this platoon, but in one that landed synchronously a hundred meters away. As its medic it doesn't use Specialist Rivera but Specialist Miranda, but among the three soldiers stumbling down to Rivera is, you guessed it, Miranda. Once, near the Adirondacks, Rivera borrowed Miranda's cell phone and, in one month, talking to Krystal long distance, ran up a $2,000 bill, and he's been lavishing a third of his salary paying off Miranda. And now his creditor teeters as though he's drunk and says not "Doc!" but "Eddie! Oh, help me!"

"Oh, shit! What's wrong?"

"I don't know. My back."

"That scares me," Rivera says. His friend can't be moved from the incoming fire if his spinal cord's hit, but Rivera runs his fingers on Miranda's bulletproof jacket—Miranda's Interceptor—and says, "There's nothing wrong with it. It's all right." But on Miranda's seat there's blood, and as Miranda screams, Rivera rips open his camouflage pants, pulls out a piece of a mortar round, a sharp piece as big (or small) as one of Miranda's teeth, says, "It ain't too bad. You're all right," and, giving the souvenir to Miranda, replaces it with sterile stuffing, with Kerlix. He then finds a scalloped hole in Miranda's right hand, some shrapnel having passed like a dumdum bullet in one side and out the other.

Then *boom!* A mortar round scores an ear of one of the two other casualties.

The two other casualties. Besides Miranda (who swathes his right hand himself), there's Sergeant Abbott and Sergeant McCleave. Abbott's the sergeant for the other platoon, where, at his instigation, everyone addresses everyone else as Brother. "Brother, can I have some polish?" "Brother, you need any cocoa?" McCleave has the cot right next to Rivera back at their base camp. Moving in, he said to Rivera, "Thank God! I'm sleepin' nex' to my medic!" and Rivera said playfully, "Well, I hope your feet don't stink." The mortars now chasing them, the two medics and the two sergeants run and stumble to a safe haven behind a small knoll, and Rivera starts ministering to Abbott and McCleave. Abbott's got a piece of a mortar round in his triceps, and Rivera treats it by the book, wrapping it in Kerlix while saying, "You're all right," but it's impenetrable what's wrong with McCleave. On his clothes is no blood, but in back of the knoll he sits as though wearing a sign saying HOMELESS. He stares as though waiting passively for a *clink* in his dented tin cup.

"Sergeant McCleave," says Rivera. "What's wrong with you?"

"Who . . . are . . . you . . . ?" McCleave doesn't say it, just looks it.

"Sergeant McCleave! Please tell me! What's wrong with you?"

"Where . . . am . . . I . . . ?"

"Sergeant McCleave!" Rivera screams, shaking him vigorously.

Some slobber comes to McCleave's lips, and he says audibly, "I . . . don't . . . know. . . ."

"Sergeant McCleave!" says Abbott, the shrapnel-suffering sergeant. "Tell the doc what's wrong with you! Or you'll die!"

Or you'll what? As slowly as worms, these words wend their way to McCleave's addled brain. "My hand . . . my back . . ."

Rivera rips off McCleave's gloves and says, "Good." He looks at McCleave's Interceptor and says, "Good." He cuts McCleave's pants, and on both of McCleave's legs, both upper and lower, he sees dozens of holes from the same indiscriminate mortar round that hit Miranda and Abbott. Now, shrapnel is painful wherever it is. Unlike a bullet, it enters red-hot, and it starts burning the flesh, fat, muscle, nerves of the boy who haplessly caught it. McCleave's state of shock isn't in any way overwrought. He can't raise either leg, so Rivera props each leg on his knee like a two-by-four that he's sawing as, with his hands, he wraps on the Kerlix, lest his good buddy bleed to death and, at their camp, his cot right next to Rivera's become unoccupied.

By now Rivera's the only medic in either platoon, or so Rivera reasonably believes. But now from the other platoon, a hundred meters away, a hundred meters of bullets, grenades, and mortar rounds raising divots, there comes a cry of "Doc!" and Rivera, as intuitively as a champion sprinter at the cry of *Go*, commences a deadly hundred-meter dash. *I'm running,* he thinks philosophically—*running for my life for someone else's life.*

• • •

He's scared. He runs anyhow. He pants, being ninety-two hundred feet high. In front of him—*ffft!*—some bullets raise dust like the bubbling mud at Yellowstone. Do any grenades come in? Do any mortar rounds come? If so, Rivera doesn't register them. The finish line, no frangible tape, is a pile of rocks behind which there lies the boy who cried, "Doc!" and Rivera dives at him like someone stealing second. He also dives at two soldiers he hasn't expected: the battalion medic (a boy who's wounded) and the battalion *doctor*, a major amazed to be at such remove from a MASH. Rivera's hundred-meter sprint wasn't in vain. The medic and doctor both have lost their aid bags, and at these guardian rocks the Kerlix, et cetera, is all in Eddie's monster. *Thank God I stuffed it*, Rivera thinks.

The casualties (by now there are two) are one boy who's saying, "I can't see!" and one boy who's gasping, "I can't breathe!" and, with Rivera's aid bag, the doctor treats both. "How you doin'?" Rivera asks them—asks, asks, even shouts from a hundred meters to the two sergeants and Miranda, "How you doin'?"

"We're all right."

"Just lay low," Rivera shouts, aware that if one of them falls asleep, his breathing might stop and he'll die. While shouting, Rivera's thinking, *Oh, God, will these casualties ever end?* No, they won't, for in this other platoon another mortar round just fell and the radio operator cries, "Doc!" The boy, PFC McGovern, is Rivera's phenomenal friend, phenomenal since each of his legs seemed wired to a separate cerebellum. "McGovern! What's *wrong* with you? You got two left feet?" Rivera agonized on countless occasions as McGovern tripped over his cot, the MRE box (meals ready to eat), or even the crack in the floor, spread-eagling. "McGovern!" Rivera agonized. "Did you not see it?" "I seen it! I thought I'd get over it!" But now (it's just about noon) no fault attaches itself to McGovern as he lies sprawled, both feet, both legs, both arms full of fiery shrapnel.

"It's burning!" McGovern cries to Rivera.

"What's burning worst?"

"My feet!"

Rivera takes off McGovern's left boot, left sock. McGovern's left foot is a shrapnel-studded caveman's club, and Rivera instinctively shields his eyes.

"What is it? What is it?"

"You're all right, man," Rivera says, his hand raised, his fingers apart, a gesture meaning *Easy. It's all right,* his head turning toward the battalion medic, his lips pantomiming, *Oh, fuck.* He wraps McGovern's foot in Kerlix, but the Kerlix becomes blood-red, and he unwraps it and rewraps it in Kerlix, then Ace. "I know this hurts," says Rivera. "But you gotta try to wiggle your toes."

"I can! But they hurt!"

"I know they hurt, buddy."

"Oh, God! I can't take it!"

"But you'll be all right." But McGovern screams, and Rivera takes out his Nubain, injecting a minimal milliliter. "The pain, this'll get rid of it," Rivera says, then starts on McGovern's other foot, his legs and arms.

"The enemy," cries an undaunted sergeant, "wants us to sing the 10th Mountain Division Song!" Around him the soldiers start it: "We are the 10th Mountain Infantry / With a glorious history . . ." *Booooom!* It's the Air Force, thank God, but all the American soldiers recoil as a cargo plane metamorphosed into a bomber drops one of its one-ton bombs on the mountain that all this affliction comes from, on the cloud-covered heads of the Qaedas. As anyone would, as soon as the Qaedas hear those horrific bombers approaching, they go with lock, stock, and barrel (rifles, launchers, and mortars) into their caves, go, if they technologically could, into the fourth dimension until the bombers depart. But during every lull, Rivera runs to his patients in both platoons, asking them, "How you doin'? Are you awake? Now, don' become sleepy on me! Don' fall asleep! You need some water? Here, have some water. Man, you're all right. Man, you're all right. You're gonna make it," at times thinking privately, *Is he all right? Is he gonna make it? I don't know.*

"Doc," all Rivera's patients ask, "when are the medevacs comin'?" The boys mean, When are the choppers coming to carry us out?

"They're comin'. They're comin'," says Rivera while thinking privately, *When are the medevacs comin'?* He radios battalion, "Polar Bear? When are the medevacs comin'? When are the QRFs"—the Quick Reaction Forces—"comin'? Where's our help? What's takin' time? We got to get these casualties out!" On this wide-ranging radio, the officers at battalion can't say, "They're tryin'. The medevacs, tryin'. The other companies, tryin'. But the LZ's too hot. The landing zone's inaccessible."

Then *booooom!* The soldiers cringe, the bombers conclude, the Qaedas, unchastened, undismayed, come from their caves, their rifles, launchers, and mortars coming, too, and "Incoming!" the soldiers shout. To shield him, Rivera lies on top of McGovern, the boy with wounded feet, legs, arms, the boy benumbed by Nubain, he puts his head on McGovern's and hears him say, "Please please please." Then *boom*, a mortar round hits First Lieutenant Maroyka. Then *ffft*, a bullet hits Specialist Almey, a boy who played basketball with Rivera, shooting, shooting the ball like some repetitive plastic toy. Then boom, a mortar round hits Major Byrne, the doctor far from a MASH and, with Rivera, the last intact practitioner here. Then boom, another mortar round hits the battalion medic, this one from two feet away. Then *ffft*—

It's midafternoon and it's still going on. How many soldiers in two platoons of Company C of the 1st Battalion of the 87th Regiment of the 10th Mountain Division of the American Army were hit? Restrict yourself, the Army adjures me, to "Casualties were light," "were moderate," "were heavy."

Casualties were heavy.

I tell people, "you're all right," thinks Rivera. *But who'll tell me I'm all right?* It's moratorium time as the bombers inconvenience the Qaedas, and all right he's certainly not. Rivera's worn out. His day began at two this morning, and he hasn't eaten since then. He's hardly had water, either. His face is charcoal-colored due to close mortar rounds, and on his hands there's blood, other people's ectopic blood. On all three browns of his camouflage clothes is this same inappropriate red. If someone cries, "Doc!" Rivera expects to run up and treat him. But can he? *Whatever I have, I'm about to lose it,* Rivera thinks. *What am I even doing here?*

And then Rivera remembers the World Trade Center. Remembers the flaring fires like Zeus' lightning bolts. Remembers the businessmen *(My God! How desperate were they?)*—businessmen and business-women throwing themselves to the plaza, eighty floors below. The towers collapsing, the ashes supplanting them, the ash-plastered people running away. The people doing the rounds of the hospitals, asking, "Did you see this man?" "Did you see this woman?" And hearing repeatedly, "No, I've not." And never discovering them. And never burying them. It's not two platoons, it's not sixty people the mourners sought, thinks Rivera. It's three thousand people! As bad as Anaconda is, Rivera thinks, *We're better off. We'll never ask, "Did you see my mom?" "Did you see my dad?" "Did you see Krystal?"*

He thinks of the wife who must have asked, "Did you see Steve?" Steve was the paramedic at a Harlem station in New York City who, after medic school in Texas, Rivera did six weeks of training with. "Do you want to do an IV? . . . Do you want to do an EKG?" *Do you want to,* Steve always asked, and Rivera always said yes. Now, Rivera has heard that on Tuesday, September 11, the North Tower collapsed on Steve, the deed of the organization on the mountain in Rivera's plain sight. And now Rivera remembers why he's here. It's for the three thousand dead. It's for their bereaved, to let them know they're avenged. It's for the heroic paramedic at the Harlem station, Rivera apostrophizing him, "It's for you. We're gettin' 'em for you, Steve."

It's then that Rivera hears, "Doc!"

Rivera springs up. He starts running. In his own platoon a mortar round has burst, and he must retrace his bullet-pelleted hundred-meter dash. He succeeds. The source of the "Doc!" is Sergeant Wurtz, a boy he's played one-on-one basketball with, Rivera teasing him, "You cannot play me, Sergeant Wurtz. You'll lose." "We'll see." But now Wurtz is lying supine as if he's been grievously fouled, his combat boot off, his foot above him, his hand holding it as if, if he carelessly let go, it would fall off. He's rocking like a child's seesaw, screaming, but as Rivera wraps his Kerlix, another mortar round comes in, the Qaedas are zeroing onto them. On one pogo-stick leg, Wurtz hops, hops, in Rivera's embrace to a safe haven higher up, the Kerlix trailing behind him. "Oh, fuck," says Wurtz, gasping. "I thought I'd blown off my foot."

"It's all right."

"I don't know. It's burnin' like hell."

"Shrapnel's hot."

"Is my foot ever gonna get better?"

"Sure, it's gonna."

"Am I ever gonna get outta here?"

"Sure. You're gonna be playin' basketball next week. But," says Rivera, "you're still never gonna beat me."

The two take refuge behind some rocks. The day's last casualty is the radio operator for Rivera's platoon, Specialist Stanton, a bullet in his right foot, and Rivera helps him hop to the wounded ward on the invaluable rocks' safe side. The ward looks like Rubens's *Massacre of the Innocents*, minus any of Herod's assassins. "Doc," a number of innocents say. "I can't feel my arms," "I can't feel my legs."

"They'll be all right," says Rivera, concealing that this means damaged nerves.

It's now six o'clock. Night's coming on, the dark's coming on, and the temperature's dropping toward twenty. Rivera's polypropylene coat, polypropylene gloves, polyester sleeping bag—Rivera's "snivel gear"—isn't with him, Rivera like most soldiers having shed it this morning on exiting the Chinook. It's many kilometers away (if it were nearer, he'd give it to patients anyhow), and all Rivera has on is T-shirt, shorts, and four-colored camouflage clothes, just what he'd wear on an Adirondack dog day. He shivers. To listen to, his teeth could be a train on irregular rails, rattling. He lies down with two patients, keeping them warm and, at least slightly, himself warm, too. It's a three-soldier night.

• • •

"The night belongs to us," the American Army says. American soldiers have NODs, night optical devices, the world around them as bright as twilight although it's a worrisome bilious green, and the Qaedas don't have them, not yet. Tonight what the Qaedas can see are the flash, flash, lightning flash of America's bombs, but not America's infrared lights, lights in a druid circle, lights the American soldiers meticulously laid out. The lights encircle the LZ, landing zone, for the medevacs, if the medevacs actually come and if, by tomorrow, the casualties will be en route to Frankfurt or Washington, D.C. And lo! at eleven o'clock appear a couple of angelic medevacs that the Qaedas, unable to see, apparently hear. The Qaedas launch a Stinger missile, and, to avoid it, the medevacs disappear again, none of Rivera's patients aboard. "I can't believe this," says Rivera, though not to his anxious patients. "They," the Qaedas, "aren't gonna let us leave! At dawn they're gonna be shootin' again!"

He prays for the first time today. In his pocket, he clutches a little white cross. "Whoever dies wearing this," the cross's embossment says, "shall not suffer eternal fire," and, as one hand clutches it, the other crosses himself and Rivera prays, "Lord, if I can't make it out of here, please take care of my mom and dad and please take care of Krystal. Krystal," Rivera continues, hoping she'll hear him as God just did, "whatever we do, to do it together's better. If we were poor, were dressin' in rags, were sittin' in cardboard boxes, we would be happier together. I love you." It's then that the medevacs return, take on the prostrate patients like McCleave and McGovern, take off, and it's one hour later that the Chinooks return, their rotors (thinks Rivera) glistening in the full moon like the pearly gates. They take on the walking wounded like Miranda and Abbott, then all of Rivera's platoon, platoons, then with an exultant roar take off, Rivera whispering, "Thank you, Lord," and saying aloud, "We made it! We made it!"

An hour later, Rivera is in his quiet, lightless, motionless tent. He sits at the stove, letting the warmth like a bowl of hot soup saturate him, then has a bowl of hot soup indeed, in thirty hours his first nourishment. On his cot he just passes out, but rest for the weary isn't his.

"Get up! Get up!" a soldier surprises him at a god-awful reveille. A soldier from Company B, he's scarcely known to Rivera. "Get up!"

"Get outta here," Rivera mutters.

"Get up!" says half of Company B, assembled at Rivera's cot. "We were at the radio yesterday, listenin' to Company C! It was like the Superbowl!"

"What was?" Rivera mutters.

"You!" say the soldiers of Company B. "You saved the whole company! We don't know how you did it! We call you Superman!"

As soon as the telephone's up, Rivera calls Krystal. She says, "Hello?"

"Hey, baby."

"Oh my God! Are you all right?"

"I'm all right."

"You don't even know. Someone called from the 10th Mountain Division. He said they'd heard a medic was hit. How bad, they didn't know, but I was cryin' like crazy. I called your mom, and she was cryin', too. She called the Red Cross. But they knew nothin', so I watched the TV news, and I just knew you're in Anaconda. I was scared."

"Baby, I wasn't hit. But now I know: I don't want to live away from you. As soon as I'm back I want an apartment with you. I want to live with you, I want to marry you, and I want to have babies with you."

"Slow down," says Krystal, laughing through tears. "I'm not ready for babies yet."

"I don't care what you're ready for. As soon as I'm home I'm makin' babies."

"No you're not."

"Oh yes I am."

"Wait till I finish school," says Krystal, still laughing. "Then we'll start doin' other things. I'm so glad you're okay."

"Oh, baby, I still can't believe it. All day we're takin' fire. All day my buddies gettin' hurt. All day my buddies tellin' me, 'Help me, Doc.' And you know what? I helped them. I was scared, and I didn't know if I'd get out, but I helped them. All that stuff that I thought I'd forget, I remembered. I did what I was taught to do. I can't believe it," and Rivera, tears in his eyes, slams his fist on the telephone table. "But baby, because I helped them, they didn't die! All of 'em, they didn't die!"

II. Company B (March 3 to March 10)

There but for the grace of God go I. No one, but no one, thought this in Company B as it listened in distant tents to the "Superbowl" and the vicissitudes of Rivera's buddies. Why, these were B's buddies, too! Were boys who B had partied with in America, had played dominoes with in Uzbekistan, had slumped on red canvas seats with on the plane to Afghanistan! All day, B sat entreating its lieutenants, "We gotta help 'em! We gotta join 'em!" One lieutenant had a friend who'd died at his desk at Cantor Fitzgerald, a desk in the airplane's flaming path in the north tower of the World Trade Center. On each of his hand grenades, the lieutenant (a former broker, too) had written his friend's five-syllable name—STERGIOPOULOS—with a Magic Marker, and B entreated him, "Please! Just get us a Chinook!"

"No, the LZ's too hot."

"Then land the Chinook five miles away! We'll walk in!"

"No . . ."

The next day, B got its Chinooks. Quite typically, B has three platoons, and in the avenging lieutenant's platoon is a boy who saw the events at the World Trade Center in real life and not on TV. He was on leave in Paterson, New Jersey, fifteen miles away, and was asleep when his brother awoke him. "Come upstairs."

In his boxers the boy went upstairs, looked out the window at New York City, and said, "Holy shit! What happened?"

"The building fell down."

"Holy shit!"

The boy's name is PFC Shkelqim Mahmuti. Born in America to Albanian parents, he's a Muslim like them. Even before the Towers fell down, a Muslim was often picked on in America. In grade school, in high school, his coevals laughed at Mahmuti, "Ha-ha! Pork is good for you! Fuck Mohammed!" Later, at United Parcel, the other drivers said

to Mahmuti, "What are you? Muslim? . . . Yes." "I'll be watching you."
All this discrimination would cease when he joined the American
Army, Mahmuti thought. It wouldn't.

His face was dark, his nose was sharp, his brows were a
Mesopotamian's: thick, black, unbroken. A *hood* is what these features
meant to many policemen in Paterson, and Mahmuti at age fifteen in
fact dealt marijuana, cocaine, crack, in New Jersey. He was often
arrested, and in April last year, telling himself, *I gotta change,* he needed
a half dozen waivers from three courts to join the American Army. He
took basic training in Georgia, took graduation leave in New Jersey,
saw the great tragedy in New York, and one week later joined the 10th
Mountain Division at its frantic camp near the Adirondacks, frantic
due to his sergeant's announcements of "Here's your packin' list!"
"Here's your malaria pill!" "Here's your orders!" "We're leavin'
tomorrow!" Were leaving to Asia, leaving to fight the—*Muslims.* One
fellow soldier asked him, "You know what side you're on?"

"Yeah. I know what side I'm on."

It wasn't the Muslim side, Mahmuti sincerely believed. He believed
he could aim, fire, and kill a Muslim even if, as he also believed, the
Muslim would go to paradise while all Mahmuti's fellow soldiers went
to Muslim hell. In his own pocket, the Koran said, "Lo! The worst of
beasts in Allah's sight are the Unbelievers," but also the Koran told
how Muslims killed Muslims without the Koran's complaint. Nor did
Mahmuti's parents demur at Mahmuti's killing another defender of
Allah. "Don't sweat it," Mahmuti's father phoned him. "To say this
isn't easy for me, but if you must kill him, kill him."

"It'll be him before me, Dad."

But one doesn't know, does one? till the Moment of Truth, the
unpredictable confrontation on Muslim turf.

To kill the Qaedas was what every soldier brooded about as, on the
first night of Anaconda, the casualties came in. Mahmuti's sergeant,
Sergeant Fuentes of San Antonio, prayed: "Take care of us, Lord. I've
got these young soldiers with me. Guide me so I can take care of 'em."
But the Lord isn't the only presence the soldiers count on. The next

day, the sergeant wears on his helmet a G. I. Joe, a doll his son mailed from Texas, and, while walking to the Chinooks, the whole platoon devoutly touches it. "He'll take care of us," say the soldiers, then the Chinooks take off, and the soldiers applaud and say, *"Yeah!"* . . . "One hour," the helicopter pilot says.

"Any way we can get there in thirty minutes?" asks Mahmuti.

At two in the afternoon, the Chinooks drop onto the same corrugated place that Rivera's did, and the sergeants cry similarly, "Get out!" With rapid heartbeats the soldiers do. But now the Qaedas on the grim mountain are (to trust the American Army) dead, dispatched by white lightning bombs, or (to mistrust the American Army) alive on snow-crusted trails into Pakistan, and the Chinooks take off, the platoon's exposed, and for the moment no one's shooting at it. Lest someone does, it starts digging what it calls Ranger graves, which are foxholes one foot deep. His digging done, Mahmuti lies in this shallow grave, the sun setting, the evening constellations setting, the Qaedas (if any) firing no bullets, grenades, or mortar rounds, but our Afghan allies firing tracers of red, orange, green, and blue at (if any) the Qaedas, and the American Air Force bombing them. At two in the morning, Mahmuti rises like Lazarus and, with his platoon, walks east until dawn, then west until noon. To quote no lesser enthusiast than Irving Berlin, *This Is the Army, Mr. Jones.*

At last the durable order comes to Mahmuti's platoon, Dig in on top of this small-sized hill.

A small-sized but oh-so-steep-sided hill, a hill for alpinists with rope. His helmet, Interceptor, rucksack, and rifle encumbering him, Mahmuti (with his platoon) climbs up, the gray shale crumbling underfoot, turning into gray dust. On top of the hill, surprise—the Qaedas rematerialize, the Qaedas start shooting at the startled platoon from God knows where. And *ffft! ffft!* from somewhere below the Americans come the Qaedas' bullets, then *boom! boom!* come the Qaedas' notorious mortar rounds. The first of them falls where the soldiers just were, Mahmuti thinking, *Holy shit! We could've been dead!* On the hilltop, most soldiers look for the Qaedas, shouting, "I don't see 'em," but some soldiers in this sudden baptism of fire just cower behind boulders, among them the soldier who in the Adirondacks asked Mahmuti, "You know what side you're on?"

Mahmuti is looking for the Qaedas. So is his Sergeant Fuentes. Borrowing someone's binoculars, the sergeant suddenly cries, "I see 'em!" Some with Russian rifles, some with Russian mortars, the Qaedas all are competent soldiers, staying apart. All are standing, walking, or running in the old corrugated valley below the Americans, reversing yesterday's hierarchy and, in consequence, reversing yesterday's odds, for now it's Americans sitting pretty and Qaedas sitting ducks. "You see 'em?" the sergeant asks a heavy-machine gunner near him.

"No, I don' see 'em."

"One's over here. Two's over there. And one's runnin' toward those trees."

"I still don' see 'em." The gunner fires blind and *kkk!* the cartridge sticks. "It's jammed!"

"Damn." The sergeant turns to another gunner. "Shoot this way!"

"Where's he at?" asks Mahmuti. He lies by the sergeant, excited.

"Son, hold these bines. I'll shoot tracers, that's where he's at." On one knee, the sharp-sighted sergeant fires at a Qaeda eight hundred meters away, and the second machine gunner fires that way. The sergeant fires at a Qaeda six hundred meters away, and (the gun functioning now) the first machine gunner fires that way. The sergeant then fires at a Qaeda five hundred meters away, the Qaeda who's running toward trees.

"I'm ready to cover your fire," says Mahmuti.

"All right, Mahmuti." It's five o'clock, and Bob (the big orange ball) is setting before them. In the valley, the Qaeda's shadow is longer than the Qaeda himself. The two rifles almost touching, the sergeant fires once and Mahmuti twice. The first bullet hits the Qaeda's chest, the second two hit his stomach, and he falls down undisguisedly dead.

"Holy shit!" says Mahmuti.

"We got him! We got the bastard!"

"That's good fuckin' shootin', Sarge."

"Good shootin', Mahmuti! I'm proud of ya!" The sergeant shakes

hands with Mahmuti, shakes hands energetically, shakes hands as if
Mahmuti, his son, has just won the Nobel Peace Prize. "Now let's get
the other shit-heads!" And with rifles, machine guns, mortars, and, to
gild this lily, a couple of B-52's the soldiers do what yesterday's soldiers, however willing, didn't: They kill the Qaedas.

A few days later, Mahmuti sees another Qaeda and, far from dis-
patching him, has a conciliatory conversation with him. The man, who
Mahmuti meets in the valley in an adobe building full of Americans, is
an American prisoner. He's shoeless. His hands wear plastic cuffs, and,
in lieu of a proper blindfold, his head wears an empty sandbag like an
empty grocery bag. By accident, Mahmuti in his combat boots steps on
the Qaeda's bare foot and tells him, "My bad."

"Water."

"You're sayin' water?"

"Yes yes."

"You're speakin' English?"

"Yes yes." Mahmuti takes off the outlandish sandbag, and the
Qaeda starts crying. *Man*, thinks Mahmuti, *I'm not gonna kill you.* But,
thinks Mahmuti, *what if you weren't the prisoner and I was? My shirt
says Mahmuti, my dog tags say Islam, my pocket carries the Koran. You'd
call me a Muslim traitor. You'd say, "So you're against the jihad!" You
wouldn't just kill me. You'd torture me.* Not reciprocating at all, Mahmuti gives the man water, socks, blankets, and asks him, "What's
your name?"

"Mehmed Tadik."

At home, thinks Mahmuti, *I've got a Muslim friend named Tadik.*
"You're a Muslim?"

"Yes yes."

"I am a Muslim, too."

He's mocking me, the Qaeda quite clearly thinks. His teeth start to
grind as if they're chewing betel nuts. "You Shiite or Sunni?"

"Sunni. How about you?"

"I Sunni." But still the Qaeda looks skeptical, looks to Mahmuti as
though, if he weren't handcuffed, he'd kill him.

Mahmuti assures him he's Muslim. He says the Arabic prayer *"Bismillah e Errahman e Erraheem"*—"In the name of Allah, the Beneficent, the Merciful." Again the Qaeda starts crying and, in English this time, Mahmuti asks him, "Are you Al Qaeda?"

"No no! I student Kabul University!"

"You're lying."

"No no! I no Al Qaeda! I peace!"

"Are you *harām*?"

"No no!" The word means sinful.

"You are *harām*. You aren't Muslim. We're pure, we Muslims. We don't go killing innocent people like in New York. That shit, we Muslims don't do."

"No no! I no kill! I student!"

Mahmuti walks away. He has little love for the Qaeda. But having met him, met Tadik, could Mahmuti do what five sunny days ago he did to another human being, another believer in Allah—could Mahmuti shoot him and say, "That's good fuckin' shootin'"? No way.

Regrets? That isn't what soldiers feel or Mahmuti feels. He thinks about the Qaeda he killed sometimes. He tells himself, *It either was him or me. I won't let Mom sit and cry because some fuckin' terrorist took me out. Just as Dad said: Who cares that he's Muslim? He's wrong.* At night Mahmuti prays to Allah, "Thank you for keeping *shaytān*, the devil, away from me. Thank you." But maybe Mahmuti has, well, not regrets, not remorse, but can I say qualms? Or why did Mahmuti protest to his sergeant one day, "We did the right thing."

"Damn right. We did the right thing."

"It wasn't for pleasure, God knows."

The seventh day out, Mahmuti and his platoon return to their camp, and Mahmuti calls up his father in Paterson. *"Unë mora nje,"* Mahmuti says in Albanian. "I took one."

"Shit!" says Mahmuti's father in English.

"Are you all right?"

"Yeah. No one got hurt. None of *us*."

"Good good." His father pauses. "Good job." Mahmuti's sergeant calls up his wife in Texas. He doesn't tell her "I took one," but tells her, "A few things happened but I'm okay."

"In my heart," his wife says, crying, "you're a great warrior now. You've earned your feathers." His wife isn't being figurative. Despite his Hispanic name—Fuentes—the sharp-sighted sergeant is an American Indian, an Aztec, much as I thought that Cortés had exterminated them all. The sergeant grew up by an Aztec reservation in Texas, where, on his return, there'll be an immemorial ceremony for him, the great warrior getting a fifty-four-feathered bonnet, the feathers dyed red, white, blue, and (for the days gone by in Tenochtitlán) environment-emulating green. "You've earned your feathers," his wife says. "You know?"

"I know," the eagle-eyed sergeant says.

III. Company A (March 18 to March 29)

Why the continued resistance to Company B? It might be Osama bin Laden is hiding there, an American commander tells an Afghan official in *The New York Times*. To catch Osama, his subordinates, or any of his foot soldiers becomes the mission of Company A of the 4th Battalion of the 31st Regiment of the 10th Mountain Division. In one platoon, known as the Misfits, are two boys who, when the towers fell, still were in Georgia learning their *right face, left face*, were in the same exact barracks and, by extraordinary chance, in the same exact double bunk. Their names, ranks, to hell with their serial numbers, are Private Andrew Simmons of Newark, New York, near Rochester, and Private Andrew Starlin of Buda, Texas, near Austin. Two Private Andrew S.'s.

A baby-faced boy, Simmons has oval glasses, scholarly-looking black rims. In high school he sang in the concert choir. The other boy, Starlin, is pink-nosed, pink-cheeked, round-faced. His innocent eyes say, *Me? I know nothing about it*. In junior high school he played in the band. Simmons and Starlin played football, too, Simmons guard and Starlin center. Last year Simmons graduated, Starlin got his GED, and, for money for college, the two joined the Army, doing their basic training together in Georgia.

The two didn't know it, but precious little of basic training would stand them in stead in Afghanistan. Saluting? Marching? Using their hands reciprocally, all in the service of *right shoulder arms*? More folderol for *port arms* and *port arms salute*? What they would do in Afghanistan Simmons and Starlin didn't learn in Georgia: running into icicle-sided caves where maybe, maybe, would be Osama, firing their rifles automatically, firing their machine guns, and throwing their hand grenades like Bata pitching machines. From Georgia they went to Kuwait, another training place for the 10th Mountain Division. There they learned to eschew all Kuwaiti women. They learned to stand aside of Kuwaiti prayer rugs. Their shoe soles they learned to expose to no Kuwaiti.

To run into caves behaving deranged—no, Simmons and Starlin didn't learn that in Kuwait.

They flew by cargo plane to Afghanistan, then by Chinook to Anaconda's sometimes disastrous, sometimes felicitous locale. The sergeants yelling, "*Get out,*" the two soldiers did—the two soldiers do, and their first thought is *Oh my God!* Their shock isn't due to bullets, grenades, mortar rounds, or any other man-made devices but to God's mountains around them. Mountains like this, the Andrews (who scarcely have seen the Adirondacks, much less the Rockies) haven't known except in *National Geographic.* Steep, snow-sided, cragged, the mountains tower above them like heaven's immaculate parapets. A soldier with them from Alaska thinks of Louis Armstrong's "What a Wonderful World," and one from Michigan thinks of Dire Straits's "These mist-covered mountains/Are a home now for me" and the song's planetary conclusion, "We're fools to make war." A soldier from Arkansas thinks of the Bible, of God cutting stone on Mount Sinai, of how some stone-blind people look at creation and don't perceive there's a God. Or how some people, like Osama, their quarry today, Osama who pleads belief in God, look at these sacred mountains and say, "A good defensive position."

The soldiers are in the Qaedas' often-visited valley. To the east is the Qaedas' notorious mountain, and to the west is a humpbacked one the Americans call the Whale. It's there that Simmons and Starlin (and all the Misfits) deploy. Their helmets, Interceptors, rucksacks on, their rifles carried like quarterstaffs, the two tenderfoots (in army argot, crispy critters) start up the Whale's precipitous side. Like marbles, the pebbles skid downward and the two critters skid with them like Jack and Jill, first on their boots, then on their seats, then stoutly stand up and retrace their route, the top of the Whale two miles away whatever they do.

On top of the Whale with guns, grenade launchers, mortars are, in all likelihood, the Qaedas. To keep them down, Starlin's squad halts, and Starlin fires an antitank missile. His squad fires rifles, rifle grenades, machine guns as Simmons's squad approaches where the Qaedas should be. A white flare (a star cluster) signals cease fire, and Simmons's squad assaults the top of the Whale. Simmons's sergeant passes a cave that a Qaeda could at any moment storm out of, his Russian rifle smoking. "A cave! Get back!" cries Simmons's sergeant. "Frag out!" the sergeant continues, tossing a hand grenade—*boom!*— and the cave anorexically collapses. "It just caved in! Oh, fuck!" cries Simmons's sergeant, seeing, on a boulder above him, a Qaeda, a man in green camouflage and, on his shoulders, a yellow blanket—*bang,* and the sergeant shoots him. "I got one!" He sees another blanketed being— *bang!* "I got another!" He sees still another—*bang!* "I got three!"

Chaos is king. Dead, dead, dead at Simmons's feet are one yellow-blanketed donkey and two Qaedas, none of whom is Osama. Farther away is a Qaeda who Simmons, *bang bang bang!* keeps firing at but who escapes behind a boulder, and in the ground is a quite provocative hole that Simmons drops a hand grenade into, a hand grenade that falls, falls, like Alice in Wonderland and, in time, emits a chthonian *bing.* Such is the Great Osama Hunt for Andrew number one.

Still downhill is Starlin's squad. It sees another cave on the Whale's side. The Misfits conclude it's a man-made bunker: three walls of inter-locked rocks, the fourth wall the Whale, the roof perhaps plywood and, on top of that, more rocks. The question is, Where's the doorway that (at any moment) the Qaedas with Russian rifles might hurtle out of?

Starlin's squad searches for it. In the interlocked rocks it sees some interstices for the Qaedas' rifles, and Starlin tosses a hand grenade expectantly into one. He cries, "Frag out!" and runs up the Whale— *bang!*—and runs downhill to another interstice to toss another grenade in. Uphill, downhill, uphill, he's on a crazy gymnastics machine at an altitude twice that of Denver. He's winded. He breathes like a dog whose tongue's hanging out, huh huh, huh huh. At last Starlin finds the Qaedas' perilous doorway. Into it Starlin's sergeant throws another grenade—*bang*—and tells him, "Go in!"

"I'll lead with lead!" The first *lead* rhymes with *deed*, the second rhymes with *dead*.

"Go for it!"

And through the doorway goes Starlin, shooting, apparently, at a Qaeda: a Qaeda's chest, a Qaeda's shirt, well, that's what the target appears to be. In comes Starlin's sergeant, shooting (shooting a shotgun) at the same man, and another sergeant shoots, too. Oh, Lord have mercy! Not falling down, the man keeps moving as Starlin and the two sergeants shoot. The smoke from Starlin's gun, the other gun, the shotgun, the crumbled rock, and, who knows? from the Qaeda is so thick it might be an hour past midnight. No one sees anything, but on Starlin's rifle, attached with duct tape, is a small flashlight, and Starlin cuts through the darkness with it. The little that's left of the target, which, it develops, is hanging by rope from the ceiling, might have been a T-shirt, blanket, sandbag, or Pillsbury flour bag but by no flight of anyone's fancy was ever a Qaeda. *Damn*, Starlin thinks.

"Holy shit! I can't believe it!" says Starlin. It's some days later, and Starlin sees something amazing. A bunker, a Qaeda bunker, is a true treasure house that Starlin, merely an American, might even envy. The tents aren't cheesecloth, the blankets aren't cotton, the sleeping bags could emanate from the U.S. Army Quartermaster Corps. In one corner is a propane stove—a cooking stove—and pots, pans, forks, spoons, teapots, teacups and saucers, and in another corner are scissors, needles, catheters, syringes, all the supplies that Rivera has plus Chap Stick and Vaseline. On the floor is no Persian carpet, but in some other bunkers (even on other bunkers' *walls*) are many, and, so help me God, in these other bunkers are Korans, boom boxes, audio recorders, audio players, video cameras, night optical devices, gymnasium bags from Adidas, sneakers, boxing gloves, punching bags, fingernail clippers, toenail clippers for Goliath, sewing machines, money—both Afghan afghanis and Pakistani rupees—a Russian sword that Starlin's sergeant appropriates, and a Casio watch with altimeter and compass that Starlin appropriates. "Holy shit!" says Starlin. "This mountain! I can't believe the Qaedas got everything up it!"

And more. In and around the bunkers are cartridges, mortar rounds, rockets, grenades that the Misfits detonate. But there're thousands, and for hours they're exploding, hitting the Whale, nearly hitting the Misfits. One rocket hits a red cedar, the tree catches fire, and the smoke floats to a Navajo soldier. He experiences déjà vu. Before coming to Afghanistan, he sat in a hogan in Arizona with a Navajo medicine man. In headband, turquoise necklace, crimson shirt, the man opened a leather pouch and on the hogan's earthen floor sprinkled red cedar shavings. He rattled a rattle, drummed a drumstick, sang a Navajo song the Navajo soldier understood, then set the shavings afire and, in Navajo, said, "Let mother nature help this boy. Let him come swiftly and safely home." In the smoke, the words rose into the soldier's nostrils, consciousness, self. And today in Afghanistan, the red cedar smoke and the words again envelop him. *It's mother nature's sign. I'll come swiftly and safely home,* the boy tells himself correctly.

To their sheltered camp come the Misfits. With time to reflect on it, Simmons is quite upset by his recollection of the two dead human beings, but Starlin thinks, *They screwed with us, so we screwed with them.* At night the Misfits use MRE boxes, other boxes, MRE plastic bags, even cargo-plane pallets to build a crackling campfire—*crack!* an MRE creamer exploding in blue-green sparks. A sergeant strums on his ukulele, singing a gospel song: "The Lord is my Light, / The Rock of my salvation / Of whom shall I be afraid? / Of whom shall I fear?" . . . "Know what I'd do if I found Osama?" a Misfit asks. "I'd cut him into little pieces. I hear they have a reward for him. I'd ask them, 'How much is each piece worth?'"

"No, you wouldn't. You'd do what you've been told to. You'd shoot him."

But really, did Simmons and Starlin ever come close? Did ever Osama live in the Whale? No one knows, although the Qaedas' paperwork showed that he scarcely needed to to account for the Qaedas' commitment. In the rubble the Misfits (and other boys in other ruins in Afghanistan) found these papers, dirty, dog-eared, charred papers in both of Afghanistan's languages and six other languages, too, and army intelligence translated them. They showed that the Qaedas came from Afghanistan and from Algeria, Arabia, Bangladesh, Bosnia, Canada, China, Egypt, Iraq, Jordan, Kuwait, Libya, Kyrgyzstan, Morocco, Pakistan, the Philippines, Russia, Somalia, Sudan, Syria, Tajikistan, Turkey, Turkmenistan, the United Kingdom, the United States, Uzbekistan, and Yemen. At their camps in Afghanistan, at 6:00 every morning, the Qaedas did exercises, averaging thirty push-ups, thirty sit-ups. All morning the Qaedas studied weapons, using, in English and Arabic, Dari, Pashto, Tajik, Urdu, and Uzbek translations, manuals from the American Army, Marines, and Special Forces and even articles from American hunting magazines. In the afternoon the Qaedas studied the Koran. They weren't taught *Right shoulder arms*, but to A, B, and C's common question of "Why were they such fierce enemies?" the Misfits found a troublesome answer. It simply is this: "We were good soldiers. And they were good soldiers, too."

Epilogue

In April the division comes home to the Adirondacks. Three boys have died, none of them in Afghanistan, remarkably. Two were killed by errant artillery rounds as they breakfasted in the Adirondacks, and one committed suicide in Uzbekistan. Another division, the 101st, from Kentucky, also fought in Anaconda. So did the Special Forces, and eight of its soldiers died. One fell from a Chinook as Mahmuti and his platoon dug Ranger graves miles away, and six boys died while trying to rescue him. Another boy died in a Qaeda ambush.

Uninjured, undead, are all the Osama-stalking soldiers of Company A. They didn't catch him, but they neutralized his caves, bunkers, camps in Afghanistan, Osama becoming an impotent individual alive (or, who could disprove it? dead) in God knows where and God doesn't care. Of the Andrews, Simmons is single, but Starlin comes home to his second son, twenty ruddy inches long and one day old. His son says, "*Wah*," and Starlin says, "Wow," astonished at this little human being, a boy who, thanks to Starlin's army, surely won't die in an unprovoked holocaust, as a two-year-old did last September in the Center's south tower.

Also uninjured, undead, are the Qaeda killers of Company B. Mahmuti comes home to Paterson to a couple of younger cousins who ask him, "Did you kill anyone?" and he answers, "No." Fuentes, Mahmuti's eagle-eyed sergeant, comes home to the Aztec reservation near San Antonio, the warriors all racing barebacked horses and, in red-, white-, blue-, and green-beaded moccasins, dancing to the sun and the moon, the bells on their ankles tinkling.

Undead, thanks to Rivera, and still in Company C are Horn, Miranda, Abbott, McCleave, Almey, and Stanton, one hugging him and one patting him as Rivera receives the army commendation medal with a V for valor, but McGovern (two toes lost) and Wurtz still aren't back. Rivera comes home to Krystal's new many-mirrored apartment close by in Liverpool, New York. He buys her a half-carat diamond ring. One night, lying together, his fingers exploring her eyelids, eyebrows, hair, as if he's just discovered them on Jupiter, he tells her the ultimate truth of Operation Anaconda. "I love you, Krystal. But also," Rivera says, "I love those guys. So much that I might have died for 'em. Even those guys in cowboy hats and big-buckled belts, I *love* 'em. I don' listen to country music with 'em. I don' do the two-step with 'em. But when they cry, 'Doc!' I run like they're my own brothers. Because they are."

And crying, Krystal, a medic herself, says, "I understand."

The Make-Believe War

by Evan Wright

Evan Wright covered the war in Afghanistan for Rolling Stone. *This article ran in the August 8, 2002 issue.*

Operation Cherokee Sky begins after dark on June 29th when a Canadian reconnaissance or "reccy" platoon departs Kandahar Air Field in southern Afghanistan. About a dozen troops aboard Toyota 4x4s set out on the seventy-five-mile journey to the town of Qalat, in the east, believed to be a secret Taliban stronghold. The reccy platoon's job is to drive into the mountains north of the town and scout landing zones for a helicopter assault on two caves, dubbed "Big-Ass Cave" and "Smaller-Ass Cave" by operation planners.

Next morning at about eight Zulu (military time), a fifty-vehicle armored column assembles outside the gates of the airfield. Its job is to drive to Qalat and then encircle a medieval fortress that intelligence analysts believe is being used as a Taliban staging area. From there, the column is to swing forty miles south and sweep through a village where Taliban forces reportedly held a conference a week earlier, which ended with them rampaging through the countryside, burning a school and shooting villagers, killing at least one. About 500 Canadians are slated for this mission. One hundred Americans are also involved, serving as helicopter crews, in Air Force Special Operations ground teams and in Special Forces, whose behind-the-scenes role is to control the entire operation.

Before the Canadians depart in their armored column on the morning of June 30th, they crowd onto a dusty spit of land for an address from their commander, Lt. Col. Patrick Stogran. He stands on a pile of dirt atop a bunker and tells his troops not to fear the enemy. "If they fuck with us, the wrath of hell on earth will be upon them," he says. "The fury of hell is 500 men in green baggy suits," referring to the forest-green combat uniforms worn by the Canadians. These seem out of place in the tawny deserts of Afghanistan and are being worn only because of a massive screw-up back in Ottawa. They are extremely uncomfortable and as such have become both a joke and a symbol of the toughness of the soldiers who wear them. Playing on this theme, Stogran continues, "If they go to hell, I want visions of green demons to be the last thing they see."

Stogran is a lean, handsomely weathered forty-three-year-old who in his dress uniform and dark-green beret bears a passing resemblance to famed British World War II Gen. Bernard Law Montgomery. Stogran is something of a character at Kandahar Air Field, where the main Canadian force in Afghanistan is posted. In briefing sessions, he jokingly refers to the Taliban enemy as "heathens." At the same time, he carries Muslim prayer beads given to him "by a mujahedin friend." When the Canadians held a tough-man fighting contest in early June, Stogran entered and took on his deputy commanding officer, a beefy man at least fifty pounds heavier. Spectators claim the vastly outmuscled Stogran attempted to cheat by kicking the deputy CO outside the ring during a timeout (still, the colonel lost). Stogran's flair for the dramatic is tempered by his directness and sincerity. In April, after four of his soldiers were killed and eight seriously wounded in an accidental bombing by the U.S. Air Force, he sat in the scarred rose garden out-side his office and cried.

Despite his grief over that loss, Stogran does not hide the excite-ment he feels at commanding an army during war. When I run into him a few nights before the launch of Cherokee Sky, he expresses regret that this will be the Canadians' final mission before going home at the end of July. "When I came home after Bosnia," he says, referring to the peacekeeping mission the Canadians have maintained in the bloody former Yugoslav republic since the mid 1990s, "civilized life seemed almost boring." He smiles. "There's something to be said about living in a place of total lawlessness and anarchy. You never know what's going to happen."

The 850-member Canadian regiment, which arrived in Kandahar in January, was involved in two major operations before Cherokee Sky. But its ambition to prove itself in combat has been thwarted by faulty intelligence assessments of where the enemy is actually located. "I thought Tora Bora was going to be something magical," Stogran says, referring to the massive hunt for al Qaeda in the caves of southern Afghanistan in January. "But in the end it was far less than we had expected. It was the same in Anaconda. We expected to find hundreds of enemy fighters. We probably encountered twenty-five."

Few American officers will speak as candidly about unmet objec-tives in Afghanistan. The last major operation prior to Cherokee Sky, the American-led Apache Snow II, entailed a massive helicopter assault on two villages north of the Pakistani border in early June. It took ten days of planning, 200 American soldiers and more than a dozen heli-copters and fighters to capture a few hundred dollars' worth of cor-roded ammunition and weapons.

The main armored column departs Kandahar at ten Zulu on the 30th. The road, optimistically referred to as "Highway One" on Coalition maps, is littered with blown-up fuel trucks, bomb craters and col-lapsed bridges. About twenty miles east of Kandahar, it starts to degen-erate into a single narrow, rutted lane. The column includes seventeen eight-wheeled Canadian armored vehicles—Bisons or Coyotes—and about a dozen American Humvees outfitted with anti-tank missiles and automatic grenade launchers. The remaining twenty-five or so vehicles are fuel and transport trucks. Overhead, Apache Attack helicopters fly air support.

In pre-mission briefings, the governor of Qalat, Hamidullah Tokhi Khan, was portrayed as an active Taliban supporter masquerading as a U.S. ally. During a slide presentation in the briefing room, Khan's name was projected on the wall beneath a warning in bold red letters, THIS GUY IS NOT TO BE TRUSTED. Cherokee Sky's mission was to surround Khan's fort, outside of Qalat, where 300 of his soldiers maintained a garrison. Stogran would then stride up to the fort's gate and demand entry.

"We know there are bad guys in there," Stogran said at the briefing. "We can expect resistance." Following an expected confrontation and possible exchange of gunfire with the fort's gatekeepers, Coalition troops would enter and conduct a room-to-room search, detaining and frisking each of the fort's occupants and arresting those believed to be Taliban.

But in the last hours before the mission starts, everything changes. During the final briefing, an American Special Forces soldier with the code name Coyote interrupts Stogran to announce a new plan. Coyote says that his men have delivered a letter to a close ally of Khan's, warning the warlord that Coalition forces will be coming to his province. Furthermore, Coyote explains that an SF team will be entering the fortress and meeting with Khan hours in advance of the Canadian armored column.

Stogran shows no reaction to the news that his surprise siege has been scuttled. Without missing a beat, he says, "Then I intend to walk in solo to the fort and do some handshaking and backslapping." Still hopeful that even his announced arrival might provoke a confrontation, he adds, "What we will do next will be determined by my pucker factor"—"pucker factor" being military slang for "ass-puckering fear," the instinct a soldier has to either stay, fight or flee. Coyote interrupts again, telling the colonel that he won't actually be walking into the fort. "Our guys are now planning to have Governor Khan send some guys to meet you outside the fort."

But even this plan falls apart within hours of the mission's departure. Soon after the convoy leaves, a fuel trailer bursts into flames because of the desert heat. Another breaks an axle. Due to the dust and mountainous terrain, radios in the vehicles cease operating beyond a three-mile range. The road is jammed with traffic—trucks carrying fuel and tires from Pakistan and cars filled with returning refugees, their roofs stacked five feet high with bags and bird cages. (Afghans, even in the worst poverty, have a mania for keeping songbirds.) U.S. intelligence analysts estimated that the ride would take four hours. Nearly nine hours after we began, we reach the fortress at Qalat.

By the time we arrive, we learn from radio chatter that "Sunray"—Stogran's call sign—has been greeted warmly at the fort by Khan. Stogran's troops, frustrated that their showdown with the Taliban has turned into a meet-and-greet, speculate sardonically on their commander's fate. "Sunray is staying inside the fort," says a voice over the radio. Somewhere in the darkness, another Canadian voice calls out, "You think they're raping Sunray yet on the hood of one of their trucks, eh?"

The governor, suddenly a friend of the Coalition, has invited us to camp that night outside his mansion in a desert plain above town. We drive several more miles before reaching a barren field in front of Gov. Khan's walled compound, which is about half the size of a WalMart. We circle the armored vehicles, post watches and sleep for three hours, then wake before dawn to rendezvous with a helicopter air assault on mountain caves forty-five minutes to the north.

Just before sunrise, the seventeen Bisons and Coyotes form a ring around a mountain dubbed "Objective North." The idea is to cut off any Taliban fleeing Big-Ass and Smaller-Ass caves, which are at this moment being invaded by 200 Canadian troops dropped in by choppers. The first Apache escorts appear overhead just as a shepherd leads a flock of sheep across the desert to a well.

But the caves turn out to contain nothing more than bat droppings. Over the radio, someone asks permission to blow up Big-Ass Cave "to deny the enemy a hiding place," though you get the idea it would also be a fun thing to do for bored soldiers with plenty of Gq explosive. The request is denied due to the fear that destroying Big-Ass might bring down an entire side of the mountain and wipe out other caves thought to contain primitive wall drawings. "It's not good if we blow up cultural stuff," our Bison commander says, just the faintest hint of disappointment in his voice.

After this operation sputters out, we pick up a U.S. Air Force two-man Special Operations team, who go by the names Dragon-1 and Dragon-6. They pile into the Bison, greeting the Canadians with warm handshakes. Special Operations soldiers annoy just about everyone in the regular Army because they tend to have the most up-to-date weapons and gizmos and get to accessorize their fatigues with cool add-ons such as exotic hiking gear and colorful local garb. Dragons 1 and 6 wear the latest Patagonia "wicking fabric" shirts and Arab head scarves and smell of coconut suntan lotion. Both are covered in grime from their adventure on the mountain—they had explored all the caves on their own, hours before the air assault—but both are handsome enough to be Abercrombie & Fitch models, dirtied up by makeup artists for an ad campaign.

The Canadians receive the young Americans with icy politeness. Gradually, though, the twin Dragons, who are so damned friendly, win the Canadians over. Dragon-6, who describes himself as "almost twenty-six years old," passes the time chattering about his favorite motorcycles back home and their relative merits in picking up girls at the mall—"Pull up in a Buell and chicks just slide onto your seat." Then he switches subjects to a vacation he took last summer in Germany. "I thought about hitchhiking," he says. "But my mom worried that it was too dangerous, so I rented a car."

Inside Khan's fort, about fifty Canadian and American soldiers have set up a camp, where they have been sleeping for the two nights since the operation began. At the outset of Cherokee Sky, the plan had been to surround, search and possibly arrest the 300 or so troops in this fort. Now, Coalition soldiers mingle guardedly with Khan's men, barefoot solders armed with AKs. Many paint their lids with black kohl eyeliner, a fashion once popular among the Taliban.

U.S. Sgt. Maj. Iuniasolua Savusa stands near a camo net strung up by the Coalition encampment. "Can you believe this place?" he asks. The fort is known to have existed since at least medieval times. Some speculate the place had been a fort since Alexander the Great moved his army through here more than 2,000 years ago.

But it isn't so much history that permeates the place as it is the smell of human feces. Khan's 300 men utilize every spare inch of dirt as an open-air toilet. In some places, dried excrement is piled six inches deep.

"My first night here," says a Canadian sergeant, "I woke up with a fucking turd next to my head."

"I don't blame Alexander the Great or Genghis Khan, whoever the hell it was, for getting the fuck out of here," says Savusa, spitting tobacco juice into the dust. "I hope we do the same."

Unlike the rest of the men, Lt. Col. Stogran is in high spirits. He stands in an impromptu command tent set up with wall-size maps and computers, about to make an announcement.

"We are going to air-assault the mountains around the village of Shinkay," he tells the assembled commanders. "We are sending our armored squadron down tonight to block exits from Shinkay. Governor Khan has agreed to provide soldiers to sweep the village."

After marathon meetings with Khan during the previous thirty-six hours, the warlord has now denounced the Taliban and declared his undying loyalty to the Coalition cause. In a few hours, Khan says, 200 of his own troops will go door-to-door in Shinkay, rounding up traitors.

Col. Mike Linnington, the American commander in Kandahar, cinched the deal when he flew in and presented Khan with a gift bowie knife inscribed with the logo of the toast Airborne Division. Through a translator, Col. Linnington explained that Jim Bowie had been an American hero who died at the Alamo in Texas, the home

state of President Bush. According to witnesses, the story had been gar-
bled in translation and Khan believed the knife was a gift from Bush
himself. No one tried to dissuade him. Laughing about the meeting a
few days later, Linnington tells a reporter, "Boy, I was good. I bull-
shitted that bastard left and right."

The final pre-raid meeting with Gov. Khan takes place later that
evening. Stogran, accompanied by a translator, the U.S. Special Forces
soldier Coyote and a handful of other SF, meet the warlord in a carpet-
lined room in his mansion. Khan, a potbellied man in his late thirties,
greets the Coalition emissaries warmly. The room smells of fresh paint.

Coyote does most of the talking for the Coalition side. "How many
soldiers are you giving us for this mission?" he asks.

"I will prepare fifty mujahedin for the assault," Khan says through
the translator. "Thirty of these come from my personal guard." It's far
fewer than the 200 men promised by the governor earlier in the day,
but he vows, "The enemy cannot escape from us. I will give you my
best commander; he will go with you because he is so smart and
knows the district so well."

Coyote thanks him profusely.

"If one American is shot," Khan swears, "five of my men will be shot."

He promises Stogran that his soldiers will turn up three prominent Taliban leaders in Shinkay. Stogran seems happy to believe this
prediction.

"Shinkay offers the possibility of excitement," he says.

Our armored column rumbles into action four hours before sunrise. In
central Qalat, we stop to pick up a passenger, an SF soldier who goes
by the nickname Halo. SF function in twelve-man teams called Operational Detachment Alphas. They display a swaggering, almost reckless
sense of humor and function as a law unto themselves. Some ODA
teams are rumored to have adopted all of the customs common
among Afghan soldiers, including the constant smoking of hash. One
ODA team I encounter pulls me aside, laughing hysterically at what
they call my "Rolling Stoned" press card. "Rolling Stoned will love

this!" a soldier who calls himself Padre says, pulling out his digital camera. "It's the best cache we've found so far in Afghanistan." Given his weirdly excited laughter, I half-expect to see photos of ear necklaces or some similar forbidden war trophies. Instead of trophy ears, however, he scrolls through the images until he finds several showing teammates holding wet, sticky buds of marijuana.

"Howdy!" Halo shouts to the half-dozen guys in the back of the vehicle once he's aboard. Without waiting for a response, he launches into a monologue about the woes of Afghanistan. "Did you know there's water everywhere here? It runs in underground rivers just beneath the surface of the desert. Problem is Afghans don't even know how to drill a well. They dig wells by hammering pipes directly into the ground. They don't understand the concept of drilling. But that's what happens when your whole country's illiterate, and if they can read, the only book they know is the Koran. They'd rather just run around in their little man jammies"—his word for Afghan native dress—"shooting each other."

Halo who is thirty-six years old, resembles the comedian Chris Elliott on steroids, and like a comic character, his taunting cheerfulness seems a thin disguise for his anti-social tendencies. Still, he seems to be having a good time in Afghanistan.

"You should see these guys try to shoot their guns," he says, laughing. "They don't even aim. A lot of them saw the stocks off their AKs because they think it looks neat. Without the stock, an AK shoots gas out the back. The only way to fire it is to hold it out and spray. They're lucky if they hit you at twenty meters. We hit 'em with ambushes at 300 meters with a sniper rifle with a silencer. All you see is one guy slump over. His buddy stands up to see what's going on, we take him out. We've taken out five guys before the rest realize we're killing 'em all."

The convoy grinds to a halt. We're now in a mountain pass—part of an old smuggler's route to Pakistan—and it's impossible to see why the lead vehicle has stopped. "It's a fork in the road," Halo says confidently. "Afghans—at least here in the south—will always stop at a fork in the road. Even if they've been down it a hundred times before, they'll have to debate about it."

As if on cue, a voice comes over the radio saying that we're stopped because Khan's soldiers can't decide which fork to take in the trail. Halo slumps against the side of the vehicle.

The convoy resumes its march haltingly, stopping for a few more forks. The third time, several of the trucks turn off their engines. One of Khan's soldiers walks down the line of vehicles, stopping at each, gesturing wildly.

Halo points to him and says, "That's Khan's commander. He's really just someone's brother-in-law." The commander draws near. "This man has a barely functional relationship with reality," Halo says. "See that watch on his wrist? That's a joke. He doesn't even know how to tell time. I've asked him what time it is, he can't tell you—his watch is upside down."

Khan's commander is asking occupants of each vehicle if they have any spare AA batteries, which are prized commodities in these parts. For the next twenty minutes the Afghan troops refuse to budge until finally we hand over batteries.

The original plan called for the armored column to take up positions behind the village of Shinkay under cover of darkness. Then, Canadian troops would drop into the mountain passes, blocking the retreat of Taliban soldiers flushed out in the door-to-door sweep conducted by Khan's soldiers. But Khan's men couldn't locate the route behind the village, and so we roll into the Shinkay valley long past sunrise. Given our lateness, Stogran orders the column to drive straight through the town.

We enter the first narrow opening in the outer wall of Shinkay just as the helicopters swoop in over the horizon. Children rush out onto rooftops. Women peek out of doors, crying. Some kids cover their eyes in fear. Our engines throw up a horrible racket as we squeeze into the narrow, high-walled streets. When we reach the western gate of the village, our Bison sets up a blocking action. We're joined by two Toyotas full of Khan's troops.

"This is going to be a dry well," Halo says. "Khan's troops aren't going to do anything."

As he speaks, several of Khan's soldiers descend from the trucks and crawl beneath them to nap in the shade.

"Khan really doesn't want to help us," Halo says. "See, two weeks ago our ODA first visited Khan. We told him if he didn't go along with us, we were going to kill him. Simple as that. He's going along with us now, but he's afraid to take on the Taliban here."

Halo climbs down from the truck to consult with his SF comrade Coyote. Several local elders appear bearing cups of hot chai tea to offer the foreign occupiers. Coyote, Halo, a translator and a portly village elder gather behind the Bison. Through the translator, the elder thanks the coalition soldiers for visiting his village.

"I've heard it all before," Halo says. "He's going to tell us the bad guys left town. They always say the same thing."

The old man stops speaking and shoots Halo a look. The translator says, "There was a bad man here three weeks ago, but he left on his motorcycle to a different village east of here."

Stogran scrubs the entire mission a couple hours later, and we withdraw from Shinkay without conducting a search. "I thought Khan's men were going to search specific locations in town," Stogran says, "but when I asked the commander about this, he looked at me, confused. He said, 'But the Taliban are over there.' He pointed east. Perhaps the problem had something to do with the commander's obvious inability to read a map."

On the long ride back to Qalat, Halo says, "We are going to talk to Khan tonight. He's got to give us something, or else we'll have to renew our offer to kill him."

Next morning, outside Khan's mansion, the warlord's commander leads a small caravan of Toyotas stacked with crates containing surface-to-air missiles—an arms cache they turn over to the Coalition as a show of good faith. In the wrong hands, the missiles could easily be used to shoot down Coalition jets or passenger liners. Twenty-six of the missiles are Russian SA-7s or Pakistani knockoffs. Three are British-made

Blowpipe missiles, precursor to the American Stinger. These are marked as having been manufactured in 1984—about the time the CIA's program to arm Afghanistan in its fight against the Soviets was hitting its stride.

A journalist from a wire service walks down to the area where the missile boxes were unloaded. "This arms cache was discovered as a result of the successful Coalition mission in this area," Halo tells the reporter. It's another victory in the war on terrorism.

Not Much War, but Plenty of Hell
by Evan Wright

The initial stages of the war in Afghanistan soon gave way to a different kind of struggle. This article appeared in Rolling Stone (July 25, 2002).

To the soldiers of the Fifth Platoon Delta Company living at Kandahar Airfield, deep in the former Taliban stronghold of southeastern Afghanistan, dawn breaks each morning with a horrible stench. Their tent is located at the southernmost end of the airfield, not far from the "shit lagoon"—the canal where all the excrement from the camp's 5,000-plus inhabitants is dumped every day. Temperatures in Kandahar soar to more than 125 degrees, and the first hot winds of the morning bear an overwhelming smell of raw sewage, spiced with the odor of disinfectant from the latrines outside the tent, not to mention occasional gusts of diesel fuel blowing off the line of helicopters on the nearby runway. Sitting on the edge of his cot, twenty-year-old Pvt. Joshua Farrar, a former surfer from South Florida, shakes a Newport out of a dust-covered pack, surveys his fellow soldiers getting up to face another day in Afghanistan and concludes, "This all sucks."

The Fifth Platoon Delta are air-assault infantry attached to the 3-187th Battalion, America's main combat force in southeastern Afghanistan. Their job is to fly into battle on helicopters, rappel down from ropes, and blow the crap out of tanks, fortifications and the enemy. But in Afghanistan the soldiers have been thrust into an ill-defined role. They mount round-the-clock combat recon patrols through former Taliban villages in the Kandahar desert. But the shooting has stopped for the most part, and now the soldiers are called on to enforce a shaky peace while serving as America's ambassadors of good will in what remains a lethal land.

As they prepare for their patrol, Farrar and a couple of the other gunners stand on top of two Humvees to mount machine guns in the turrets. Lt. Donato D'Angelo Jr., a twenty-six-year-old from Ramsey, New Jersey, leans on some sandbags outside, studying a plastic-encased patrol map.

The first thing you notice about D'Angelo, the platoon leader of Five Delta, is his physical power. He is about five feet eleven and weighs 195 pounds, with much of that weight carried in his shoulders and massive biceps. A week ago, he set a regimental record in Kandahar for his weight class by bench-pressing 325 pounds. D'Angelo played soccer at West Point, boxed for three years and completed Army Ranger school, during which he survived a lightning strike that killed the man next to him.

"Today," he says, "we will drive through some minefields and drink tea with village elders." He looks up with a sort of grin or snarl. It's tough to tell. D'Angelo is the son of first-generation Italian immigrants. "I'm like the black sheep of the family for being in the Army," he says. "My brother's twenty-three. He's a bond trader in Manhattan, making $120,000 a year, and I'm making $35,000 living in a tent in Afghanistan with fourteen other guys."

"Step aside, sir!" a soldier shouts. "Dust devil coming." From across the parking lot, a brown cyclone whips up from behind a row of por-tajohns; D'Angelo steps back five paces while the funnel slips by. "You get used to the dust here after a while," he says. Most afternoons, forty-mile-an-hour winds kick up dust storms that blow into the air-field like a thick fog, reducing visibility to a few yards.

"Do people at home still care about the job we're doing over here?" D'Angelo asks. He speaks softly, but emphasizes every syllable, as if laboring to make himself absolutely clear, just in case you happen to be a dumb fuck. "Are they still patriotic and all that, or have they forgotten about us?"

D'Angelo spits a thick stream of brown juice and adds, "You know, I took it kind of personally when the Towers fell. That was my back yard. To say I wanted to put my life on the line for America is too abstract. I came to Afghanistan to protect my mother, my sister and my little brother."

There are about 4,000 soldiers based at Kandahar Airfield, as well as an additional 1,000 coalition soldiers, most of them Canadian. The three-square-mile encampment at the base, seized from Taliban control last year, is the one piece of land in southeastern Afghanistan the United States controls absolutely. The barbed-wire perimeter is heavily forti-fied with machine-gun nests, bunkers and guard towers. Of all the per-sonnel stationed here, less than 1,000 are actual infantry soldiers. The rest serve various support roles—truck drivers, computer technicians, inventory accountants—and this is the only Afghan soil they will ever set foot on.

In the six months since the Americans took over, Kandahar Airfield has gone from a mine-strewn ruin to a makeshift thriving city. Life inside the wire has its own peculiar rhythms. Americans at the camp inhabit their own time zone—the Pentagon's worldwide standard, known as Zulu Time, which is four and one-half hours behind local time, meaning dawn breaks at about 12:30 a.m.

At this hour, the bombs usually start going off as part of the work done by the ordnance removal teams, and you begin to see early-morning fitness nuts jogging, toting grenade launchers and pistols—everyone is required to carry their weapons at all times. By 4 a.m. Zulu, the local Afghan workers show up, including a team of former mercenaries supplied by the local warlord, who tend the old rose garden outside the terminal while armed guards keep a watchful eye, lest one decide to hide a bomb in the bushes. All day long, huge C-130 and C-17 transport planes disgorge steel shipping containers and mountains of supplies. (It takes two daily C-130 flights alone to keep the PX stocked with items like chips and salsa, Eminem CDs and thousands of cans of warm soda.) At two in the afternoon, when the sun starts to set in Zulu Time, officers hack golf balls at a primitive driving range built on the threshold of an old minefield. At about three in the afternoon Zulu, soldiers begin to crowd the "morale, welfare, recreation" (MWR) tents to phone home and watch the shows *The West Wing* and *Fear Factor* on big-screen TVs. Then, at about 6 p.m. Zulu, they hit their tents, where they are rocked to sleep by the thunder of mortar barrages from night maneuvers on the near practice range.

Despite efforts to offer the comforts of home, life at the camp is mighty unpleasant. The food is awful—a combination of premanufactured T-rations and MREs (meals ready to eat). Temperatures inside the tents hit 130 degrees in the day, the portajohns are foul and beastly hot, dust sifts into clothes and sleeping bags, and showers are available for only limited use. Add to that constant bouts of dysentery and the ever present threat of rocket attacks—none successful so far—and you can understand why the soldiers have bitterly dubbed the post "Ass-Crack-istan."

Among the stringencies the soldiers complain about most is General Order Number One, which bans possession or consumption of alcoholic beverages by U.S. soldiers in Afghanistan. "There's a way around everything," says one enlisted soldier. "Some of the guys like to huff," he says, referring to the tried-and-true brain-frying high of sniffing inhalants. "I was against it at first, but we got a good high from Glade."

Sexual relations are banned on the base, but stories of forbidden conduct abound. In April, an Apache attack-helicopter crew, monitoring the camp through night-vision equipment, picked up a couple having sex in a vehicle. And several women have been flown home after it was discovered they were pregnant. Assignations are not unknown at a place dubbed "Terrorist Terrace"—a blown-up bunker at the south end of the airfield. "I hooked up with an enlisted girl at the MWR tent," says a young officer. "We borrowed a Humvee and drove out to Terrorist Terrace. We'd never met before. We talked for a few minutes, and I said, 'Listen, do you want to fuck?' And she said, 'Um, OK.' When I came back and laid down in my tent with her gunk all over my dick, I knew I had done a bad thing. Then I thought, 'I can't believe it. I just got laid in Afghanistan.' "

The Fifth Platoon go by a roguish call sign. Over the radio they are the Hell Hounds of the Tank Killer Company Wolf Pack, or Wolf Pack Five for short. But, gathering in their tent in the final hour before their patrol, they look more like a smalltown baseball team than combat soldiers. The youngest is nineteen, and most of the rest are in their early twenties. The oldest, Platoon Sgt. Patrick Keough, is a thirty-six-year-old father of two. Despite the mad tattoos many display on their backs and arms, the bunch still give the impression of hometown innocence—one that is reinforced by frequent proclamations of how much they all care about one another. "All of us are brothers," says Pfc. Andrew Wiser, a twenty-year-old from Conneaut, Ohio. "I'd die for any of these guys." Their intense feeling for one another results in an almost naive faith. "Nothing bad is going to happen to any of us in Afghanistan," Wiser says. "We'll do anything it takes to look out for each other."

Wolf Pack Five showed up in Kandahar last March, ready for battle. "I expected to start shooting as soon as we stepped off the plane," says platoon section leader Sgt. Paul Quast, a beefy thirty-four-year-old with a shaved head and hard, deep-set blue eyes. Some of the soldiers, like Pfc. William Ballard, have been disappointed by the lack of action. A slender, soft-spoken, squinty nineteen-year-old, Ballard says, "I thought there'd be more war in Afghanistan, more like Vietnam." When he came to Afghanistan, Ballard brought along a custom sniper scope for his M-203 weapon—a combination grenade launcher and assault rifle—telling Keough he needed it to "shoot Afghans." Keough made him send it home to his father in Reno, Nevada.

The Fifth Platoon's only glimpse into the horrors of war occurred early on the morning of April 18th, when they pulled guard on the gunnery range—"Osama House"—after four Canadian soldiers, serving as part of the U.S.-led coalition, were killed in a friendly-fire accident. It happened at about midnight when an overzealous American F-16 pilot dropped a 500-pound bomb on the Canadians, mistaking their gunnery practice as hostile fire. "I saw a torso," says Farrar, who spent a whole day with the platoon guarding the accident site. "That was enough."

Farrar, fair-haired and a lanky six feet one, moves with a slowness that's both lazy and deliberate, and says he joined the Army to get money for college. "I never thought there was going to be a war," he says. "There were guys at Fort Campbell who squirmed out before we deployed—like a kid who developed 'dizzy spells.' I thought of doing that, but fuck it." Farrar holds an unusual position in the platoon. His superiors consider him one of the platoon's best soldiers, but he is also the lowest-ranked. About a week after he arrived, he was busted down two ranks to buck private when an infraction he'd committed back at Fort Campbell, Kentucky, caught up with him. Farrar is sketchy about the details but allows it had something to do with a urine test. (Bad luck seems to dog Farrar. On a recent mail call, while his buddies opened letters and boxes of cookies from home, Farrar received a parking ticket. "This girl didn't write me for three weeks," he says. "I told her to pack her shit and get the fuck out of my house. Now she's got my car.")

At about 0600, the platoon strap on about sixty pounds of protective gear and equipment apiece and climb into three Humvees. They drive out the front gate of the American camp and go less than a mile, to a former Taliban command post surrounded by fourteen-foot-high mudbrick walls, that belongs to America's ally in Kandahar, an army called the Anti-Taliban Forces.

The Fifth Platoon stay here for days at a time while running patrols, sleeping in beat-up Marine Corps pup tents set up in a dusty field opposite the ATF command post. Pulling into the fort, the men scramble out of the Humvees and make for the tents, each racing to find one that has the fewest rips and, ideally, zippers that work. You would think staying in the fort would be a hardship duty, but spirits are high. Spc. Armando Ramos, a twenty-year-old from Bakersfield, California, who has a three-year-old daughter back home, says, "Dude, this is the only place where we have the privacy to jack off."

Farrar groans, "I am so sick of beating off." Ramos adds, "I see a stick figure of a naked chick someone drew in the latrines, and I'm ready to go."

Before the first patrol, D'Angelo assembles the men for a briefing held beneath a parachute strung up in a corner of the walled fortress for shade. Once they sit down, D'Angelo turns to the new guy, Pvt. Jason Swinehart, a nineteen-year-old former high school football player from Ohio who arrived in Afghanistan only five days ago, his bag packed with George Strait and Kenny Chesney CDs.

"Private Swinehart, where are we?"

Swinehart looks around, grins, turns red. "I don't know, sir."

"We are outside the wire," D'Angelo says in his most patient, speaking-to-a-dumb-fuck voice. The Kandahar desert is basically one vast, unmarked minefield. Three ATF soldiers were killed several weeks earlier when their Toyota pickup hit a mine less than a mile from the ATF fort. Two more died in a mine blast just beyond the perimeter of the air base. The American and coalition soldiers have been luckier. In April, a Canadian patrol hit a mine, but they were in an armored vehicle and no one was hurt. D'Angelo turns to Swinehart again. "What do the occupants of the lead vehicle do if they hit a mine?"

Swinehart sweats it a moment, squeezing his eyes shut in deep thought, then answers: "Everyone exits through the hatch, sir?"

"Very good, Swinehart," D'Angelo says. Swinehart's ability to quickly adapt to conditions in Afghanistan proves one of D'Angelo's pet theories about young soldiers: It's easier to train the ones who don't have a lot of education. "See," D'Angelo explains as the men start getting into the trucks, "if you took a nineteen-year-old philosophy major in college and gave him Swinehart's job, that guy wouldn't know what to do. We put Swinehart on top of the truck with a machine gun in his hands and drive him into a village where people have their own personal weapons—shotguns, AKs—and they start waving them around." D'Angelo spits a long stream of black Copenhagen juice into the dust. "What do you do if you're Swinehart? We have very simple rules: You don't shoot unless he aims a weapon at you. I trust a guy like Swinehart to follow the rules. If you put that machine gun in the hands of a nineteen-year-old philosophy major, he might think too much. We don't want that. In the Army, everything is decided for you. Just follow the rules."

Sgt. Quast, the thirty-four-year-old platoon staff sergeant, leads the initial patrol of the day from the first Humvee. A second Humvee follows about seventy-five yards behind. The basic crew of each consists of the driver, the turret gunner and the TC (truck commander), who also operates the radio. The patrols also include an ATF translator and a medic. For several days the soldiers have been excited about the prospect of driving new "up-armored" Humvees recently shipped in from the States. Up to now, patrols were conducted in conventional thin-skin vehicles providing little protection against land mines. The new Humvees are fitted with 3,500 pounds of armor protection. But it's not the safety features that have the men talking; it's the fact that these new vehicles are rumored to have air conditioning. All morning, Ramos has been repeating, "Dude, we're gonna be cruising in the up-armors with the AC on full, windows all up and shit."

The AC unit blasts with the noise and ferocity of a leaf blower, but hot air and dust pour in as usual through the open roof hatch where the gunner stands. The added armor interferes with the global-positioning-navigation unit, called a Plugger. The TCs now have to hold the Plugger about two feet out the window for it to operate.

There are other problems. The secure radios mounted in the Humvees cease to work once they get a few miles into the desert. So in order to communicate with one another, the soldiers ask friends and relatives to send seventy-dollar Motorola walkie-talkies you can buy at any WalMart in the States. "The Army issues us its own walkabouts," says Quast. "But they don't work worth shit."

One of the ATF translators has told the soldiers that there is a McDonald's in downtown Kandahar. It's nothing but a cruel joke, but since no one in the Fifth Platoon has ever seen Kandahar—a war-torn city of medieval bazaars and dirt roads clogged with donkeys and chickens—they have no reason to disbelieve the report. "What we ought to do," says Quast, straining to see the trail ahead through the vehicle's two-inch-thick armor windows, "is send one of the ATF guys into Kandahar and do a run on the McDonald's."

He shouts up to the turret. "You hear that, Swinehart?"

Swinehart leans down, hands still on the machine gun. "Yeah!" he shouts. "Get me Supersize everything!"

The desert is littered with the silver hulls of Russian fighter planes, wrecked tanks and missile trucks. Mosques, old Soviet barracks and schools lie in ruins everywhere. You can tell who blew up what by the style of destruction. Russians and warring Afghans flatten structures and whole villages through massive artillery and aerial bombardment. Buildings hit by the U.S. Air Force tend to have one neat blast down the center, leaving the four corners standing.

The destination for Quast's patrol is the village of Mowmand, about seven miles up a dry riverbed. Homes in Kandahar villages are made of mud brick and stucco, shaped like beehives and nestled between a maze of walls the color of the dust that blows in the wind. The land strikes the Americans as so alien that some have nicknamed it Tatooine, after the planet of mud-hut villages in the *Star Wars* movies. The soldiers call Afghans "Habib," similar to the way "Charlie" was used to describe friend and foe in Vietnam. They goof on Pashto, imitating it with the sound "abadabadaba." But their attitude toward the people is more complex and decent than their prankish humor might indicate. American soldiers are more willing than other coalition forces in Kandahar to mix with the locals. Canadian recon units, which conduct their patrols in tank-like armored vehicles, seldom stop unless by prearranged plan. Master Cpl. Steve Marty, a soldier in a Canadian patrol unit, says, "We know what they did to the Russians. They'd invite them in and give them food laced with hepatitis. The Afghans in the villages still have all their weapons. If we got into a fight, it would be six of us against a whole village. We don't stop unless we have to."

The soldiers in the Fifth, many of whom share dog-eared histories of the Russian defeat in Afghanistan, are as aware as anyone else of the dangers posed by the villages they patrol, but their wariness is tempered by the particularly American faith, bordering on naivete, that most people can be brought around if, as Quast says, "you treat them with respect and dignity.

"First time we came to one village, the Canadians had been patrolling before us," says Quast. "A man hopped out on one leg, giving us the finger. Kids came out with rocks. Our gunner locked and loaded the .50-cal on a little kid who was aiming to hit him with a rock from a slingshot." The soldiers defused the tense situation by taking a direct approach. "We had our translator ask what they were so mad about. Turns out the patrols had been speeding through the village, kicking up dust, waking everyone up." The Fifth Platoon promised to drive more slowly through the village.

The Humvees stop about seventy-five yards from Mowmand's outermost wall. While Farrar and Swinehart remain in the gun turrets of each Humvee, Quast steps out of the lead vehicle. Following procedure, he will stay here and send in a couple of soldiers to make contact with a village elder. Sgt. Jeremy Ludweg, 24, from Louisville, Kentucky, will go on, along with the ATF translator and a soft-spoken twenty-four-year-old art-school dropout from Detroit, Spc. Sean "Doc" Murphy, the platoon medic.

Murphy normally doesn't tell villagers he is a medic. "I don't have enough supplies for villagers," he says. But during a previous patrol, a man who lives outside the village invited Murphy into his house, telling him his children were sick. At first, Murphy kept quiet, but then the man's daughters came into the room. Their hair had fallen out, and their scalps were bleeding. "They just needed some iodine," Murphy says. "So I decided to bring some."

Even though more than a thousand people live in Mowmand, a spooky silence radiates from the village walls, broken only by the braying of donkeys. Ludweg has never been inside Mowmand before and doesn't trust locals as much as some of the other men do. A wiry redhead who wears small gold-frame glasses and speaks with a mild Kentucky drawl, Ludweg is famous in the platoon for nearly calling in a strike on two rabbits running through the perimeter of the Kandahar Airfield, which he mistook in his night-vision scope for Al Qaeda infiltrators. Ludweg is due to ship home in fewer than twenty days, leave the Army, marry his fiancée, finish college and find "a job where I never wear a uniform again." For obvious reasons, he wants to play it safe. "Doc, we're not going in, are we?" Ludweg asks, scanning the village uneasily, holding his M-203 high in front of his chest.

Murphy explains to the translator, Mohammed Abdullah, that they don't want to go into the village. "Of course, sir," Abdullah says, gazing at the village with a serene smile. He is a pudgy man, about twenty-five, with a fidgety gap-toothed smile. He's unfailingly polite and always appears eager to please the Americans. But like other ATF translators, he often seems not to listen to what the Americans are saying. "I will take you into the village, sir."

Murphy and Ludweg reluctantly follow. Weighted down with about sixty pounds of body armor, ammo and weaponry apiece, their boots whoof up knee-high clouds of dust with each step. Beneath the Americans' helmets, sweat pours down their faces. In the extreme heat, fair-haired Americans develop a strange complexion. Their skin burns red in blotches, but underneath it develops a sickly white pallor, especially on Ludweg. He hangs back, fuming. All the color has drained from his face, except for his nose, which is bright red, almost blinking like a clown's.

By now, children are streaming out of spider holes in the buildings and walls. About twenty boys and a couple of girls, with fly-covered smiles, approach the Americans with their hands out, chanting *"Kalam!"* which means *pen*, and begging for candy, even cigarettes. Basic items such as pens are novelties in many poverty-stricken Afghan villages.

After a few minutes, two men emerge from the village, followed by a young girl missing most of her hair. She has an oozing, red sore across the bald portion of her scalp. Murphy gives the men about ten dollars' worth of iodine solution and gauze, and explains how to use it. The two villagers shake his hand, then touch their hands to their hearts, a traditional Afghan show of affection.

Up by the Humvees, a small riot has broken out among children surrounding it. Swinehart and Farrar stand in their turret, hands on their machine guns, faces bright red and sweating. Theirs may not look like the most interesting job in the world, but in moments like this, you realize that holding a finger on the trigger of a machine gun in an alien village half a world away is a fairly profound responsibility. The weightiest challenge faced by the average college student their age is usually on the order of figuring out whether he'll get laid more or less if he goes vegan.

Quast orders Swinehart to throw a plastic water bottle to the side of the vehicle to draw the kids away. As soon as he throws it, two boys, each about nine, race over, and both grab it, then start beating the shit out of each other. A man in a black turban, once the Taliban uniform, approaches out of nowhere. He has a scythe slung over his shoulder, with an enormous blade sticking out. Murphy, Abdullah and Ludweg walk up just as the man in the turban comes their way. Ludweg, nose beating red, drops his M-203 on the guy and stands back. The man in black cuts to the side of the Humvee where the boys are fighting and whacks both of them in the side of the head with his open fists.

It is late in the afternoon when the patrol returns to the Wolf Pack compound inside the ATF fort. D'Angelo calls them together for debriefing. Water bottles chill on a giant block of ice in a plastic chest. The ATF guys control an ice machine in Kandahar and trade the U.S. soldiers blocks in exchange for copies of skin magazines.

"Swinehart, what did you learn on your first patrol?" D'Angelo asks.

"I never seen a camel before, sir."

"What else did you learn?"

"Them kids fighting over a bottle of water. I never seen anything like that. I'll never forget that." He shakes his head, grinning. "I saw another kid; he put his fingers over his mouth like he wanted a cigarette. Kid couldn't have been more than six years old. And already smoking cigarettes?"

Farrar cuts in, saying to Swinehart, "Over here, six years is already like a third of a person's life span. It makes sense to start smoking at that age."

The men in the platoon, like most other American soldiers, are in the almost unreal position of belonging to a seemingly victorious army that for the most part hasn't fired a shot. Battle-hardened ATF soldiers regale the young Americans with hair-raising tales of shooting down Soviet helicopters, slaughtering Al Qaeda fanatics with grenades, carving Russians up with bayonets. During meals at the Wolf Pack compound, the Americans pass around these secondhand tales as reverently as if they were their own.

But something about their ATF brothers-in-arms confuses the Americans. They are not only the most macho fighting force they have known, they are seemingly the gayest. Open affection between men— and even what might be defined as pederasty back home—is fairly common in Pashtun culture. Traditional Kandahar love songs frequently revolve around themes of love and flirtation between a boy and a man. Even when there's no sexual connotation, Afghan men tend to hold hands and touch each other a great deal.

Sometimes the ATF soldiers will try to explain to the Americans that a life with women only is an unfulfilling one. "When I told my counterparts in the ATF that I'm married," Keough says, "some of them have asked me, 'Is it a marriage of love?' They say, 'Women are for having children. Men are for love.'"

The first time Ludweg came to the compound, he thought he had established a rapport with one ATF soldier, talking to him about the relative merits of the AK-47 vs. the U.S.-issue M-4, when Ludweg happened to comment on the nice flowers growing in the lawn. The soldier leaned into Ludweg's face and said, "You have pretty eyes."

Some of the American soldiers refer to their ATF counterparts as "the butt-pirate army," but again, as in the relationships with villagers, their feelings about them are more complicated and open-minded than you might expect. In their free time, some of the soldiers in the Fifth Platoon stop by remote ATF checkpoints farther out in the desert, throw down their weapons and sit around for hours in the primitive guard huts playing cards and watching pirated Jean-Claude Van Damme DVDs. "Their culture is different," says Keough, "but they're soldiers, which makes them our brothers."

Still, the contrast between the Americans and the Afghans couldn't be sharper at night in the ATF fort. When the sun goes down, the ATF soldiers gather on a small, meticulously kept lawn in front of their command post and sit under lamps made from old Soviet bomb casings, stuck upright in the lawn and wired with colorful lights.

ATF soldiers, who run their own patrols by putting as many as three men at a time on tiny Honda 125 motorcycles, zoom in and out all night. Others loiter on their small lawn, wrestling for hours, then holding hands, arms draped limply over shoulders and AK-47s, swaying as they listen to songs blasted from a boombox. Occasionally they hire boy singers, usually about thirteen or fourteen, who sing and dance on the lawn. The older soldiers, bearded men with black, craggy smiles, stand around gazing like fans at a Britney Spears concert.

On the American side of the fort, those not on patrol sit around on upturned crates bullshitting. One of the most striking aspects of infantrymen's life is the intimate relationships they are forced to maintain with shit. The topic is never far from conversation. At the airfield, the smell of sewage is a constant factor, and everyone has to take his turn on the "shit truck" detail, emptying the base-camp portajohns. But it's on this patrol where the subject of excrement becomes a near-obsession. Every other day or so, shit here is disposed, a truly disgusting procedure that involves mixing excrement with diesel fuel and setting it on fire. The disposal process requires constant stirring and relighting, which all takes about an hour. "The trick to it," says Keough, "is stay out of the wind so you don't get that shit smoke in your clothes."

They debate the best ways to dig shit trenches (the basic communal toilet first used at Kandahar Airfield) and whether the best source of "field-expedient toilet paper" is to cut off one's T-shirt sleeves or use the upper portion of a sock. They laugh about the time that turbulence from a low-flying C-17 blew over the shitter on the perimeter with an unlucky grunt in it. Or the time Keough laughed so hard about Ballard's bad case of the krud—as the local dysentery is known—he shit his own pants. It's a good time at the ATF fort. The Americans talk about shit, then jack off in their pup tents. The ATF soldiers party with boys on the front lawn.

One morning just past dawn, the Fifth Platoon is ordered back to the airfield. The men are told they will be taking part in a helicopter assault on two villages near the Pakistani border. For the next thirty-six hours, the men practice field drills while battalion commanders speak confidently of taking on "a significant concentration of Al Qaeda forces." But Apache Snow II quickly runs into difficulties, and the Fifth Platoon is cut from the assault. (When Apache Snow II is finally launched ten days later, the 200 U.S. troops who land in an armada of choppers find villages filled only with women and children, a few boxes of rifle ammunition and three rocket-propelled grenades given to them by a village elder. A suspicious facility in one village, which military-intelligence analysts speculated might be a terrorist weapons plant, turns out to be a lumber mill.)

After being cut from the mission, the soldiers in the Fifth feel let down. "We just want the chance to do what we train for," says Ramos. Alone in the tent, D'Angelo seems the most disappointed. "I joined the Army to do extreme things," he says. "In this kind of war, the Air Force comes in, blows the shit out of everything. The Special Forces does their thing. The infantry comes in and we just guard what's already been taken." D'Angelo spits a stream of brown tobacco into an empty Gatorade bottle. "I think about leaving the Army and going into the real world. But sometimes I think the corporate world is cold. You won't measure up, they fire you. In the Army, if you fail at something, they try to rebuild people. Once you're in, they'll always find something for you. The Army is almost addictive. Everything is taken care of for you. My brother was telling me I should become a cop in the New Jersey Highway Patrol. I wouldn't know how to do that. If I saw someone was speeding, I'd just shoot him."

When the platoon goes back onto patrol, military intelligence passes down a report to D'Angelo that the route they had used to deliver medicine to Mowmand was mined after they left. According to the intelligence report, a man was spotted planting a mine on the road and told a local villager, "This mine is for the Americans."

Quast volunteers to take a patrol to a village near Mowmand to inquire with the locals if they have heard anything about mines being planted.

Within minutes of reaching Morgan Kechah—the village where they hope to obtain intelligence about the alleged mining incident—Quast and his ATF translator find a villager named Abdul Raheem. "He wants us to come to his house for tea," Quast tells Ludweg, the other TC on the patrol. "We can't turn down an Afghan's hospitality. It's an insult."

Quast insists that all the men come, including Ludweg. They squeeze through the low, four-foot-high entrance to Raheem's adobe home and are joined by two bearded, turbaned elders. Ludweg flashes a curt smile and hunches lower on his M-203.

Quast peels his armor off as he sits on the floor. Raheem reaches up to a high shelf molded into the adobe wall and takes down a plastic bottle of Khoshgovar, an Iranian brand of cola. A young man, out of breath from a sprint to a neighboring village, brings in ice in a bucket made from an old antifreeze jug. Raheem picks up several glasses. He ceremoniously inspects one glass and observes a spot. He cleans it by delicately clearing his throat and hocking some spit into it. He wipes it on his dirty robe.

Ludweg's eyes bug out. But when the beverage is served, he and the other Americans soldiers raise their glasses and drink. After exchanging awkward pleasantries, Quast brings up the topic of land mines. He asks

Raheem if he knows about anyone planting mines to kill Americans. Raheem appears shocked by the story. He and the two elders debate for a long time in Pashto. "The story is not true," he says in halting English. "Impossible." Then, through the translator, Raheem says, "We want Americans to stay. We want to protect Americans. If you leave, we will have more war. We want you to keep coming to our village."

When the Americans say goodbye and walk back to their Humvees, Raheem follows. He becomes agitated, eager to say something, but uncertain of how to express himself. He grabs one of the Americans' arms and asks, "How do I show my love?" The Americans look at him, puzzled.

"In my country," Raheem starts, "I show love to my friend by hold his hand or put my hand on his shoulder. How do I show love to Americans?"

Quast takes his hand and shakes it goodbye.

By the time Quast's patrol arrives back at the Wolf Pack compound, the second squad of the Fifth Platoon is preparing for its own patrol. Farrar grabs his helmet and groans. "The first thing I do when I get out of the Army is, I'm going to get some piece-of-shit job, go in to work the first day with my uniform fucked up, French fries hanging out of my mouth, all blazed, and they'll say, 'You're fired!' And I'll say, 'Fuck you, too,' and walk out of there laughing. You can do that in the civilian world."

One of the men asks Quast about that run to the Kandahar McDonald's they've been talking about for days now. Quast steps up: "I've got some news about the McDonald's in Kandahar." He stares ahead, his deep-set eyes expressionless. "The translator who told us about that . . . turns out, he lied. There is no McDonald's."

The soldiers stare at the sergeant while the news sinks in: There are no Happy Meals in Afghanistan. One naive belief has been shattered, but the others, deeply held among the men in the Fifth Platoon, remain intact—their faith that brotherly love will protect them against the worst evils of war, and that by behaving with characteristically blind but generous American decency, they will triumph in Afghanistan where all others have failed. No one believes in the latter more than D'Angelo, the platoon realist. Though he often complains bitterly about his failure to engage the enemy in combat, he occasionally brings up his father's experience in Italy during World War II. "My father's family hid in a cave when the Americans invaded and fought the Germans. My father was seven, and his face was bleeding from a cut. They could hear the Americans outside, and my grandmother wanted to take him out to get medical attention. My grandfather said no, but they took him anyway. The Americans fixed his face up and gave them food." D'Angelo stretches out his sleeve, showing off the flag and his patches for Ranger and Air Assault school. "Those were American soldiers."

from McCoy's Marines: Darkside Toward Baghdad

by John Koopman

Former Marine John Koopman covered the United States invasion of Iraq for the San Francisco Chronicle. This selection is excerpted from a six-part series that appeared in November 2003.

The Kut

The Marines are driving through the outskirts of Kut. It's about 100 miles from Baghdad. Everyone is anxious to get there. Take Baghdad, end the war. Kut is the closest large city, and there's been fighting in and around it.

McCoy's battalion is to provide more violent supremacy and militia suppression.

At dawn, 155-mm howitzers shake the earth. They're launching high-explosive rounds into the outskirts of Kut. Three-Four moves toward the city, following a path taken by another regiment. Death and destruction are everywhere.

Bodies lie on the side of the road, jackets covering faces. Iraqi military vehicles are smoking ruins. A herd of sheep lies silent, adding to the putrid smell of death.

For a long time, I see no live Iraqis. Armored vehicles, tanks and artillery pieces are on the road and in nearby fields. Marine tanks blew holes in everything. Just in case.

We come upon a T-55 tank, still burning. Something inside the tank explodes. The crew hatch on the top of the turret blows off and hurtles 30 feet into the air. Following it, through the circle of steel, is a perfect smoke ring that wafts 20 feet straight up before dispersing.

It's beautiful.

For all I know, three or four Iraqis were roasted inside that tank.

We keep moving toward the center of Kut. This is an industrial area. Warehouses and repair shops. Tanks blast and machine guns rattle now and then.

War is loud.

Howell's humvee is right behind a tank, and I watch its turret move back and forth. I try to anticipate when the big gun will fire so I can plug my ears. The tank stops and the turret turns to the right. Howell listens to the radio traffic, says the tanker saw movement in a building.

I plug my ears and, at the last second, see a dog in the dirt halfway between the tank and the building.

"Boom!" The explosion rocks the building and a terrible shock wave hits the dog. The dog howls and screeches, runs around in the dirt trying to catch its own tail and then runs yelping into the brush. A half mile down the road, I spot the dog running with a slight limp.

The Ambush

As we move farther along, the sergeant major stops the Humvee and tells me to get in the front, in the passenger seat, so he can get in the back with his rifle. I do as I'm told, but it makes me nervous. The Humvee door is made of canvas. If we take fire from the night, I have no protection.

We come to a stretch of road with a wide-open, sandy patch to the left and a palm grove to the right. The roadway is elevated, and there's a 10- to 15-foot embankment facing the grove.

It's an ambush.

The Iraqis are dug in. They let most of the tanks pass. Then open up with machine guns and rocket-propelled grenades.

I see bullets hit the last tank in the column and the Amtracs. We're directly behind the last Amtrac in the column.

Someone fires an RPG at the Amtrac close to me. The shot comes from close range. It hits the armor, then bounces off and explodes in midair. Apparently, it hit the vehicle before the warhead was armed. Otherwise, it would have opened up that Amtrac like a soup can.

The Amtrac pulls to the side of the road and parks at a 45-degree angle. The turret gunner starts pouring .50-caliber fire into the woods.

Evnin pulls the Humvee behind the Amtrac. I get out and get behind the Humvee.

The Amtrac driver drops the rear ramp of the AAV and 3rd Platoon of Kilo Company pours out. They hit the pavement and go down that embankment, into the teeth of the Iraqi machine guns. And start to return fire.

The grove is filled with gun smoke. You can hardly see. The last two tanks in the column are still close enough to fire. They shoot their high-explosive rounds directly into the groves. The blasts cut palm trees in half. All I can think is: God help anyone underneath those blasts.

I squint and peer into the grove, trying to spot Iraqi soldiers. There, behind a stump, I see movement. A head pops up. I see a teal blue shirt.

A tank gunner sees it, too. He opens up with his .50-caliber machine gun. The tree stump, a tree next to it, the dirt all around—they come alive with a flurry of bullets.

The Iraqi bounces up, then slumps over the stump. Dead. Half his face is gone.

Behind me, the sergeant major is telling Evnin to get his M203. The 203 is a hybrid weapon, an M-16 with a 40-mm single-shot grenade launcher attached to the underside.

Moreno is on the roof of the humvee with his sniper rifle, looking for targets in the smoky grove. The action is so close, he doesn't need a spotter.

Evnin gets his weapon and the sergeant major leads him to the rear of the Amtrac in front of us.

"There's an RPK firing out of that bunker back there—try to take it out," Howell tells Evnin. But Evnin can't spot the bunker in all the smoke. Howell takes Evnin's 203 and loads one grenade round into it. He fires at a mound at the far end of the grove.

"Right there, right about where that hit," Howell yells over the din of gunshots. "You see it?"

Evnin nods and takes back the weapon. I'm standing by his side, to the right of the Amtrac, looking at the raging firefight, as he reloads. He fires a grenade into the trees and steps back behind the Amtrac to reload.

I step away and move to the other end of the AAV, to take a look at the battle from that side. I still can't see much. Too much smoke. I go back to see what Evnin is doing.

But he's not shooting anymore. He's on the ground.

Evnin had stepped out to fire his grenade launcher when an Iraqi in the grove cut loose with a burst of machine-gun fire. Evnin is hit in the upper thigh and abdomen. About an inch below his protective vest.

Howell drags him over the pavement about 20 yards to an area behind a small mound of earth. Trying to get cover.

He loosens Evnin's trousers and calls for a corpsman.

Time moves slowly and sights are blurred. I walk over—with no protective cover—to where Evnin lies. I watch the sergeant major and the medic working on him. How can this be? It's Evnin. He can't be shot.

Evnin's pants are down. I see two bullet wounds, one on the right and one on the left side of his gut. Just inside his hip bones.

It doesn't look bad. Not a lot of blood. I look away.

Evnin is awake and alert.

The corpsman prepares Evnin for evacuation. A Humvee roars to a halt on the road next to them.

Howell looks down at the young corporal and smiles. "Hey, Evnin. Look at the bright side. You won't have to ride with me anymore."

Evnin looks up and says, "Sergeant major, you're an a—."

Four Marines pick up the wounded man and push him into the back of a Humvee. The vehicle speeds off to the rear, toward the battalion aid station. And, presumably, to a helicopter out of here.

Meanwhile, in the grove, two other Marines have been hit. Corpsmen take them into an abandoned trench and bandage them.

"God, it hurts," says a young Marine, gritting his teeth, his arm in a bloody sling. "Kill some of those motherf—— for me, sergeant major."

In the grove, the battle rages on.

Lance Cpl. Dusty Ladendorf is an 18-year-old kid from Oroville. Later, in Baghdad, we talk about that battle. It was his first big fight. "There were two seconds of shock and after that I just started going through the motions," he says. "Just do it. Don't think about it. Get out of the track, start shooting. Cover your buddy, find the enemy, maneuver, close in on him. And kill him."

Ladendorf and the others start working their way into the palm grove. The squad comes upon a bunker. They see a hand come out holding an AK-47, spraying the area with bullets.

A Marine throws a hand grenade into the bunker. The Iraqi picks it up and throws it back. It lands 7 meters from Ladendorf. The grenade has a "kill zone" of 5 meters. It goes off. No one is hurt.

They throw another hand grenade. The Iraqi throws it back.

Finally, someone takes a grenade, pulls the pin and waits a couple of seconds. Then throws it.

The grenade goes off in the bunker. No one comes out.

Over the next half hour or 45 minutes, the platoon works its way through the grove. Bob Nickelsberg runs past me, trying to get in front of the Marines to get their pictures. Crazy bastard. I look around. Howell is busy, there's no place for me to be. So I walk into the grove alone, about 30 meters behind the nearest Marines.

It's hot. Smoke fills the air and I'm scared. I don't know who's dead and who's alive. There are bunkers everywhere, and I expect an Iraqi to come out of one shooting.

I pass by a large fighting hole and look inside. Two dead Iraqis are lying there, both curled into fetal positions. They're facing each other, heads almost touching. They look like friends, or brothers, sleeping together. It's intimate. Horrible.

The sun beats down on the grove, and we all sweat under the heavy gear. The Marines find weapons and ammo and throw them into a pile. They set fire to it, which adds to the heat. Bullets crackle and pop as they cook off in the fire. The platoon reaches the far end of the grove. Officers are screaming at sergeants. Sergeants are shouting at privates. Adrenaline pumps and bullets go off. Everyone yells.

Any Iraqis still alive run out the back of the grove and disappear. Some try to swim across a stream and are cut down by machine-gun fire from Marine armor.

The fight is over. I go back to the road, still wary of the bunkers, but more confident now. Surviving that kind of hell gives you confidence.

Up on the road, two Marines bring out a prisoner, his hands bound tightly behind him. He wears green pants and a black sweater. Not the uniform of a regular soldier, or Republican Guard. He speaks English, but he doesn't have much to say. Just that his arm hurts. It looks broken.

Moments later, four Marines bring out another Iraqi. He's in bad shape. His left leg is twisted and turned 180 degrees. He's bleeding. He's either unconscious or dead.

The Marines drop the Iraqi on the ground next to the other prisoner. The first one raises his head and looks around. A Marine sergeant shouts at him to put his face in the dirt. He does, for a minute, then raises it up again. The sergeant grabs the prisoner's head and shoves it to the side, facing the dying man.

"Keep your f—— head down, or I'll put a sack over it!" he says.

The man nods. I can see him looking at the other man. Their faces are about a foot apart. The second one has his eyes closed. His body convulses. I think he's dead. But then he brings his arm up from his side, to his head. And lies still.

He, too, is taken to the aid station.

With the fight over, Howell drives back to check on Evnin. As we approach the aid station, we see a transport helicopter in a field to the right. Running toward the helo are four Marines carrying a stretcher. On it is a body bag.

God, don't let it be Evnin.

It's the Iraqi.

He's dead.

The doc at the aid station doesn't say much about Evnin. Just that he was stable when he was put on the helicopter.

But we feel OK about him. When a wounded person is alive and alert when he gets medical attention, he usually makes it.

In the Humvee, Howell sees that Moreno is wearing Evnin's pistol belt.

"It's OK," Moreno says. "Mark and I always said, if one of us gets hit, the other gets to ratf—— his gear. I told him I was going to take the holster."

"Evnin's got it made," Howell says. "He's out of this hellhole."

"He'll be getting a sponge bath from a pretty nurse tonight," I add.

We drive back to the front of the column. The tanks are sitting by the side of the road.

I find McCoy in his Humvee. He says we missed a suicide run. Six or seven Iraqis had got up from their fighting holes in the sand and run across open ground toward the Marine tanks. They carried only AK-47s. The tank gunners mowed them down like wheat.

The 7.62-mm AK bullets bounced harmlessly off the heavy tank armor, barely scratching paint.

In one of the fights, the tank company commander caught a round in his hand. He was in the turret hatch when a machine gun raked his tank. The bullet entered just behind his index knuckle and came out near his wrist. It cut through tissue but didn't hit any bone or tendon.

"It hurts like a mother, but I got real lucky," says Capt. Brian Lewis.

The fight is over. Three-Four moves out of the city, to a staging area, to spend the night.

We get to the area and set up camp. I dig into an MRE and have some warm water. Howell asks to speak with me in private.

We go behind the Humvee. The sun has set. It's dark. "Evnin didn't make it," he says.

The Compound

Faces are grim the next morning. We leave Al Kut and head northwest again, toward Baghdad. Hundreds of men stream down the road in the opposite direction.

They wear the long shirt and sweats favored by Iraqis. Most are young. There are no women.

The Marines think they're Iraqi soldiers, maybe Republican Guard, who are running away from the fighting. They're headed toward Kut. Some wave and smile.

Some are sullen. Some limp. They swarm abandoned and shot-up vehicles to strip them of any valuables. One man rolls a tire in front of him.

The guys are too tired and too mad to care. Losing Evnin was tough.

The sergeant major says little about Evnin. It's hard to read him. He's not exactly a touchy-feely, it's-OK-to-cry kind of guy. But he'd been tough with Evnin. He rode him about his appearance, about his driving, about keeping the Humvee clean. But it was just sergeant major stuff. Not much different than he was with any of the Marines. I got the sense Howell wondered if he'd been too rough on the kid, and now couldn't take it back.

Three-Four drives to the outskirts of Baghdad. No resistance. McCoy gets orders to raid a military compound. This is a sprawling, forested area with new buildings and a high fence atop an earthen berm.

The Marines fire a line charge over the fence. A hundred pounds of C4 explosive set off a teeth-rattling blast. Now there's a huge hole in the fence.

They go in and find nothing. Not a single person. Just a couple of old, empty armored vehicles and ancient anti-aircraft guns. The Marines pop them with grenades and look around. The search takes most of the day. It's another hot one. The Marines are about to head out when McCoy gets a call from an officer. They've found a suspicious building.

Darkside drives over, followed by the sergeant major. There in the middle of the woods, in broken-down, dirty Iraq, is a nice, clean complex of buildings. The offices are modern and nice. They have air conditioners, but the power isn't on. Some of the interior offices are still cool from the air conditioning. There are pressed-wood cabinets, the kind you find at Home Depot.

Every single work space has a painting or photograph of Saddam.

Outside, in the sand, are high-tech metal-working machines. They're covered with plastic tarps and surrounded by sandbags. Someone was trying to keep the machines safe from falling American bombs.

No one wants to go inside. Through the windows, the Marines see plastic tarps and bags filled with something. Maybe a lethal chemical. So the place is secured and the Division is notified.

The battalion intelligence officer, Capt. Brian Mangan, goes in with his interpreter. Simon and I follow. The Marines kick down doors and rifle through desks and file cabinets. There's little there. It is too clean. Not a single document. And few personal effects. But suspicious enough to be declared a "sensitive site."

We find bottled water in a secretary's refrigerator and discuss whether it's safe to drink. Mangan wonders whether the Iraqis poisoned the bottles on the way out. Paranoia is good thinking, but I'm hot and thirsty. I figure the Iraqis couldn't have been nefarious enough to booby-trap a water bottle. So I take a sip. I'm still standing a few minutes later, so the other guys divide up the water and start drinking. It's cold enough to be good.

We'd been inside for more than an hour. When we get out, the Marines are freaked. And mad. There are stories about underground tunnels and Iraqi agents.

They thought we'd disappeared, or been captured.

Howell and I have a major fight. "You don't do that again," he shouts, as if I were an errant schoolboy.

I point out that I was with a Marine officer and that I had a responsibility to investigate. If there were chemical weapons or evidence of such, better that a journalist be on hand to avoid later allegations that the goods were planted by American troops.

"Besides," I said. "It's my neck. I know the risks."

"I don't care," Howell yells. "You put Marines at risk with that kind of s——. You know we'd have to come looking for you."

We argue for some time, neither giving ground. And both of us right, in our way. But I also know that Howell is right. We should have come out sooner. I say so and offer an apology. I also tell Howell that I'll leave his Humvee if he wants.

The sergeant major isn't used to dealing with civilians. He accepts my apology and then tells me he's sorry for yelling. And he doesn't want me to leave his vehicle. Now that we've patched things up, he wants to know more about what we found in the offices. I give him a sip of water, and explain afterward where I got it. He spits it out.

That night we sleep among perfectly groomed rosebushes in the courtyard of the complex.

Rockets' Red Glare

The next day, Three-Four sets out for the bridge over the Dyala Canal. The bridge has major military implications. The entire 1st Marine Division is about to attack Baghdad from the east. There are only two bridges that allow eastern access. Both have been damaged by the Iraqis. McCoy's bridge has a hole in the middle; nothing can drive across. But the Marines have to take this one so engineers can build a pontoon bridge across the canal. Basically, the entire division is waiting to cross. Right here, right now. The war depends on it.

The battalion drives out the front gate of the military compound midmorning.

It's already hot. The main gate opens onto Route 6, which leads to the bridge a couple of miles away. And then on into Baghdad.

To the left of the road is a tall berm. On the other side, more trees. Kilo Company spreads through there and moves west toward the bridge.

To the right of the road are buildings, houses and shops. It's a crappy, cramped urban area. And it's swarming with Iraqi Fedayeen.

The Marines have moved about 100 yards down the road when fire comes in from the buildings. Iraqi snipers firing from rooftops. Rocket-propelled grenades (RPGs) rain down like the Fourth of July.

An RPG is an ugly, nasty little thing that has killed U.S. troops in every war since Vietnam. It's like a large bottle rocket, fired from a shoulder-held tube. It has no aiming mechanism. So it just goes straight off and either explodes on impact or detonates in midair above a target.

You hear "pfffffsssssssstttttt" and then "boom."

The sergeant major has a new driver, Lance Cpl. Kevin Norcross from Orange County. He drives the Humvee behind an Amtrac, moving slowly down the road. I sit in the back, in the open, with Moreno.

"Pffffffffssssssssssttttt! Boom!" An RPG round explodes 20 feet over our heads. There's a puff of black smoke. We hear bits of shrapnel hitting the pavement around us.

I get down from the back of the Humvee and take cover on the side opposite the shooting.

Pffffffffssssssssss! Boom! Another RPG goes off overhead.

Boom! And another. Boom! A fourth RPG.

"I think someone might be aiming at us," Moreno says.

"You think so?" I ask.

I hear that Pffffffffffsssssssssssttttt again and dive straight for the dirt. Boom! Another one directly overhead.

For the first time in the war, I think I might die.

Norcross' hands are shaking as he drives the Humvee to the left side of an Amtrac, almost scraping the paint off, to get some steel between us and the RPGs. We sit there and hide.

I look up and see two Marines sitting atop the Amtrac. They're calmly firing their M-16 rifles into the buildings. They seem neither afraid nor desirous of cover.

"Did you see that guy in the window?" one asks.

"I saw something move. I was just shooting into the window and all around it. I was hoping."

"Yeah, he never popped back up. I think you got him."

"Could be."

They keep firing. Bullets are plinking off the armor and off the pavement. The Marines have a serene, internal calm. The violence, the threat of death all around them, seems to mean nothing. They just sit up there and shoot.

Someone told me once that the trick to keeping your wits in battle is to imagine that you're already dead. Or that you certainly will die. If you survive, all the better.

I try that now. It doesn't work.

From behind us, I hear someone shouting. Iraqis are near the front gate of the military compound, trying to flank the Marines. A .50-caliber machine gun in an Amtrac opens up and pours a stream of fire down the street. I can't tell if they hit anyone. But the shooting continues for a long time.

The column keeps moving and eventually Norcross pulls into a courtyard behind a building, on the other side of the shooting. I sit in the sand and heat, wondering why I'm here.

McCoy comes and goes in his fast Humvee. He sees the fight from a higher vantage point. He's getting reports from commanders all around. And it's good. No Marines dead or wounded. McCoy says the Iraqis are employing "Chechen-style" guerrilla tactics. Much like the resistance fighters opposing the Russian Army, they gather in seven- to 10-man "hunter-killer" teams. Armed with RPGs and machine guns, they try to set up ambushes. They aim to strike quickly, with deadly force, then disappear.

But the Marines have studied this and have trained to work against it. They're chasing down groups of Iraqi men and challenging them, and getting into firefights.

"We really put the wood to them," McCoy says.

The Marines are getting more and more tense. They see unarmed men walking around. Sometimes these men duck into a building and come out firing. The troops figure the Iraqis have weapons hidden here and there. They know, or hope, the Marines won't fire on unarmed men. The Iraqis go from cache to cache, firing, dropping weapons, firing again.

It's a rugged couple of hours. The Marines creep slowly down the roadway. Machine guns rattle and tanks blast holes in buildings. We're all sweating like pigs in the chemical suits.

At times, the air is a solid wall of sound. M-16 rifles, M-60 machine guns and .50-caliber heavy machine guns pour fire into alleys and windows. The smell of cordite, or gunpowder, fills the air.

The Marines say they killed 15 to 30 Iraqis. I hear about one sniper who recorded eight kills from across the canal.

I can't see any dead. They're scattered in and among the houses and shops.

The Bridge

Finally, we reach the bridge. This is a dirty, ugly part of the Baghdad metropolis. There's garbage on the street. Abandoned restaurants are caked with grease and dirt and smell like barnyards. Food left in shops is rotting and smells like hell. A corner store has been torn open, and a couple of Marines step inside to look around. There are cartons of cigarettes, bottles of juice and candy. The sergeant major yells at everyone to get out. "You're Marines, not looters!" he says. Two minutes later a journalist runs up to the Humvee and gives me a bag full of cigarettes and candy he's taken from the store. The sergeant major shoots me a look, but I turn away and start giving the stuff out to passing Marines.

I hear shooting coming from the bridge.

The Marines come under heavy fire from Iraqi army and militia on the other side. All evening, Marine artillery and mortar fire rain down on the Iraqi side. The Marines shoot rifles and machine guns across the canal into buildings and cars.

When I finally make it to the bridge, I see the body of an Iraqi on the span, close to the U.S. side. He's in civilian clothes. He's been shot in the head and chest. On the far side, a small Japanese-made car burns brightly. Thick, black smoke rolls from it. On this side of the bridge is a cluster of buildings around a courtyard. In front are three shacks, sitting at the top of the embankment leading down to the water.

A couple of tanks are parked to the left of the shacks. I'm standing inside the little building, peering out a window, the tank cannon about 10 feet away. I hear the shout, "Tank's firing." I try to duck, but the big gun goes off. The force of the blast lifts me 6 inches off the ground. My ears ring for an hour.

The 120mm cannons tear holes through houses on the other side.

Incoming

Digging my fingers into my ears, I walk into the courtyard. In that space, about 200 square feet in an L-shape, Kilo Company is getting ready for an assault on the bridge.

Marine artillery pounds the far shore. Simon and I stand in the courtyard and watch the thunderous bursts land in a palm grove. Shell after shell. You see a bright flash and a burst of smoke, and a second later the sound hits you with a shock wave. On the radio, I hear someone say the bridge assault will start in 15 minutes.

We watch an artillery shell land short. It hits the water and sends up a huge spray. A couple seconds later, a shell lands on the U.S. side, down the canal bank to the right.

And then, time stands still.

I hear—or feel—an enormous blast directly behind me. I know it's an artillery shell. I'm thinking it's an American shell that landed short.

A hot, hard wind blows past me. The air turns dark. I duck my head and hold onto my helmet. God, don't let any shrapnel come my way.

Hot, burning engine oil sprays my back. I turn to see the impact. The shell has struck an Amtrac parked next to the courtyard wall, about 3 yards from me. Simon and I duck into the nearest building. I'm nervous. I don't know if another shell is on the way. Maybe someone is targeting this building. We have no idea whether we should stay or run. So we wait a half minute. No more shells.

I look out the window and, to the left, I see the charred, smoking wreckage of the Amtrac. Men are shouting. I'm afraid for what I'll find outside.

The Screaming and the Dead

The blast made a smoking, twisted crater on top of the Amtrac. It shot fire and bodies out the back end. I walk around to the back side. Blood and oil mix with the dirt. Two crumpled, still bodies lie in the dirt.

"F——! F——!" some of the Marines are screaming. "F——!"

Other Marines lie moaning on the ground. Corpsmen and buddies huddle around them. Gunnery Sgt. Jean-Paul Courville and 1st Sgt. James Kirkland organize medical help. Then tend to the dead.

The bodies of Lance Cpl. Andrew Aviles and Cpl. Jesus Medellin are tucked into their sleeping bags. "I was standing just 10 feet away," says one Marine, shaking. Blood streams from his lip.

What follows is a half hour of shock and confusion. Corpsmen work on wounded men in the dirt. One Marine is deaf from the sound of the blast. Another is screaming and writhing in pain. In the middle of all this, I see McCoy. His jaw is set and he looks grim.

He says the artillery shell came from the Iraqis, not the Americans. I don't believe him.

Marines sit huddled in the courtyard. They look haggard and drawn. Reports come in that Iraqis are targeting artillery fire on this position. Everyone scrambles for cover.

I find a hole and make myself small, waiting for more artillery to come down. None comes. After a while, I go back to the courtyard. Kilo Company is gathering for another run at the bridge.

Bloodlust. I now understand bloodlust.

Bloodlust starts with anger. Anger at the situation, anger at the heat, anger at the Iraqis, anger at whoever started the war. Then there's pain. Pain from the blisters on your feet, pain from the armored vest that rubs your collarbone raw, pain in your back from sleeping on the ground every night. Then confusion, over what's going on and why and when. And then there's blood. Blood that's been spilled. Your friend's blood. That combination of anger, pain, confusion and blood leads you to do things you wouldn't otherwise contemplate.

For Marines, it might be fighting harder, shooting sooner. For a noncombatant, it might simply be taking chances, not caring what happens to you.

Bloodlust will make you do strange things, like look inside a burning car to see charred bodies and watch the flies eat dried blood on the face of a dead man.

McCoy knows he has to get a handle on his Marines and prepare them for battle. It isn't easy. Order and discipline and training have to kick in when all seems lost. Guys have seen their buddies blown to bits.

He talks to some men individually. His officers talk to others. Here's where leadership kicks in. There is a sense of urgency. Despite the deaths, the fight has to go on.

A half hour after the shell hit the Amtrac, Kilo Company masses at the bridge. And prepares to cross.

A team of combat engineers goes first, carrying metal scaffolding to place across the blown gap in the span.

McCoy and Shealy stand by the front shack. The colonel is about to run across the bridge when the sergeant major stops him.

"We can't afford to lose you," he tells McCoy.

McCoy stands back and contemplates the situation. He takes the radio handset from Shealy and starts calling his officers, checking their progress.

Kilo, meanwhile, starts running onto the bridge. They bunch up at the far end and pour fire into everything. The sound is deafening.

But the Iraqi defenders are either dead or gone. There is little, if any, return fire.

Heavily armed infantry Marines run into nearby houses, kicking in doors, looking for a fight.

I see two Marines crouch near an alley. One peers around the corner, then goes back into a crouch and readies his weapon. "Ready, crazy?" he asks his buddy. The other man nods and they leap into the alley. A possible ambush. It reminds me of the final scene in "Butch Cassidy and the Sundance Kid." The two Marines sprint into the roadway, rifles at the ready. No enemy fire comes. Along the shore near the bridge you can see fighting holes and bunkers. Large piles of clothing and personal effects—notebooks, pictures, blankets—are strewn about. As are dozens, maybe hundreds, of AK-47s and RPGs. This is where the fire had come from the day before.

The Look Of Death

McCoy says 50 or 60 Iraqis were killed in the two days of fighting. Many of the bodies are on the road on the Baghdad side of the bridge. Inside a smoking wreck of a car are a clump of charred bones. Farther up, an older man, maybe 55 or 60, is slumped over the steering wheel of a delivery truck.

Across the road, a soldier in the uniform of the Republican Guard lies face down in the dirt, a circle of dried blood next to his head.

In the palm grove are craters made by American artillery shells. Holes in the dirt are chest deep and 8 feet wide.

In the aftermath of the deadly fight for the bridge, the ugliness of war gets worse. I follow a group of Marines north down the road that leads to the heart of Baghdad. They stop about a mile away from the bridge. The burned-up wreck of a car is on the road. A body lies next to it, also burned. The man is in a push-up position and stiff with rigor mortis.

Down the road, a car drives toward the Marine checkpoint. Someone fires a shot, then another. The car screeches to a halt. I see from a distance two men getting out of the vehicle, their hands held high.

"Look at those people," one Marine officer says, "driving around like there wasn't a war going on."

The Snipers and the Civilians

This is how the Marines deal with oncoming vehicles. A sniper is stationed near the checkpoint, atop a roof or on a vehicle. He fires warning shots in front of vehicles. If a car doesn't stop, the sniper fires a shot into the grill or engine area. And if that doesn't work, the Marines light the whole thing up. The driver and passengers are often killed.

The Marines are unapologetic. They believe the Iraqis are coming to attack. Better they die than a Marine.

But the situation now seems static. Marines are stopping cars, no fighting is going on. I'm standing with journalists, some embedded and some unilateral who tagged along with the battalion. We're in a doorway to a courtyard next to the palm grove. A dead Iraqi soldier is lying right next to us. I keep trying not to look at the blood next to his head.

I decide to return to the bridge. I want information on the artillery shell that hit the Amtrac.

I don't buy McCoy's explanation that it was an Iraqi shell. The timing was too close to the American bombardment. Everyone figures it came from a Marine artillery battery. I want to talk to people, get firsthand accounts of what happened.

So I don't see what occurs on the road after I leave. Some of the other journalists stay.

They tell me later that Iraqi cars keep driving toward the checkpoint only to get shot up by nervous, trigger-happy Marines. They say men fire on cars before the snipers fire warning shots. They say officers and snipers keep shouting at the Marines to hold their fire, but some do not. And civilians die because of it.

But the Marines tell a different story. Crazy, suicidal Iraqis drive cars and trucks straight at the checkpoints, or at Marines, or tanks. They ignore orders to stop and they ignore warning shots. The only thing to do, the Marines say, is to kill them.

The Marines have been warned constantly about suicide attacks. On the way to Baghdad, the 5th Marines lost a tank to a suicide truck bomb. The men of Three-Four saw the M1 Abrams vehicle burning fiercely as they drove past it to the city.

The day of the bridge assault, word comes over the radio that Iraqis are using ambulances with explosives to make suicide runs.

The order comes down: You see an ambulance driving fast toward you, shoot it.

Whatever the reason or rationale, a lot of people die on Route 6 that day.

Marines and journalists tell other wild tales of that day. A van is shot up and a family inside is killed. The van sits silent all night. In the morning, a man and woman crawl slowly, carefully, out of the wreckage. They had sat in that shot-up van all night, among their dead relatives, afraid to come out for fear of getting shot.

The woman had been shot in the toe. A Navy corpsman bandages her, and she and the man leave.

A black Mercedes Benz drives straight at a checkpoint. The Marines shoot it up. They look inside to find a man and woman dead in the front seats. In the backseat is a young girl, maybe 5 years old. She's alive and clutching a stuffed bear.

That wrenches hearts. Even tough Marines sympathize with a child, now an orphan. And no one can say why the parents died. Was it a horrible mistake, or was it suicide?

"Imagine that, making a suicide run when you've got your kid in the backseat," says one Marine who witnessed it.

Battalion communications officer and 1st Lt. Paul Keener chokes up when he sees the girl. He's got a baby daughter at home.

He puts down his gun and picks up the girl. He holds her close, as close as he can with his body armor and ammo pouches. But close enough to give her some human contact on the worst day of her life. He personally takes her to the battalion aid station. Later, she's gone. Into the system, wherever that is, where war orphans go.

A day later, I'm riding with the sergeant major and we drive to the front of the Marine advance. Tanks and infantry are fanned out near a military compound. Machine guns are firing. But it doesn't seem like a major firefight.

I find Simon standing next to McCoy's Humvee. Robinson says he just witnessed a suicide attack. A small white car drove straight at an American tank. He says the Marines fired warning shots but the car didn't stop. So they lit it up.

"I watched them shoot up this car, and they killed the driver and passenger," Robinson says, somewhat shaken. "It was an attack, I can tell you that for a fact. But when we looked into the car there were no guns and no bombs. Just two dead bodies. How do you figure?"

The Inquiry

When Simon and I return to the rear, to look into the blast that almost killed us, we find Marines who heard explosions from other artillery rounds that landed on the American side. When we say that the official word was that they were Iraqi rounds, the guys just shake their heads and say "no way."

It's not uncommon for howitzers to go off course, or rounds to land short.

A couple of days later, McCoy finds Simon and me and tells us that an official Marine inquiry found that the artillery was Iraqi.

Military intelligence had been monitoring Iraqi radio traffic, he says, and reported hearing Iraqi officers calling for artillery fire on Marine positions near the bridge. And hearing that the request was approved.

The Marines have something they call counter-battery radar. It sees enemy artillery shells in midflight and can track their trajectory. The inquiry found that counter-battery radar detected Iraqi artillery shells before they hit the Three-Four positions.

Officials also conducted a "crater analysis" of the wrecked AAV. The angles of twisted metal confirm, McCoy says, that the round entered from a forward direction, meaning Iraqi positions.

The official line is that the Marines were hit with a 155mm shell from an Iraqi GHN-45 artillery piece.

Baghdad

After the battle for the bridge, we're in Baghdad. It's different than I imagined. Relatively nice, relatively new. The buildings are two- and three-story houses. The architecture European. Stonework and squared-off shapes. Most homes have balconies in the rear, along with clotheslines and TV antennas. It was an affluent area before the war. There is no one here.

It's spooky. We're in Saddam's backyard now. Who knows what will happen? We're still waiting for the Republican Guard to show up. An ambush could be right around the corner.

The Marines find scattered groups of militia fighters. There are sporadic firefights. Nothing of consequence. No Marines are shot. They say they've shot several Iraqis. I don't doubt it, but I don't see many bodies.

The battalion moves down the main road for blocks at a time, running the Afak drill. They move in and deploy. Grunts knock down doors, snipers get on the rooftops and shoot at anyone with a gun.

The sergeant major is especially good at this.

Howell goes into the buildings while Moreno, Norcross and I wait in the Humvee.

There's a stack of soda bottle crates in the back and I desperately want a soda. But I can't bring myself to steal.

The sergeant major calls for Moreno to come to the roof. I'm bored and hot. I figure I'll go up, too, take a look around. Moreno and I climb a fence and scale a wall to get to a backyard balcony and then take stairs to the rooftop.

I see Marines looking into abandoned backyards down an alley. Closer in, I see a stack of AK-47s found in a house and then piled in the street.

Howell points to a building about 600 yards away. He says he saw someone moving in and out of a window. He thinks the guy had a rocket-propelled grenade launcher (RPG). Moreno looks through the scope, but sees nothing.

"Well, keep an eye on it. I'm going to take a look around. John's coming with me."

I don't argue; I figure I can use the exercise. Howell jumps over a wall and onto the next building and I follow. We move up one building and down the next. This is like something out of *Lethal Weapon*. We're going in and out of balconies and rooftops, under clotheslines and around smokestacks.

The sergeant major climbs onto the top of a wall and jumps 5 feet onto a rooftop. I climb onto the same wall and look down. There is a gap between buildings, and we're five stories up. It's a long way to the pavement and a short jump to the other roof. I should just turn around and go back.

But I jump. For 10 minutes we work our way through buildings, some that had been under construction before the fighting. Howell leads the way, poking his M-16 into everything, ready to shoot. I've got my notebook in my pocket, ready to run.

No one is here. Not a thing. We get to the ground and Howell climbs up another wall and keeps going.

And that's how it goes for another day. The temperature is rising and it's getting more and more uncomfortable. The only excitement comes when the Marines go into the Baghdad Institute of Technology and find some industrial-type chemistry sets, lathes for making artillery warheads and some empty howitzer shells.

Putting two and two together, it looks as if the Iraqis were using the place to make chemical artillery weapons. But there is no evidence, and the military higher command doesn't have enough people to send experts. So we bed down for the night in the main courtyard.

The next morning orders come for more of the same. By this time, I'm worn out. Tired of the war, Iraq, the Marines, everything, I just want to go home.

But we move out, down the road past bombed and burned buildings. At an intersection, we find the remains of a firefight. Shot-up and burned cars and charred Iraqi bodies. Under a highway overpass are Iraqi fighting holes with blankets, canteens, helmets and weapons. We go up the road and wait while the snipers climb yet another building. And wait some more.

A car approaches an intersection guarded by a tank and a Humvee with a .50-caliber machine gun. The driver hits the brakes and stops.

"If he drives past that light pole, you can shoot," Warrant Officer Gene Coughlin says to a sergeant next to him. "If he keeps coming in the face of all of this, he knows what he's getting into."

The car backs out of the intersection and turns around. "He doesn't know how lucky he is," Coughlin says.

The Press Corps

The Marines move out again.

Only now, something changes. The Marines were finding a couple of militia or Fedayeen guys to fight here and there, but now there is nothing. Nobody.

We drive down the road faster and go farther. Marines stop and dismount and take the high ground.

And now, something new. People. Civilians on balconies just a few feet above our heads. They're laughing and smiling and waving and clapping.

Our Humvee pulls up beneath a low balcony, and the sergeant major gets out to scout the place. Women and girls are smiling shyly at him and waving. A big grin splits his craggy face, and he offers a tentative wave back.

Someone hands down a water bottle. He doesn't want to take it, but it would be an insult to decline. He takes a swig. Now he's smiling even more. It's the women.

"Remember this place," he tells Norcross. "We might have to come back."

We mount up and move down to a large traffic circle. Still no shooting. I get down to stretch my legs. On the other side of the circle I see people in blue armored vests with the letters "TV" in white tape. It strikes me: We've found the international press corps.

I go over and introduce myself to some British reporters who have been in Baghdad during the war. They were under the control, and protection of, the Iraqi government until the previous day. But the government collapsed and the Iraqis left. Which means the journalists have no protection from looting and angry mobs. They heard a Marine unit was moving up the road and they came to meet it.

I find a reporter from the *Los Angeles Times* and ask about *The Chronicle*'s man in Baghdad, Rob Collier. The guy says sure, he's around here somewhere. We find Rob talking to another reporter. "Collier!" I shout. He and I hug. It's a strong, I'm-glad-you're-alive hug.

Meanwhile, McCoy is on the radio with Ripper 6. Regiment tells McCoy to move down to the Palestine Hotel, where the journalists are staying, and provide security.

Weird. Baghdad promised to be a bloodbath of urban fighting. But it seems safe. The Marines stay tense and on alert, but the threat appears greatly diminished after the battles already fought.

The Statue

The battalion moves to the Palestine, which is adjacent to a large traffic circle enclosing a small park. The area is dominated by a statue of Saddam Hussein atop a marble pedestal.

The Marines encircle the square and the Palestine Hotel. Tanks and armored vehicles block side streets. The grunts dismount to set up security on the sidewalks.

Iraqis are everywhere, maybe 300 or 400.

"Saddam NO! Bush YES!" shouts one gleeful-looking Iraqi boy.

The Marines don't know whether to shoot them or hug them. Mustachioed men who look like the enemy are dancing and laughing and shaking their hands. Kids ask for money, which most of us don't have, and when they don't get it, they ask for water. There is precious little of that.

The kids put flowers in the pockets of the Marines' armored vests and shake their hands. The war is over.

We don't know this yet. But you feel it in the air. There's too much happiness, too much celebration. What the liberation of Paris must have felt like.

"There's still a lot of fighting to be done," McCoy says. "But this is a momentous day."

A couple of Iraqis climb onto the pedestal of Saddam's statue to the cheers of the crowd. They tug on the statue, but it must weigh tons. Someone tosses up a rope and they tie it around Saddam's neck. The crowd pulls the rope, but there aren't nearly enough people to do the job.

The men get down, and a huge Iraqi man walks up carrying a sledgehammer. The guy has a big gut and massive shoulders. He looks like an Olympic weightlifter. He starts swinging the hammer against the marble pedestal, but after 10 minutes he has chipped maybe an inch off.

I go to McCoy's Humvee. He's on the radio with Ripper 6.

"Ripper 6, this is Darkside 6. I got a whole crowd of Iraqis over here who want help bringing the statue down. Request permission to give them a hand, over."

McCoy talks more with the regiment and then signs off. He calls the tank commander and says simply: "Do it."

Tanks break down and they need maintenance to keep going. They go everywhere with a monstrous tracked vehicle called the M-88 tank retriever. It has a 1,300 horsepower engine, a crane and tools. Everything you need to topple a statue.

The tank crews drive the M-88 over the curb and up the concrete steps, crushing them. They drive up next to the statue. The crew works for half an hour or more, trying to affix various cables to the statue.

At one point, one of the Marines passes an American flag to another man above him and he wraps it around Saddam's head. I'm on the other side of the plaza, so I can't see exactly what's happening. Some people say that some of the Iraqis are mad at the appearance of the U.S. flag. Others say they cheered, but then quickly asked to replace the American flag with a pre-Saddam Iraqi flag.

Whichever the case, the damage is done. The image of the U.S. flag in Iraq is beamed around the world. The American military is angry because they'd made great efforts not to make the war look like an American invasion. Members of Congress are angry, anti-war protesters are angry. McCoy gets calls from high up the chain of command.

Meanwhile, Iraqis are jumping on and off the tank retriever. Marines are trying to keep back the crowd so the statue won't fall and hit them.

Finally, the enormous vehicle belches black smoke. The engine rumbles like a steam locomotive. It moves back and the cable goes taut. The statue rocks an inch. With more power, the retriever rolls back a couple of feet and the top of the statue starts to sway. It moves in a slow downward arc.

And then, Saddam is parallel to the ground, about 15 feet off the deck. The retriever gives one more jerk, and the whole metal mess comes crashing down.

The crowd is on it in an instant. Dozens of people kick and punch the fallen statue. One man takes off his shoe and smacks the metal Saddam in the head. I'm told this is a great Iraqi insult.

I go to my backpack and get out my last two Cuban cigars. I find the sergeant major and give one to him. We light up and touch cigar stems in a toast.

"It ain't over yet, you know," he says.

Artillery rumbles in the distance. A moment later, shots ring out on the edge of the plaza. A Marine has spotted an Iraqi with a gun and fires off a couple of rounds. The crowd ducks and scatters, then comes back.

Not everyone is pleased by the spectacle. A handful of peace activists, human shields, argue against the war to anyone who will listen. One woman walks up to a group of Marines and calls them murderers.

Most guys ignore her. Or laugh. But it gets to some.

"I didn't bury two of my fellow Marines just so someone like that could call us murderers," says one Marine corporal who helped remove the bodies of those killed in the Amtrac. "They died for this country."

The celebration continues until after dark. McCoy works to set up security, coordinate with regiment and talk to the never-ending press corps. Later, as the light is just about gone, he takes a seat on a concrete step in the middle of the square. He sighs.

Young kids and their parents stop by to shake his hand and say something in Arabic. One man kisses his cheek and hugs him, saying "U.S. Army, good."

McCoy smiles and corrects the man: "Marines."

The Palestine

I find Collier in his room at the Palestine. He and I write our stories late into the evening. He has beer in a small fridge. It's lukewarm, but I don't care. It's the first drink I've had in two months. He also has running water. Not hot, but I haven't bathed in weeks. So I take a cold-water bird bath in his tub.

Then I sack out on his spare bed. And sleep like a dead man. I wake early in the morning. I have no idea where I am. Or how I got there.

The elevators don't work, so I walk down 11 flights. I meet McCoy in the stairway. He hasn't had any sleep. He has been doing

TV interviews all night, CNN, Larry King, all the big names. McCoy's a household name.

The lobby of the Palestine is a madhouse. Hundreds of reporters, photographers and producers come and go, chatting up Marines, trying to set up interviews. Iraqis come to look for work. Marines set up security outside.

News comes in gulps. The army is roaming western Baghdad. Saddam is nowhere to be found. The Iraqi government has withered. The U.N. ambassador says, "The game is over."

That's good enough for me.

The Marines are still on edge, worried about ambushes and suicide bombers. Not far away, a suicide bomber sets off an explosion that wounds three Marines. The Iraqi's body is cut in half.

About the same time, a squad searching a building finds suicide bomber central. It looks like a factory. There are vests and explosives and detonators. And some empty hangars that, apparently, once held bomb vests. A Marine shows me a note he found inside, with Arabic writing, offering instructions on how to blow yourself up.

The Right Thing

It's dangerous in Baghdad. The streets are jammed with people, especially around the Palestine Hotel, and the hotel across the street, the former Sheraton. Gunshots can be heard every couple of minutes. Some shots are close; others far away. Shooting is so common no one bothers to check it out. You can sit in your hotel room with the window open and hear automatic gunfire. Sometimes it's just a couple of shots; sometimes an exchange of fire.

I'm in a room at the Sheraton with a reporter from *U.S. News and World Report*, Kit Roane. We hear shots coming from outside, near the banks of the Tigris River. We ignore them. More shots. We look out the window. Marines are running, but are they running fast? With urgency? Not really, so we go back to our conversation. More shots. Now there is sustained automatic gunfire and mortars going off. We can see the splashes landing on the other side of the river.

"You suppose we ought to go down there?" I ask.

Kit rolls his eyes. "I suppose we ought to check it out."

By the time we get downstairs, the shooting is over. It's nothing. Someone set up a machine gun in a building on the other side of the river and took shots at the Marines on this side. They responded with about a thousand rounds, until there were no more shots from the other side. As usual, we have no idea whether anyone died. Maybe the Marines have killed whoever was shooting. Maybe the shooter just ran away to shoot again another day.

Sometimes people get shot for no good reason. One day, a man tries to enter the battalion compound. The Marines at the gate tell the man to get back, but he keeps trying to climb over the fence. The Marines shout and yell and try to push him back repeatedly. But he keeps coming.

Finally, a Marine shoots the man dead. There is no weapon on him. No one knows whether the man was prompted by desperation or fear or hatred. "It's a tragedy, really, but the Marine did the right thing," the sergeant major says.

Fighting and Dying

Three-Four sets up security outside the Palestine for a couple of days and then moves down the road about 3 miles to a former municipal complex. They dig in their tanks and armored vehicles in the courtyard and send others to guard a local hospital.

That's when the fifth Marine is killed.

Cpl. Jesus Gonzalez was a tank crewman. He had climbed to the top of the tank when an Iraqi came out from hiding with an AK-47 in his hands. The Iraqi shot the corporal in the back. The corpsman says the bullet entered the Marine under his armored vest in the rear, went upward through his heart and came out the front, lodging in the Kevlar material.

The Thug Patrol

Marines are given the task of conducting civil affairs in nearby communities. This is a huge departure for them. They're more comfortable smashing and bashing and destroying things. There's no way to sugar-coat it. They fight, they kill. Now they're told to make nice and help the civilians.

Second Lt. Milan Langella leads patrols of eight to 10 men through the city streets. The Marines don't want to do this. The Army, he says, is better suited for it.

"Marines should either be fighting or on liberty," he says.

Langella says the locals call him "Tom," but he doesn't know why. He likes that they recognize him, though. Sometimes he takes the guys out on a specific assignment, to look for a sniper who fired on a patrol the night before. Sometimes they just go looking for trouble. The big problem is the lack of electricity and running water. People stop and beg the Marines for these two essentials. But there's nothing the Marines can do. That's an issue for higher-ups.

Life is harsh in Baghdad. Garbage is left in the streets and people try to cope with it by setting it on fire. Black rivulets of raw sewage course down alleyways.

"We have no electric, no water," says one older man with a beard but no mustache. "We have no petrol, no gas for the cooking. Please tell the people we must have water, we must have electric."

Mostly, the Marines look for thieves, looters and snipers.

I go on a couple of patrols with Langella. His men use C-4 plastic explosive to blast locks off doors, then thunder inside, looking for snipers. It's rough, dirty work. Sometimes the Marines and Iraqis get along; often the Marines are rough with people and they leave hurt feelings, as well as bruises.

McCoy sees himself as a protector of the weak. He's especially fond of his "thug patrols." Two burly, beefy tank crewmen go out looking for the meanest, toughest Iraqis and mete out street justice.

The first time is at a gambling den. Locals point out the place and say the men who go there have been robbing and threatening people. So the Thug Patrol pays them a visit. No one will say later exactly what happened, but the Marines apparently beat the hell out of some Iraqis to send a message: Leave these people alone.

"We're out-thugging the thugs," McCoy says. "We want them to know there's a new game in town. We're introducing them to the Marine Corps."

The patrols go day and night, and it's here that the sixth and final death occurs in this battalion.

On April 14, Langella's patrol goes out at night. I don't go with them this time because it's hot and it's a night patrol and much more dangerous. They're trying to find the Iraqis who reportedly were using an abandoned mosque as a base for thieving and robbing.

A couple of Marines go up on a roof. Cpl. Jason Mileo takes off his helmet. No one knows why. You're not supposed to. For one thing, it protects your gourd. For another, it identifies you as a Marine. The men all wear, more or less, the same outfit, right down to goggles strapped to helmets. But it's hot in Baghdad.

A Marine sniper on a rooftop sees a man with no helmet carrying a weapon and looking down into the street where the Marines are supposed to be. Apparently, he figures it's a bad guy, about to shoot Marines. The sniper pulls the trigger. And Mileo falls dead.

The Ice

It's hot. I'm tired. My feet are killing me.

It's time to leave Baghdad.

The war is over. There's more work to do in Iraq, and more stories. But I've had enough; I've been gone for more than two months. I want to go home.

I go to the battalion one more time, to say goodbye. It's hard. I've been living with these guys for more than a month. I want to get out, but it bothers me that they have to stay. The only consolation is that they have orders to leave Baghdad and head for a staging area in the south. They might still be in danger, but probably not.

I shake hands and exchange e-mail addresses with the guys I know best. Kevin Smith gives me a big hug and then presses something into my palm. It's a rosary. "I carried that with me the whole time over here, for luck," he says. "Now you keep it."

I want to protest. He's in a lot more danger than me. But it's a heart-felt gesture, so I keep the rosary.

Howell and I share a "meal, ready to eat" (MRE), and I tell him I feel like a slacker for leaving while the Marines are still there.

"Don't be an idiot," the sergeant major says. "If you have a chance to get out of here, take it. I would."

That's a lie, but I appreciate the thought.

The next day I get on the truck and then a helicopter. Baghdad is beautiful from the air. The buildings are all caramel and cream color, and the architecture stands out. So do a dozen fires filling the sky with smoke.

I'm flying with a dozen other journalists on their way out. A couple of crews from the BBC and Fox News are with us. They've each got about 50 pieces of luggage and gear, and we all have to help them load and unload it. Another reason to despise television news.

We pile into a C-130 cargo plane bound for Kuwait City. The plane is so loud, the crew hands out ear protection. I nod off in the jump seat, my helmet gently knocking against the steel beam on the bulkhead.

The entire trip from Baghdad to Kuwait City takes 12 hours. You can drive it in eight.

I get to the Kuwait City Hilton late that night. It's air-conditioned, with beautiful stone floors and marble bathrooms.

I order room service: a cheeseburger and Diet Coke with ice. The guy forgets the ice. I give the room-service attendant an extra $6 and ask him to go back for the ice. I need that ice more than air itself.

The Return

The 3rd Battalion, 4th Marine Regiment, spends the next month in the desert, near Diwaniyah. The Marines hold a memorial for the six dead. The entire battalion comes together in formation. Six rifles are stuck into the ground with bayonets. Helmets rest on top.

Every man in the battalion passes by. They touch each helmet, and say goodbye.

Then they sit in the searing sun and wait to go home. Hundreds get sick with a stomach ailment. It might be poor hygiene. It might be the water, which they get from the river and boil. In any case, they're blowing out of both ends for several days.

Maj. Matt Baker, the executive officer, calls it "The Epicenter of Ass."

The battalion returns to Twentynine Palms on May 23 and 24. Mothers, fathers, wives, girlfriends, sisters and brothers go to a parking lot outside the base gym for a sweet, emotional reunion.

Flags fly. The Marine band plays the national anthem and "The Marines Hymn." It's hot in the desert sun.

I see McCoy and Howell, Matt Baker and Kevin Smith. There was a swirl of camouflage uniforms as the Marines get off the buses and are swamped by family members.

The married guys, and guys with girlfriends, get off the bus and find their women right away. They go into a 10-minute lip-lock, break free and sprint to their cars, with barely a nod to their buddies on the way out.

Mothers cry and hug their sons. The mother-son bond is strongest of all.

At Twentynine Palms I meet wives, mothers and sweethearts of the Marines I've been writing about. I've known them only by e-mail, and now we place faces to names.

Karen Gentrup of San Jose was the first mother to contact me. Her son, 1st Lt. Eric Gentrup, had told her a *Chronicle* reporter was supposed to go with the battalion, and she looked online to find a story I'd written from before the war. We've been corresponding ever since.

"There are no words to express how I feel right now," she says, as Eric's bus comes into view. The family moves off, toward their cars. Karen holds back, turns and looks at me and mouths the words "Thank you."

The Rattler Bar

Some guys get off the buses and no one is there for them. They go to the barracks and drop off their gear, then head to town. They want to get roaring drunk for the first time in 2003, and maybe get lucky with the local women.

One man came back early with the advance party. He met his wife at the parking lot. They went home and she handed him divorce papers.

So he and I now make for the bars, with a group of other Three-Four Marines. We end up at the Rattler, a dive with a live band and several pool tables. Marines who weren't in combat buy drinks for those who were, and apologize for not having been there. That's how things work in the Corps. Combat veterans outrank those who haven't been to war.

Women, too, seem to gravitate toward the combat vets. Women dance with the Marines and flirt shamelessly. I'm thinking this is a genetic throwback to the time of the caveman.

We close down the Rattler, and one of the women invites us to her house.

She lives at the edge of town. Her bungalow has a lawn of sand. Her adult daughter is inside watching TV.

The woman calls a couple of friends. I volunteer to drive over with the woman and my friend to pick them up. We can't find the apartment right away. It's dark and late. We stop and my friend gets out with the woman to scout around. He's still in protective mode.

"If you hear me shout, you drive to the end of the street and run an Afak drill," he says. Roger that. But there is no trouble. We find the friends and go back to the woman's house.

At one point, one of the Marines disappears into the bathroom with the woman. She's nearly twice his age. Her daughter laughs and says, "That's Twentynine Palms. The week before you all got back, the bars were full of women looking for a good time."

I stay until close to 6 a.m. I don't want to leave my soon-to-be-divorced friend alone. There are other Marines at the party, buddies of his. But they're all drunk and I can see trouble. I leave the next day. Driving down Highway 62, I connect with Interstate 10 and turn west. It's a canyon at that juncture, and looking in the distance I see a dark cloud. It's a sandstorm headed my way.

Epilogue

I talk to Sgt. Maj. Dave Howell sometimes. Evnin's death still weighs on him. He wonders if he did the right thing. He's bothered by the fact that the last thing Evnin said to him was to call him an a——.

"But you know, it wasn't really traumatic," he says. "It was profound. But it wasn't traumatic. What do you think that means?"

"It means you're an asshole," I tell him.

I see Darkside, too. Life has returned to normal for him. He's still running the battalion, and preparing to take it on a seven-month deployment to Okinawa. Training is different now, though. Most of the men are combat veterans. So they know about life under fire. But some are too salty, and McCoy and Howell have to work harder to keep them in line.

"I tell these guys that being in combat isn't all that special," he says. "My backpack has been through combat, so that doesn't mean much."

And life goes on for Three-Four.

Mark Evnin's mother, Mindy, has become my friend. We've met and talked and e-mailed each other. She wanted to read everything about Mark's death. "I keep wanting to stop the clock and keep him alive," she says. "I just think as time passes, and the shock wears off, I feel the pain more. I hate it, but there are no other good choices. So I'll read the article, cry, save it, and be OK."

Shortly after I returned from Iraq, someone told me I'd gotten the war I wanted. I was stunned. I'd never wanted a war. I just wanted to be a witness if one occurred. But I will admit this: I'm glad I went. I wanted to see the worst in humanity. I wanted to know if I could live through combat.

Darkside understands the pride, almost elation, that comes with survival.

"The greatest euphoria," he says, "comes when you've been shot at and missed."

I think about the war all the time.

But here's the strange thing: I don't feel anything about it.

I don't have nightmares. I don't wake up with cold sweats. I don't see the faces of the dead. I don't jump when I hear loud noises.

Maybe I should. But I don't. I tell people it's because I've been a reporter for a long time. You go to murder scenes, you take information from cops over the phone. It's all sterile. You put what you see or hear in a part of your brain that files it away with the story. How many times was the victim shot? Where, in the head? How old was the child who got raped? Is that a body part in the bushes over there?

So I tell myself: That's what men do with war.

All Kinds of Metal Was Flying Through the Air

by Phillip Robertson

Phillip Robertson covered the invasion of Iraq for Salon.com. This piece, which describes an early skirmish in Northern Iraq, appeared April 4, 2003.

APRIL 4, 2003, NEAR KHAZAR, NORTHERN IRAQ—Twenty men are moving quickly across the green field toward a bunker of red earth on a hill. The hill overlooks the town of Khazar, and beyond Khazar is Mosul. We can almost see the city. The sky is overcast, but the sun is behind the clouds, and they make a bright screen. Until now, everyone has been looking down the road to the west because that is the direction the front is going. As recently as Wednesday night, Iraqi regime soldiers were retreating away from Kurdish-held territory, back toward Mosul on this road. In the morning, the Kurdish fighters known as peshmerga were happy when they talked about how the Iraqi lines collapsed during the night. Crowds of Kurdish men celebrated when the Iraqis pulled out of the ridge near Kalak. But now the situation has done a Jekyll and Hyde.

It's 10 minutes to 4 on Thursday afternoon and bad things are starting to happen.

We are just about to leave, to get back in the car and drive down the road away from the front lines, because it's quiet and that is OK with us, when from our place on the hill, I see the 20 or so peshmerga running across a wheat field toward us. I turn to Sion Touhig and say, "Tell me, what does that look like?"

Sion, a photographer from Wales, has this Delphic sense for when a situation will break open, so I'm taking the temperature as we stand on the edge of the hill. Sion's ESP comes with a built-in alarm for when to jackrabbit, to bolt without dignity or restraint, which is why I'm asking is this a retreat or what, even when the answer is obvious. Our car is down the road and isn't easy to get to. As we scan the fields, more peshmerga are leaving their positions and heading back toward the road where we are.

I try to keep Sion in sight all the time as a defense against evil, but he moves around and it's hard knowing where he is. "We might have to leg it, mate," is what he says when he thinks it's not working out. "See those guys?" Sion points at some U.S. Special Forces nearby. "When they go, I go."

Here's a freakish axiom: Twenty Kurdish soldiers running toward us through a field, a field we had just crossed, is a retreat, and the invisible thing making them run is fear and something else, and just behind the fear there are other men coming who are herding them with machine guns and rifles and rocket-propelled grenades—Baath party members or Fedayeen Saddam, because who else would do something that bold? Sion is also sure the peshmerga coming across the field represents a retreat, and just as we figure this out, the state of the world does its silent flip from OK to not OK, and then the shooting starts, bringing with it all the attendant demons of the air and their hideous sounds, cracks, zips and detonations.

Sion says "Fuck this" and jumps into the Special Forces perimeter, which is now full of confused peshmerga who are trying to get out of the way of all the stuff flying through the air. They retreated to a raised square 30 feet on a side made of dirt berms. It sits on the top of a hill and below the hill is the road to Mosul; across from it, green fields. The American soldiers take each corner of the perimeter, load their machine guns and look out over the fields for targets. Inside the perimeter are deep foxholes reinforced by sandbags, but no one is in them yet.

The defensive perimeter, a popular principle in the age of shock and awe, is right where we want to be, and everyone who's anyone has one. If you don't have a defensive perimeter, find somebody else's and get in. So we get in. Sion does it first, then me, and that was it. Inside the perimeter I saw the men lying on their stomachs and peering over the edge into the fields, while all kinds of metal flew through the air over us. The perimeter made a red-earth edge against the sky.

We forgot about standing up. That wasn't going to happen. And we also forgot about trying to make it back to the car. That wasn't going to happen either.

We found the first battle of Northern Iraq the way everyone else did: We drove there after breakfast.

On Thursday we woke up and did the usual things. Sion ate an egg in the dining room of the Shireen Palace and argued with the waiter while I sat down and talked over plans with Baravan and Rashad. Rashad is our driver and Baravan is a lawyer from Dohuk who translates for us. They are old friends and can't be separated. They work with us, not for us.

Baravan and Rashad are Kurdish independent operators. Baravan has this joke, which isn't really a joke, where he says, "Mr. Phillip are you ready for Mr. Chicken?" when he wants to know if we're hungry. "What about Mrs. Rice? Oh, you know Mr. Chicken loves Mrs. Rice." He laughs insanely at this one as we drive down the road in a station wagon that reeks of gasoline and fresh bread. Because Baravan loves the Mrs. Chicken riff, Rashad loves it, and talks about his chicken farm outside of town. Rashad, a solid man in a chocolate suit, is a former peshmerga who keeps Mr. Kalashnikov in his station wagon with several clips of Mrs. Ammunition. They will go anywhere.

During the previous night there were air-strikes and thumps and bangs, but we don't pay attention to them any more because they are normal business, like power failures. The thumps and bangs are the U.S. airstrikes on Iraqi positions near Kirkuk and Mosul, the major oil cities in the north of Iraq. For most Kurds, Kirkuk has a kind of holy status—it is the urban center of their culture. It is also true that when the Kurds take Kirkuk, Kurdistan, their quasi-independent state, will become instantly oil-rich. Kurdish people don't speak about Mosul, a city built near ancient Nineveh, with the same reverence and longing. Kirkuk means both money and history in equal measure—a state of affairs which greatly upsets the Turks to the north.

After eggs, we checked mail, and finally piled into Rashad's car and headed out toward Kalak from Arbil, looking for the new front. On Wednesday night, the Iraqi army had withdrawn from positions over-looking the town of Kalak, on the Zab al Khibir river, to Khazar, about seven kilometers away, and it seemed like it was worth a visit, even if we were getting there late.

The drive from Arbil doesn't take long—about half an hour—and Kalak's old bridge over the Zab al Khibir is still there. The town itself is there. Everything looks the same, except there are no Iraqi soldiers camped out on the ridge that rises up over the town; the emplace-ments are empty. We drive up to the ridge, past celebrating Kurds, until we reach the site of the Iraqi camp. Iraqi documents are flying, drifting across the muddy plain; boys are busy looting the weapons from the half-destroyed bunkers, cracking the crates with pieces of twisted metal. When we pull up, Sion sees a kid beating an unused mortar round with a stick.

Rashad finds an Iraqi military map of Kalak in a ruined bunker and pockets it. As we walk around the former front line zone, we find another bunker in the back that has scores of oblong boxes covered with orange stickers. Baravan translates the lettering and says the black boxes are sealed chemical weapon antidote kits. We get back in the car and keep driving west toward Mosul, looking for the last peshmerga checkpoint.

When we get there around noon, the TV networks have already set up shop, and there are media people milling around from all over the world. All the Land Cruisers are parked at the side of the road, and the peshmerga won't let us go any closer. It's a massive traffic jam. Worse, we can see that there are a few journalists a half mile down the road watching a battle, but we can't see it from where we are, and we want to go see what's happening.

Sion starts walking down the road, and a Kurdish soldier catches up to him and stops him. A couple of others try the same thing and they get stopped. But then all of us are trying to walk down the road at the same time, and there aren't enough soldiers to deal with everyone going at once. Sion gets into a scuffle with a peshmerga, which he wins, and keeps walking down the road. I remember a camera pointing at me—some cameraman saves me by filming the two soldiers holding my arms. Then after they take off, a fresh pair of soldiers tries to stop me—they're young guys who I know, and they are laughing. I tell them, see that battle? Yes, they say, yalla, and they are still laughing, which is good. And I say let's go, and they give up, and then we are all walking down the road toward the hill that overlooks the town of Khazar.

Just as we get there, two U.S. soldiers are walking back down the road, and they say to us, "You people have no sense."

Up on the hill that overlooks Khazar, the U.S. Special Forces were being mortared by the Iraqis just down the road. The mortars were coming closer, moving toward us as the Iraqis refined their aim. A U.S. soldier with a radio called in an air-strike, and after the explosion went off in the town of Khazar, it quieted down for long time.

The Americans then relaxed enough for the commanding officer to give an impromptu press briefing on the hill. He said that the Special Forces had gone down into the town at 7 a.m. to push the Iraqis back toward Mosul. Instead, they were pinned down and had to retreat to where they were now—an open bunker on the top of a hill overlooking the town. The commanding officer spoke clearly, without any action-movie bullshit; his mind was clear and he didn't resent the journalists hanging around.

At the rise in the road, there were eight or 10 Americans in nominal command of several hundred Kurdish fighters. In the briefing at 12:30, the commander told the cameras, "The Iraqis don't care how many of their soldiers die, but they just leave them in certain places, and we have to slow down to remove them." Somebody asked him where the Iraqis went and how many were out there and the officer said, "They seem to have withdrawn. I don't know how many there are."

During the afternoon, there is shooting, but it's sporadic, most of it pointed at the TV cameras. We get used to it and make sure we aren't exposed and easily hit, and after a few hours of that, we think that it's time to head back, because there's nothing new in sporadic shooting. At 3, everyone else is on the road to Arbil to write their stories or file video, and instantly the place clears out, except for the soldiers, who are still up in their redoubt on the hill. Sion says, "Do you want to go?" I want to stick around, though without any well-defined reason. We drift around until quarter to 4, and we are standing on the hill where the Americans are dug in when we see the retreating peshmerga. Then it breaks loose, and we can't go anywhere.

I get little bits of conversation among the men in the perimeter, but I can't move around. Sion is taking portraits of the soldiers and they are letting him do it, making sure that he isn't in a place where he can get hit. Then the gunners move out to each corner of the perimeter and load their machine guns. They start sighting through the telescope sights and get ready to fire on distant targets, but they're having trouble figuring out where all the bullets are coming from. More bad things are coming toward the perimeter, and the Americans are getting nervous— not so much that they couldn't deal with it, just tense frustration.

Kurdish fighters kept running up to one gunner, saying, "Don't fire there, those are peshmerga." The gunner tells the Kurdish soldier, "I know where I'm firing and I know those are peshmerga. I don't shoot peshmerga, I'm shooting at that bunker behind them." The gunner lets the Kurdish fighter look through his sight to make sure. Everyone is confused and firing weapons, but the incoming gets steadily worse. The American soldiers seem focused, careful about their targets. The peshmerga inside the perimeter just wait around with their Kalashnikovs.

The commanding officer gives a soldier near me some ammunition and says, pointing to the man's gun, "Are you any good with that?" The officer speaks to his men without yelling—just talks to them, checking in. "Why don't you go over there and see if you can draw a bead on that motherfucker," he tells the westward-facing gunner. The air above us is a bad place, and the soldiers are not standing; they're running from place to place in a crouch. It's getting much worse. Confusion reigns. The U.S. soldiers have to translate every question or command several times, and the translation varies. "Where are the bad guys? Are these the bad guys?" the commander wants to know. They lose time. The firing on our position is coming from two directions now—not just from the west, but also from the south. Iraqi gunners are moving around abandoned peshmerga positions in a flanking maneuver, trying to cut off the Americans, and they are making steady progress. It is a counterattack. The Iraqis are coming back.

For a second I think that rounds are coming from the north as well, but I'm still not sure if that really happened. It feels like we are on the way to being surrounded, and there is no way to get back to the car more than 200 yards down the road. I can still see it, because Rashad had stuck around and parked it below a rise.

Sion says that he thinks the Americans are thinking of retreating, because he sees them pack up their gear in their vehicles. Instead, they decide to call in a series of intense air-strikes on the Iraqi positions. The commander gets on the phone and calls in the location. This takes time, and we wait for the shriek of the planes and the bombs. When the sound comes, it's good, and when the bomb hits, I think, Jesus, I hope that did it, I hope that solved our problem.

The American soldiers are keyed up and working at finding the targets without hitting the Kurdish fighters by mistake; they do it by straightforward, elementary means—looking and using compasses. After the first air-strike, which is earmarked for the Iraqis to the west of us, there is still all kinds of fire coming from the south. A few minutes later, a pair of fighter jets circles and drops cluster bombs that scatter over the ground, crackle and light up an entire wheat field—a sick Chinese New Year. They do it again, screaming and diving. We are right there with the jets, cheering them, because we want the situation to back off, and if there's a fuck-up, a bad coordinate, a bungled retreat, anything like that, we'll be running across the green fields without much in the way of a chance.

I watch the eight soldiers get it right, solve the problem. The sheet of cluster bombs falls across the road, not far away at all. After that, it is quiet again, and we can leave.

With the Invaders
by James Meek

James Meek is an English novelist and reporter. His cov-erage of the Iraq war reflects his views about American aims and methods in Iraq.This piece appeared in Granta *(October 2003).*

One Thursday in early July, just before midnight, I was on a London bus taking me home through rainy darkness. I was listening to a song by Gillian Welch, 'Revelator', which I'd often played in Kuwait and Iraq during the recent war. I suppose it was the song which made me remember something I had seen on my journey out of Iraq in April, when, it appeared, the fighting was over.

We were an odd convoy leaving Baghdad that morning. There was Ghaith, my new-found Iraqi assistant, and myself in the driver Haider's worn taxi, a Cadillac of 1980s vintage, followed by two frightened young mechanics in a tow-truck of about the same age. Hitched to the truck was the nearly new Mitsubishi Pajero which I had rented in Kuwait before the invasion, promising not to take it into Iraq. The Pajero, which had been broken into, ransacked and immobilized by looters in

Baghdad in the days immediately after the fall of Saddam, still carried the livery which the photographer Paul O'Driscoll had adorned it with before we crossed the border: mud, gaffer tape covering the lights and chrome fittings, and orange patches and chevrons to signify to US and British forces that we were not hostile. I'd parted company with the colleagues I'd travelled from Kuwait to Baghdad with—Paul, who worked with me for the *Guardian*, had returned home via Jordan, while the *New York Times* team of Dexter Filkins, James Hill and their interpreter, Mandi Fahmy, were still working in the city.

Towing the car over 400 miles from Baghdad to Kuwait was tiresome. The tow-truck had four punctures. Twice the mechanics were threatened by armed men, once by US troops, once by vigilantes with Kalashnikovs; on both occasions the mechanics were assumed to have stolen the Pajero. But in the early hours of the journey we sped south under grey skies along a smooth, quiet motorway.

At one point, we passed a man and a boy walking along the side of the road close to some wheat fields. The man, dressed in a charcoal *dishdash*, strode forward without looking to the right or left. The wind making his tunic flutter was only a light breeze, yet his gait was suffused with weariness, as if he was moving against a gale. His face was heavy with anxiety and suffering. He held up his head proudly, but just to do so seemed to be an act of giant strength. The boy, about nine, was his opposite. He was jumping and skipping around the man in eccentric circles, laughing and talking, trying to attract the man's attention, losing interest, running on, running back.

When people go as correspondents to follow armies at war, as Paul and I did when we followed US and British troops into Iraq in March, they are supposed to keep only the sombre adult, grimly fixated on the horror, and leave the frisky child behind. But the two will not be parted. Without childlike curiosity, without a love of the momentary, the trivial, the surprising, the scary, the bright and the loud, what would be the point of going on? And without an awareness of the bloody burden of all the wars men make, how could the child ever come to understand the dark nature of the journey? I kept a diary.

March 21, road junction north of Safwan, Iraq
We've fallen down a whole flight of steps in the economic league, just by travelling across a line on the map, out of Kuwait and into Iraq. The first people we see are looters, picking their way through the rabble on the edge of town—ruined by this war, or the last one, we never found out—and looters are everywhere, coolly plundering equipment from every state institution going. We drive through a litter-strewn main street and women in black and boys in ragged grease-stained pullovers and tunics look at us with stares that say: 'Who are you looking at? What are you going to do for me?' They aren't unfriendly. Nor are they particularly inquisitive. Some of the guys smile and wave.

We drive on through, past the pictures of smiling Saddam and Saddam in Bedouin sheikh garb that the marines haven't got around to taking down, and try to find a quiet spot to park the cars and take stock without attracting a crowd.

We're faced with an emotional scene in the courtyard of the first house we go into, a tumbledown mud brick place opposite a great dry field covered in scraps of black plastic fluttering in the wind. An old couple who lost their son to Saddam's goons two years ago welcome us into the yard and spread rugs on the ground for us to sit on. It is a mad scene, hysterical, dozens of children crowding in, thin bright-eyed men standing looking into the group with their hands behind their backs and darting in to interrupt with their comments and stories, and Mandi, our interpreter, not knowing where to look and what to translate. The old man sobs and we are close to tears too. He says we have come too late, and for his son, of course, we have.

March 22, Rumaila oilfields
It becomes apparent that Basra is not going to be taken quickly, either by the British or the Americans, so we are uncertain what to do or where to go. Initially we strike out east from Safwan towards Um Qasr. We pass British tanks and troop carriers from the 7th Armoured Division. We drive between their gun barrels and the so far invisible enemy. It is an uncomfortable feeling. We head north up the motorway

towards Basra. The Iraqis have made no attempt to destroy their transport infrastructure by blowing up bridges or mining roads. Occasionally the Iraqi army leaves signs of its presence, a blown-up tank which didn't have a crew in it when it was hit, a slinking scorched ditch which the Iraqis had filled with crude oil and set on fire in the mistaken belief it would confuse US imaging systems, a pile of grubby blankets and stale bread rolls under a bridge where soldiers hid. But these are little installations of failed, halfhearted defence in an otherwise empty, undefended landscape controlled by the US and the British.

We talk to various soldiers, mainly American, and I build up a story I think might work, about a farcical tank battle some marines had been involved in two nights earlier. The tank crews were restricted in the kind of ammunition they used in the oilfields for fear of damaging oil installations. They were not restricted in the number of Iraqi soldiers they could kill.

Just before evening we find a camping place with a group of British military policemen from 16th Air Assault. They can't do enough for us. They give us water and food and cover our cars with a piece of hessian so that we won't leak light. I'm so tired, I can hardly make out the words I'm writing. In the oilfields, despite the marines' tender care, some of the wells are burning. After dark, the military police on duty are silhouetted against the orange glow as it brightens and fades. Their bulbous helmets make them look like aliens.

At about 9 p.m. the MPs call for Mandi to translate. An Iraqi family at the checkpoint is trying to tell them something. I follow her and start talking to the MPs. One of them comes back from the group at the car and says: 'I almost shot a kid.' He'd told the people to get out of the car, and they had, and then he'd seen a movement out of the corner of his eye, and almost pulled the trigger; it was a child.

Today reports start to come in of journalists being killed, reports which turn out to be true. I call my wife and my parents to let them know I'm okay. I let the military police make personal calls on the *Guardian* satellite phone. Most of them call their mothers.

March 23, west of Nasiriyah, waiting to cross the Euphrates
Basra has not fallen; fighting continues. It is the tomato season in these parts and we talk to farmers with their trucks heaped with crimson fruit from plantations round Zubair. They are still going to try to make it to Baghdad. They are brave men. It is their livelihood.

Everywhere there is evidence that Iraqi soldiers never went on campaign without a change of civilian clothes: the gaunt young men in cheap shoes and a bottle of grey, scavenged water walking home after tearing off their boots and uniforms and running away from the war. When they talk to us about how many hundreds of kilometres they have to walk to get home it is without indignation or surprise. That is the way things are. I wonder how many of them will die of hunger or thirst or disease by the roadside, trying to make it back.

We swing west on the road that leads to Nasiriyah and eventually Baghdad. There are six lanes and the marines are using all six in the same direction, thousands of military vehicles pouring forward at high speed. At one point we drive up on to a bridge over the motorway for a better view. Paul and James take pictures but the point is in the motion. Very few civilians will ever see anything like this: a modern-day blitzkrieg, a motorized horde taking over a road which, though it runs through the desert, otherwise looks like any European motorway, and using it to rush into battle at commuter speed.

March 24, US Marine supply base near the Euphrates
Our fourth day in Iraq and two preconceptions look shaky. One is that we would be entering Iraqi towns; the other that we would be living and working away from US and British troops, with Iraqi civilians, in 'liberated' areas. Basra still has not fallen and fighting continues in Nasiriyah on the Euphrates east of here. We cannot reach either place. The marines have no interest in urban areas. They want to avoid them. This means these towns are under Ba'ath Party control, however tenuously, and are not safe for us. Left in open, mainly desert country, unnoticed, much of it considered a free-fire zone by US air power, and without access to working petrol stations, shops or markets, let alone

hotels, we have no choice but to seek the protection and assistance of the marines. To our everlasting gratitude, they provide it. All we can offer in exchange, which is not a small thing, is use of our satphones. On that basis Paul manages to blag 120 litres of petrol from a marine refuelling dump.

I want to see the legendary Euphrates, so in the morning I leave where our cars are parked, where the tarmac of the finished section of the Basra–Baghdad motorway expires, and walk forward through the fine dust of the unmade section, past queues of drab olive amphibious tracked vehicles—Amtraks—trucks, tanks and Humvees stretching for miles. The dust is continually thrown up and ground finer by convoys moving forward, but for the time being I have given up any thought of being clean.

The Euphrates is a disappointment: a narrow channel barely forty yards wide with a few palm trees along its banks. The marines newly dug in around a bridge express their scorn for the reality of the fabulous river. I walk a little distance away from the bridge—like this section of the motorway, it is not fully built, and can take only one tank at a time, or a convoy going in one direction—and crouch down by the bank. With my back to the bridge, I can imagine the marines are not here. The river does not seem so small, and it moves powerfully enough. This is at the western edge of the Marsh Arabs' old lands. In front of me is a thicket of delicate green reeds rising from the puckered surface of the water and bending in the wind. A high-prowed canoe shifts like a vane on its moorings and, on the far bank, there is a reed hut with an arched roof. It is peaceful for a moment, before a pair of marine Cobra helicopters the colour of cigarette ash chug low overhead.

We spend the day here, talking to marines and Iraqis. Already there is bad blood between them. Irregular Saddam loyalists have been taking the occasional potshot at the marines—a pea to an elephant— and the marines have been arresting locals, confiscating their domestic Kalashnikovs, searching their houses. A pathetic cluster of Iraqi captives in civilian clothes sits cross-legged in a circle of razor wire under the bridge. At another stretch of razor wire, the boundary between the marines' domain and the way to Nasiriyah, Mandi tries to mediate between the mutually uncomprehending marines behind their machine guns and scores of Iraqis who are trying to get through. One Iraqi family brings a woman with cancer, under the impression that the Americans will help her. They can't, and she is taken back. An Iraqi who works in the hospital in Nasiriyah says US aircraft have killed ten civilians and wounded 200 in an air raid on the town.

In a house a few hundred yards away, Iraqis give us strong sweet tea, a heavenly drink to us at this time. We sit in a big quiet bare room with rugs on the floor, lit by the doorway and a small triangular window in the whitewashed mud wall. One of our hosts says that it was the nature of his country which called forth Saddam, not Saddam who made the country. 'If in Iraq there's a leader who's fair, he'll be killed the next day,' he says. 'Iraqis have hot blood. If he's not tough, he dies the next day.'

March 25, the Basra-Baghdad motorway, just north of the Euphrates

We're parked in what the marines call a herringbone pattern on an unmade stretch of the highway. Herringboning is a tactic to prevent an attacking aircraft being able to destroy an entire column in a single run. It is a good idea, except that Iraq doesn't have an air force any more.

We've been on the road since 7 a.m. Woke up at about five, listened to the BBC for a while. The World Service's coverage has been disappointing. I haven't heard a single interview with an Iraqi civilian or a Western soldier on the ground since the invasion began five days ago. Even though the embedded correspondents have no idea what's going on beyond the units they're embedded with, the BBC deals with them as if they do, and presents their deep, narrow perspective as if it is deep and broad, in the worst traditions of twenty-four-hour rolling television news. There's no sign that anyone from the BBC is operating outside the embed system in southern Iraq, although some of them surely must be.

Our days are like this. We wake at about five or six. I make hot water on a little camping stove we bought in Kuwait, and give some to our neighbours from the *New York Times*, so we can all have coffee. We're down to our last twelve or so litres of water; Paul and I are using about three litres a day between us, mainly for drinking, but also for cleaning our teeth, washing our hands and shaving. Shaving in cold water is a long exercise in painful scraping, especially if you've let a growth set in. We haven't had showers since we left Abdaly on Friday morning. It's now Tuesday. The worst is the hair, which is carrying so much dust that it's solidified into the kind of stiff, abrasive, matted pad of wire wool you scrub pans with. I can't drag the comb through it any more. We eat breakfast from what food we manage to pick up along the way plus what we brought from Kuwait—tins of processed cheese, biscuits, chocolate.

We spend the day interviewing and driving, and scrounging from the troops. At night, the marines ask us not to show white light, even from a torch or a laptop screen, because, they say, it gives snipers something to aim at and it blinds the marines' night-vision equipment. The evening meal is US military MREs, Meals Ready to Eat: fat brown plastic packets containing stodgy shrink-wrapped cakes and biscuits and processed cheese. The centrepiece of the MRE is a green plastic envelope with a hot dish inside, one of twenty-four possibilities, which you slip inside another envelope containing a thin sachet of chemicals. You pour a little water into the envelope, fold the top over, lay it on its side, and the chemicals start to react and fizz, producing heat. It heats us the pottage in about fifteen minutes. It's not great food, but our condition is such that we look forward to it.

Later. A sandstorm. Everything stops. The car rocks on its springs. For what seems like hours there is a crinkling sound as millions of sand grains strike the rear of the vehicle. We try to open the door a little but every time the wind forces it wide open and dust rushes in. The edges of the road disappear on either side and the vehicles in front and behind become invisible. I feel afraid for the first time since coming here, an echo of an old, irrational fear which has nothing to do with the fear of being hurt or killed. It is a fear of going too far and not being able to find the way home again.

March 26, south-east Diwaniyah

We've arrived at this forward supply base in the desert which in a short time grows from a few trucks and Humvees to a park of acres of fuel trucks, ammo trucks, trailers, bulldozers, generators and tents.

On the other side of the road, behind a sand wall, in a long deep ditch and along a catwalk, lie the bodies of dozens of Iraqis, most of them untouched by bullets or shrapnel; a blast must have killed them. They died after what, despite some marines' attempts to claim otherwise, was a feeble, ineffectual ambush. The marines crushed them effortlessly. With the sandstorm and the rain their faces and bodies have been covered with a fine coat of mud, making them look less like dead people and more like clay models, or like the dead Romans at Pompeii. In the article I write today I say they look peaceful, but this is because I don't have time to think of a better word. Eternal would be a better word. They look as if they have been there forever and have just been uncovered by the wind, the same wind that will shortly cover them up again. I walk along the catwalk, clocking the stuff they have left. Little parties of marines are here, souvenir-hunting, but all the good stuff, such as pins and badges, has already been taken by the infantry, who were on the scene earlier. What are left are helmets and filthy blankets and canteens. I think about taking a canteen, they look fine and almost new, but decide it would be too bad karma.

We're guests here of Colonel John Pomfret, the US battalion commander who smokes cigars in the evening and says things like 'I love the smell of diesel in the morning,' and 'I think we're all serving the same constituency,' and 'I believe in honour and nobility.' His mother was a refugee from the Kuomintang domains of China. I have a feeling this war is going to take a long time.

March 27, south-east of Diwaniyah

It's 8.30 p.m. I'm sitting in a tent with the other journalists, in our gas masks and NBC suits (nuclear, biological and chemical), in the second gas alert of the night. Everyone is trying to keep calm. Finding vials of mustard gas treatment on the dead Iraqi troops in the ditch across the road made the idea of them using chemical weapons seem more real. Looking at the map the other night I saw we were about ninety miles from Babylon. I remembered the nursery rhyme:

How many miles to Babylon?
Four score and ten
Will I get there by candlelight?
Yes, and back again.

Back again would be good.

March 28, south-east of Diwaniyah

The marines announce they are confiscating all Thuriya satphones on the grounds that the Iraqis can track them and take a grid location they can use for targeting. It's bad, though not the total disaster it appears. Paul files using another satphone system which I can use, though it's hard to get through. We still have the Thuriya hidden in the glove compartment of the car, turned off.

We're thinking of switching battalions to a unit closer to combat, namely the 5th. We speak to the commander, Colonel Dunford, and he seems to be happy to have us travelling with him. I'm beginning to think that, rather than regarding accompanying journalists as a nuisance, the marine field commanders see them as trophies. Until prostitutes get 4x4s and war accreditation, we are the nearest to camp followers the battalions are going to get.

The US advance seems to have ground to a halt. Colonel Pomfret says as much today. 'What we are going to be in is an operational pause, to rearm, refuel and rest. It doesn't mean we are stopping.' Or rather, it does. The ambushes on US convoys have freaked the marines out. Dunford doesn't mention it but his driver tells me he got shot at yesterday.

Over by one of the Hueys parked at the 5th I see a girl I assume is a journalist. I say girl not woman because she seems like the torchbearer of all-Californian (she *is* from California) girlhood, with straight shiny blonde hair sticking out under the brim of her bush hat, a glowing red-brown tan, snub nose and bright blue eyes, and an expression that says 'Hey! What's going on?' before she does, which she does. I assume she's a journalist, yeah, leaning there insouciant and apparently idle against the 'copter doorway, but she is a crew chief. Sarah Wilson is her name. She stands behind one of the two big machine guns in the doors of the Huey. A few days ago she'd been behind the gun while the bird was clattering over Nasiriyah, pumping .5 calibre bullets into a house, a house thought to be full of Iraqi resisters. A tank had called for help and she was on to them, 'Like, which house? Fire your gun at it or something so we can tell.' So the tank fires and the helicopter crew sees the house, and they try to fire their rockets, but the rockets haven't been loaded properly so they don't fire, so they bring their guns to bear, and the bullets hit the building, and the forward air controller tells them: 'Good hits.' Sarah's glad to have been busy, the first marine crew chief to have been in combat, because she didn't think she'd end up doing anything.

March 29, south-east of Diwaniyah

This is a down period now, after those first days of driving forward through Iraq, always forward every day; now we've stopped and it's frustrating. More for us than for the marines. They seem glad of the chance to do their laundry. Sports news, non-war news, is beginning to creep on to the BBC. Pomfret tells Dex he's grateful that his report in the *New York Times* about his 'operational pause' remark, which, was raised at a Pentagon press conference and impatiently denied by the spokesman, didn't name him. My report named him, but neither he nor the Pentagon seems to know that.

I've been trying to work out what this mighty force of marines is lacking; what their billions haven't bought. The answer is language. It is not just that there's never more than one Arabic speaker per battalion, not just that they haven't put more money and effort into making more of their troop multilingual by conventional means, but that they haven't even tried to apply their ingenuity, their technological and organizational genius, their gift for systematizing life, to language-learning. They're afraid of enabling elements of another culture to enter the minds of the men and women, and the cost is high, to them and their opponents. They can't meet each other except by fire. An Arabic speaker in each platoon: they could slip into the cities in small groups and talk to people. They could ask questions first, and shoot later. But to get there their American minds would have to travel a little way into the mind of Arabia, and that is a journey that seems particularly terrifying to the institution of the US military.

March 30, Camp Pomfret, south-east of Diwaniyah

I go with James and Dex to watch Major Stainbrook and Major Cooper, the civil affairs duo, trying to help some farmers start the pump to put water into their irrigation system. There's Cooper, first language Irish Gaelic, second English, trying to communicate with the aid of a device called the Phrasealator. It isn't much better than nothing. The end result is that the pump starts working and water gushes out of a foot-wide pipe. It is a joy to see it move, white and cold and alive, through the channel of parched, cracked earth towards the barley fields.

March 31, Babil Province

We move forward at last, heading for the River Tigris. We are entering the Iraqi heartland. At dusk we come across a group of marines who have found a civilian trailer parked under a tree with two surface-to-surface missiles in the back, abandoned by the Iraqis. If they are leaving equipment like this behind, surely it signifies the final collapse.

April 1, Babil Province

In the morning we leave Colonel Pomfret's benevolent cavalcade and switch to the hard-riding 5th Regiment, whose headquarters battalion camped overnight at an unfinished petrol station by the motorway a few miles down the road, past the trailer with the missiles. We stop off there for a while; a group of intelligence experts has arrived to examine the weapons. They pull down the side of the trailer and we can see the name of the missiles is written on the side. In big blue Arabic letters it says: 'Al Samoud'. None of the intelligence experts knows this, because none of them can read Arabic, not even the letters. Mandi and Hussein, a Kuwaiti journalist embedded with Colonel Pomfret, enhance their intelligence for them.

A terrified Iraqi farmer, whose farmhouse is right next to the missiles, creeps back to the home he has fled in order to get some things. There is a stand-off between him and a group of patrolling marines because he is afraid, with good reason, that they might shoot him if he does the wrong thing, and he cannot understand what they are saying to him, and the marines don't speak a word of Arabic. He stands cowering and quaking and flinching in the middle of the yard, not knowing whether to lie down, put his hands up, go back, go forward, or prepare for death. Mandi steps in to translate. The marines tell him they're happy for him to go back and live on his farm, but the farmer doesn't believe them, or doesn't trust them. In all fairness, he is right; these marines may want him to move back in, and want to help him, but later other US troops will come who do not know him and his family, and who knows what could happen in the confusion of the night when heavily armed men are all around and two peoples do not speak each other's language.

There are two grey marine Chinooks parked at the petrol station. They are supposedly there in case they are needed for casualty evacuation but they are also used to transport Oliver North in and out of the marines' area of operations. The colonel is embedded with this helicopter unit for Fox News. He spends much of the day at the petrol station, as we do. He sits around telling young marines bloodcurdling tales of Saddam the torturer—'. . . and he said, "I want him to last nine days" [before he dies of torture]'. North urinates ostentatiously in full view of everyone in the centre of the petrol station forecourt, holding an aircraft navigation map to conceal his prick, while carrying on a shouted conversation with a group of marines a few yards away. The marines love him. He does a live two-way to New York with one of the medics who went to the village. I go over to say hello and he asks me whether I work for the *New York Times*. I tell him no, I'm from the *Guardian*.

'Who owns it?' he asks.

'The liberal conspiracy,' I say. No I don't. I tell him it owns itself. He's furious with the *New York Times* for quoting Pomfret's 'operational pause' remark. Later it transpires that some officers didn't want the journalists travelling with them after Dex quoted a regimental sniper describing how he had killed a civilian woman. 'The bitch wouldn't get out of the way,' was what the sniper said. The objectors were overruled.

In late afternoon, when it is already getting dark, the part of the battalion we are to travel with prepares to move. There is a drivers' briefing. The drivers are told what they should do in case of direct fire and in case of indirect fire. Later, when we're in the car, Paul says: 'What's the difference between direct and indirect fire?'

'I suppose direct fire is when they're shooting at you and indirect fire is when they aren't shooting at you but hit you anyway.'

April 2, near Numaniysh, on the River Tigris
Back from a trip with Major Broton to the Saddam Canal bridge, shot up by marines who went forward ahead of us last night. Broton went to help a man whose friend was killed by the marines because he didn't put his hands up. The corpse is lying in a shallow hole. The dead man's friend keeps thanking Broton, who comes up with a couple of old black plastic bin bags to cover the two ends of the body and helps manhandle it into the back of a small car. He writes a *laissez-passer* for the friend on a page torn from my notebook.

The company crosses the bridge and moves towards the Tigris. We pass through villages where the residents seem surprised to see us; not by the military presence, since we can't be the first to have passed through, but by the sheer quantity and purposefulness of the convoys. They wave at us if we wave at them first. Most of the roads here are built on embankments running alongside deep irrigation channels, through corn fields alive with larks and plovers. Despite its state-of-the-art navigation systems, the company gets lost for a while. As soon as we stop, baby goats dive under the Humvees for shade and the marines lovingly coax them out.

We find our designated night stop, a fallow field, and while the marines are setting up we go to the river, a couple of miles further on, to watch a pontoon bridge being built. An F18 comes down low overhead and performs a barrel roll, scaring the Iraqis watching from the far bank, who think they're going to be bombed.

Apart from the F18, it is quiet. This bridge-building has nothing in common with film portrayals of Second World War bridges being built with shells splashing in the water around. A tank captain at a checkpoint nearby, Ted Card, complains that he and his men are bored by the Iraqis' failure to resist.

April 3, north of Aziziyah

We drive across the Tigris and on the main highway from Kut to Baghdad join another episode of blitzkrieg as the marines race each other along the tarmac at high speed. We stop short of Aziziyah while Cobras and tanks clear the road through the town, ruthlessly blasting anything that remotely resembles resistance, while avoiding any responsibility for aid and order in the town itself. For hours we watch the helicopters passing through the smoke and hear the thud of automatic fire and the crack of artillery. There are two gas alerts. Eventually, after many requests, we get an escort forward into the town and are able to talk to civilians, who tell contradictory tales of who has been hit and hurt by the US attacks, who is in hospital; some say Iraqi fighters, some say civilians, some say both. The Americans, says one man, Abdel Karim, sent bombs like silver rain.

Our company drives past and we slip in with them and drive forward in the twilight. We pass shops gutted in the fighting and see figures dancing on the roof of a burning building, trying to put the fire out with buckets. Dozens of vehicles are on fire, but it is not the scene of the aftermath of the titanic clash between the marines and the Republican Guard we had been led to expect. It is beginning to look as if the guard is evaporating. A tank burns in a palm grove, the trees, lit by the flames, reflected in the still water of a pool. We stop for more than an hour close to where something vile is smouldering, a smell so pungent and toxic-seeming that I put my gas mask on. The frogs are not affected. They cheep lustily.

April 4, near Baghdad

Paul goes forward wearing a baby-blue flak jacket and an old US helmet from the Gulf War which is too small and makes him writhe and curse as he drives. I'm not much better, in an old Israeli-made flak jacket with worn Velcro and a helmet which is to my body as the cap is to a mushroom. 'Hey look!' screamed a marine the other day as I drove past. 'There's a guy with a fucking kayak on his head!'

There can be no doubt now. For those on the streets, at least, the welcome for the Americans, the smiles and the waves, are genuine. For the first time today I see someone attack an image of Saddam Hussein; a young guy, alone, hurling stones at a portrait of the dictator not for anyone's cameras or for the US military's benefit but for his own release.

The marines' lack of linguistic skills continue to make them enemies. We see them destroy a harmless car with heavy machine gun fire because the occupants got out of it and, with no idea what the Americans screaming at them wanted them to do, ran away, leaving their vehicle. There has been a lot of fighting here today. Another first was seeing a burnt-out US tank, an M1 Abrams.

April 5, south of Baghdad

So many of the embedded reporters we see are paunchy old guys with hunter's moustaches and big camper's coffee mugs, whose families and friends are doomed to be bored with this war for decades to come. It seems to me I saw a big fellow sitting in a camping chair wearing a pair of waders the other day, but this is not possible. My wiser self has to keep pointing out to my vain self that I don't want to be one of those men. My wiser self also knows that wisdom is not the end and the answer to all things and that ultimately wisdom can only uncover the dual nature of existence, the irreconcilability of states which is reality but which we strive, with our narratives, to hide.

Yesterday the marines sent Omar on his way with his shirt and trousers covered in the blood of his family. His mother and father, his uncle, two sisters and one brother were shot dead at the crossroads checkpoint. The marines said their coach hadn't stopped and had accelerated when warning shots were fired. I guess in the darkness when people are shouting at you in a foreign language and shooting at you it's hard to know whether to stop or whether they've just missed and you only have a few seconds to escape. What do civilians know about warning shots in the dark? So there was Omar, crying and lost, all covered in blood, and his baby brother behind him with his face shot up. Omar was looking at us, and the marines standing around exhausted by shame and fear and fatigue, and feeling even worse now because the reporters were writing it down.

What do you say to Omar? How do you look him in the eye? What comfort can there be? These marines weren't going to be punished or investigated. Dex wrote it up for the *New York Times* and I wrote it up for the *Observer*, and both papers ran it, but so far as I know it went no further. The marines killed eight civilians at this checkpoint, three of them children. What do you say to Omar? The fact is that his family have been murdered for no reason that was good for him. A supporter of the war would say that there will be greater happiness for all surviving Iraqis as a result. But they couldn't say that to Omar, because it is meaningless to him. That is the duality that we can never find our way around. In speech, we are all purists; there is the good, the bad, the must-be-done and the cannot-be-allowed. In our hearts, we are accountants. I wrote about all those who died last night, the Iraqi general lying in the dirt behind the white Japanese family car, Omar's family, the marines, being petty cash in Donald Rumsfeld and George Bush's grand accounting. But the truth is we are all accountants, and the balance is not only in how good or bad this is for me, my friends, my family, my folk. It is: 'How close do I have to get?'

The reason old men can make wars is that they don't have to get close to it. Those who take responsibility don't have to look into Omar's eyes in the morning when he's drenched in his parents' blood, and those who have to look into his eyes don't have to take responsibility for it. It's a sweet scheme. I wonder what George Bush had for dinner last night. His fork must have been clinking on the china just about the time when his marines were killing Omar's family. It must be nice for the President to realize he doesn't have to say sorry to all the people who've lost the people they loved in this war. He doesn't have to say sorry to anyone.

April 7, Baghdad

The 5th is not going to cross the river into Baghdad today. The roads turn out not to be what they looked like on reconnaissance and satellite pictures. We leave them and drive south, looking for another regiment, the 7th, which we have heard is going into the city. We find one of their battalions poised to cross the River Diyala, queued up on the highway south of a bridge at midday. The troops are pumped up with aggression. Most of the lower-ranking marines have painted their faces with black and green camouflage paint, but they have made it war paint, reaching into their memories of trick-or-treating and horror films to make themselves look frightening. There are homages to *The Last of the Mohicans*, to *A Clockwork Orange*, to *Apocalypse Now*. More than one marine has contrived to make a direct tribute to Death by painting on his flesh an image of the skull within.

Hundreds of looters walk past, pushing generators and motorbikes stolen from a warehouse. The marines watch, concerned only that the looters are not a threat to them. They aren't bothered about the crime; their only response is to applaud the looters sarcastically. Hours pass and the adrenalin and testosterone begin to lose their potency. Dex is on tiptoes with frustration at being so close to Baghdad but not actually in it.

The colonel relents on his original refusal to allow us to drive forward and we cross the bridge over the Diyala under escort from Major Milburn, an English-born marine. The Iraqis tried to blow it up and had placed mines on either side but the marine engineers managed to clear the mines and bridge the gap with a folding bridge of their own.

We find ourselves on the Baghdad side of the bridge, just after marine tanks were machine-gunning something a few hundred yards away, and suddenly the marines are gone and it is getting dark. Paul wants to go back across the bridge, Dex and I want to go on to the battalion's overnight halt. But we reckon we can't stay by ourselves where we are. Paul is particularly anxious not to go on because there is an anti-personnel mine on the road which hasn't been cleared and we might not be able to see it in the half-light. As it turns out the choice is made for us. The battalion begins pouring across the bridge, blocking it, so we can't go back to the other side of the river, and all we can do is tuck in with the convoy and hope they stop for the night after a short distance.

We pull in between a couple of Amtraks and set off through the deserted industrial landscape with the glow of burning oil to our right. Paul is driving the *Guardian* car, Dex the *New York Times* car in front. No lights, so we have to make our way by the outlines of the vehicles in what ambient light there is. There is just enough to see the mine and drive around it. We press on and everything seems to be fine. Then we see something burning, up ahead, and hear a popping and a banging. It is an ammunition truck on fire, and the ammo on board is exploding. We can hear the bullets whizzing and pinging in all directions. We stop about fifty yards short. The armoured vehicles we are with just squeeze past the truck as fast as they can, but we aren't armoured, we can't go back, and we can't stay where we are. But if we try to scoot past the truck, we risk being blasted. We see Dex gesticulating to one of the Amtraks going past and then moving off. We see what he is trying to do—drive past the truck at the same time as the Amtrak, using the armoured vehicle as a shield. The two vehicles lurch forward, the Amtrak almost squashing the 4x4 until the driver realizes what Dex is doing, the *New York Times* car half off the road. They make it. Then it is our turn. We go past the truck with our Amtrak, same deal, the two vehicles squeezing past the truck. You can feel the heat from the flames in the truck. Just when we are parallel with it, the three vehicles together, our car half off the road, I see a bunch of concrete fence posts up ahead, blocking our way on the right. I warn Paul and we have to stop for a few seconds, though it seems longer, to let the Amtrak go by before we can go on. So we make it through and on to a side road, where we halt and crawl forward, halt and crawl. Helicopters are overhead and machine gun fire on the other side of a rise to our right. The sergeant in charge of one of the Amtraks, the one who realized at the last moment what we were doing to get past the truck, comes up to find out who we are and what we are doing. He is very friendly but in the course of the conversation it emerges that his unit isn't heading for a night encampment at all, it is going into combat, and we are going with it, in the middle of the night, without night vision equipment, radios or armour. The Iraqi military barracks up ahead are going to be bombed, then the marines are going to clear what is left building by building, then they are going to hit an airfield in diamond formation, tanks on the outside, soft-skinned vehicles in the middle. The sergeant offers us pistols. We need to be further back. They get on the radio and arrange for us to drive back down the column to where the colonel is, seventeen Amtraks down.

We drive slowly, counting the bulks of the Amtraks, slightly darker than the night, and find the colonel. He is furious. 'What happened to not crossing the fucking bridge?' he says. 'You're not fucking riding into combat with my boys.' He wants us to go back, but he is afraid we'll get whacked by the hair trigger his people are on for suicide bombers, seeing these two strange civilian vehicles in the night. So he has to give us an escort, which he is really pissed off about too. As he is being angry, though, he cools down and realizes that he did give us permission to cross and that there wasn't much else we could have done.

April 8, Baghdad

Wake up this morning to the smell of death. It could have been from the dead Iraqis a hundred yards up the road but more likely from the long-dead dog just a few yards away from where we stopped last night with a few light armoured vehicles, LAVs, parked around. The wind must have changed, because last night the air smelt good, and there weren't any insects. Now it stinks and the flies have incorporated us into their sphere of putrefaction around the dog. It's 7:10 a.m. We're by the bridge over the Diyala we crossed yesterday. Sitting by the road-side on James's camp bed, it's beginning to spit with rain, I can see Constablesque trees blowing in the dusty wind, a dark grey speeding cloud behind them from where some kind of oil installation got hit, or the Iraqis set it on fire. Mandi's helping mediate the passage of refugees across the bridge. Refugees, no, just people trying to go about their business without getting shot. A lot of bombing in the distance, a continuous thunder, but I feel safe here.

We've reached built-up areas already, clusters of yellow box houses. The houses closest to the marines have been searched by them and their inhabitants told to keep away. Marines have taken up firing positions behind piles of bricks and in foxholes, guns pointed towards the houses. We walk in over the dirt, past the raggedly laid bricks of the houses with their frayed black and green Shi'a flags flying. On the street we meet men who have just been arrested and tortured by Saddam's people, before the Americans came and the tor-turers fled. One has a fresh cigarette burn on his chest. While we are talking we stop cars to ask them for petrol. We find one guy who lets us siphon almost twenty litres out of his tank. He refuses to take any money. Another guy, a taxi driver, takes $10 for the same amount. Someone brings us strong sweet tea in little glasses on a tray. It is good.

April 9, Baghdad

We hook up with one of the marines' psychological operations (psyops) vehicles—a Humvee with loudspeakers on top—and head out, a convoy of four vehicles. Quickly we are in the city, in a built-up area with big city roads. We come to a junction where there are already some marines and there is a crowd, and traffic, and shuttered shops, and a red double-decker bus. Iraqis are looting a duty free warehouse nearby, pushing boxes of Dimple whisky out of there in shopping trolleys. Before we have much of a chance to talk to anyone the convoy is off again. I am driving and Paul makes me stop for a second while he jumps out and persuades one of the looters to give him a bottle.

The convoy's destination is the UNMOVIC (United Nations Monitoring, Verification and Inspection Commission) headquarters. The marines arrived after the looters. Everything inside the building is stolen or smashed. The marines are helping themselves to boxes of rations the UN left so we take some too, a change from MREs. Some of the marines come over and ask for whisky and I pour them measures according to their cups. We climb up to the roof of the building where two marine snipers lie watching the multi-storey buildings opposite. An aircraft drops a single bomb on a building a few blocks away, raising a tall cloud of cinders. Colonel Toolan, of the 1st, is on the roof looking thoughtful. The war is turning into something that isn't a war. It is beginning to look as if there is no enemy, and no real fighting to be done.

We go downstairs to find journalists from a different world, with clean flak jackets and pressed shirts, journalists who have recently showered, Brits from the Palestine Hotel, where only the previous evening Saddam Hussein's government had ruled, with all its apparatus of fear and corruption ticking and grinding in bloody greedy circles. These guys, from ITN, tell us that in the morning their old Information Ministry minders fled and that they'd simply gone with their drivers the couple of miles from the centre to UNMOVIC. The road is open. The regime has collapsed. All the fears of block-by-block street fighting, like Grozny, indeed all the hopes by Saddam Hussein of block-by-block street fighting, like Stalingrad, are gone. Very few fought. This has been a kind of rebellion against Saddam, a rebellion of not-fighting. They went to fight for Iraq, and they ran away for freedom. While we are speaking to the ITN guys we come under sniper fire and the marines shoot back, but it doesn't take away the sense that the shooting war is substantially finished.

We drive on a little further with Colonel Toolan and watch him with some of his tank commanders unfold a map of the city on the bonnet of a Humvee and discuss deployments for the rest of the day. They talk about whether they have enough tanks, but enough tanks for what? They no longer need any tanks, except for effect. Their opponents have thrown away their boots and uniforms, ripped off their badges, hidden their weapons, stuffed the cash in their holdalls, revved up the getaway cars, gone sadly home to their families, gone into shock and denial, turned to God. The mob is looting. The city is burning. It is time to say goodbye to the US Marines, who have been so kind, who have fed, watered, fuelled, sheltered and protected us and guided us to our destination. It is too bad they are trained, equipped and organized in such a way that they killed so many civilians, men, women and children, along the road. Their night-vision goggles can turn night into day but they have nothing to see other cultures as clearly. They can see Iraq only in so far as it deviates from the norm, and the norm, the only possible norm, is America.

Beyond Baghdad

by Paul William Roberts

British writer Paul William Roberts is a critic of the United States' policy in Iraq and Afghanistan. This article appeared in Harper's (July 2003).

Hey George Bush
What was the rush
When all you've done
With your planes and guns
Is replace one Saddam
With a million madmen?
      —Roughly translated, the latest popular chant

The Iraqi people were free. And, first and foremost, free meant the freedom to loot. Driving around Baghdad during that first week in April, I saw handcarts, flatbed trucks, cars, mules, even baby strollers, laden with choice items—gigantic vases, photocopiers, TVs, silk carpets—from Saddam's palaces and the various luxurious outposts of the Baath Party ministries. I saw a wheelbarrow piled high with cash: The banks were being looted. Admittedly, they contained only Iraqi dinars—$500 to the wheelbarrow—since Qusay Hussein and his mother had removed all the euros, U.S. dollars, and gold bullion with three tractor trailers two days before the war began.

I also saw a shoot-out between bank robbers. It seems three brothers did not agree on the division of the spoils and ended up killing one another over a skid of banknotes.

Next up were the hospitals. Sister Bushra of the Dominican nuns who run the Al-Hayat maternity hospital gave me a list of the items looted and for which the hospital is now in desperate need. It includes:

Patient beds
Operating-theater ceiling light
Operating table
Anesthetic machine with accessories
Stethoscopes
Scissors for operating theater (all sizes)
Incubator
Surgical gauze
Antiseptics
Antibiotics
Surgical sutures
Surgical gloves
Syringes

All the looters left, it seems, were the building and its patients.

Bombs

"What am I to do?" asked Ayad Fardis, a professor of engineering at Baghdad University. "I have nine persons in my family. Who will pay my salary? I hear from no one. No one knows when university will open."

His students were due to present their theses, but he did not know where any of them were now, if they were alive or dead. It was a wasted year.

His house had also recently been demolished by a large bomb, whose shock waves had shattered the windows of every house in a residential area half a mile square. Were there military installations or missile launchers nearby?

"No, there was nothing military in the area," he reported. "Nothing at all."

The bomb was dropped at 11:45 a.m. Everyone was home. I imagined the blast must have been deafening, but Professor Fardis, the scientist, explained that at the center of an explosion you hear nothing, because the sound waves travel outward. There had merely been a tremendous shuddering as the building cracked apart around them. I could not recall ever having heard this fact about the sound waves before, but, of course, one tends not to encounter many people able to testify on the subject.

What seemed most remarkable was that of the ten people home only one, a son, sustained any serious injuries. To explain this miracle, the professor had come up with something like an equation that combined the various locations of family members at the time of impact with the reasons for their precise whereabouts. The solution to the equation, though, was somewhat less scientific: "God. Only the God can do this."

God had clearly devoted so much time to positioning the Fardis family pawns that He had been unable to devise a similar scheme for the professor's sister and her family in the adjacent house. Of thirteen people, two were dead and eleven seriously injured.

"Here are my books, my research, my hopes and dreams," said the professor, indicating a charred pile of hardbacks, binders, and ashes. "What am I to do?" His eyes brimmed with tears, but then he pulled himself together

"We are a strong people. We have seen many war . . . many. We will survive. We will rebuild. And we want nothing from the pocket of America. We have our own oil and that will be enough. Don't worry for us."

Oil

General Al-Mokhfar and I are now in the oil business together. We're partners. He used to get a concession from the Oil Ministry of two million barrels a month. If he can get the same concession from the new Oil Ministry—when there is one—we will split 2 percent of the profits, for the general cannot travel to make deals, and I can. No Iraqis can now leave Iraq. The so-called coalition has turned this country into a vast concentration camp.

The Media

We were up at the U.S. Army's front line for the highway north. There had clearly been some recent and very heavy fighting going on. The road was littered with shell casings, some of which punctured our tire. As we stopped to repair it, I realized that what I'd taken to be oil garbage was in fact the blackened corpse of a man whose upper torso—arms, head—seemed to have melted into a tarlike puddle. Beyond him were more such flash-fried humans. Many more. The nauseating, somewhat sweet odor of dead human flesh permeated the air. Local villagers were doing their best to carry off the bodies, or body parts, to a hastily dug mass grave. The hard machines fared no better than the soft ones: Iraqi tanks, wherever I saw them, were charred, crumpled skeletons.

Limping down the highway toward us was a motley crew of men holding a black flag. They were neatly dressed in tracksuits but wore no shoes.

"Deserters from the Iraqi army!" announced the reporter for a leading Western newspaper. "They discarded their boots so no one would realize they were Republican Guard."

I pointed out that the black flag and lack of shoes probably indicated Shia pilgrims on their way to Karbala for their grieve-in—long banned by Saddam—to celebrate the martyrdom of Husayn, the Prophet's grandson. This Shia Easter was now unbanned and imminent.

"Well," said the reporter, "for readers of the ———, they're going to be deserting Iraqi soldiers now."

He instructed his photographer to capture these scenes of dispirited desertion.

But the moment we had retired to our rooms in the Al Arabee Tourism Apartments—whose rates had inflated 100 percent in three days—behind the Palestine Hotel, the reporter's editor back home decreed that the day's most important story was not deserting Iraqi troops. What readers wanted was an update on the state of "Stumpy."

"Stumpy" was the media term of endearment for a young boy named Ali, who, in a rare and unfortunate incident of collateral damage, had lost his entire family, both arms, and received severe burns on 35 percent of his body. Some days earlier Ali had been a celebrity victim—indeed, U.S. military spin doctors were encouraging the media to visit the hospital bed in legions, which created the impression that Ali was perhaps the only tragedy of collateral damage this war had produced. Had its chief architect, Donald Rumsfeld, not spoken, on March 21, of "the humanity" that now goes into the implementation of America's weapons of mass destruction?

But Ali's celebrity had swiftly waned. Bureau chiefs directed their ground troops to the wholly more appealing celebrity of the fetching Jessica Lynch, whose heroic story every reporter I discussed it with found dubious. For a start, her injuries were inconsistent with the shoot-out that allegedly caused them but were consistent with a crash rumored to have occurred as a result of careless military driving.

Either way, news audiences, it was believed, had tired of Stumpy. They wanted no more of him, let alone news of the hundreds of other Alis bleeding in the corridors of a dozen Baghdad hospitals whose contents had been looted and whose staffs were heinously overworked and totally unpaid.

Yet, it seems, readers of the ——— were more moved by the plight of young Ali than readers elsewhere. A fund had been established to help compensate for his loss of arms and family.

So the reporter and his photographer were ordered to proceed immediately to the Saddam City hospital where the forgotten Stumpy still languished.

When they returned I was told that doctors were not optimistic about Stumpy's future.

"He's going to die of septicemia," said the reporter, mournfully.

It was not the story his editor wanted, but it was a story. The photographer went to work on his images of the bereft boy, emailing them off to his photo editor. I had seen a few of the ones he sent. They were heartbreaking.

An hour later the photographer came to my room.

"Do you know what my editor asked me?" he said.

Naturally, I did not know.

"He said, 'Don't you have any of him smiling?' "[*]

The Good Man of Samarra

Samarra is a pleasant, sleepy little city 100 kilometers north of Baghdad whose chief claim to fame is a unique spiral minaret dating from the ninth century. The town in between Tikrit—Saddam's hometown—and Baghdad, Samarra was never exactly keen on Saddam or his Arab Stalinism.

Omar T. Ali al-Samarrai, to whom I had been introduced by mutual friends, had invited me to Samarra. By now I'd grown tired of the media circus around the Palestine Hotel—the events staged by the military for a gullible media—so I accepted. The journalists I knew said I was crazy to go alone, yet when I invited them to come along they refused.

There were no Americans in Samarra when I showed up there with Omar. The fact distressed him. Because Omar claimed to have done a courageous thing on behalf of the so-called Coalition: he had freed seven U.S. POWs—two pilots captured in Karbala and five soldiers taken during the fighting in Nasiriyah. The captives had been brought to Samarra by "Chemical" Ali Masjid, believed erroneously to have been killed in Basra. The orders from General Ali were to kill the

---

[*]A day later, Stumpy was airlifted to Kuwait for treatment and to retain the appearance of a happy ending. There may yet be pictures of him smiling.

POWs, but Omar had instead freed them and reported the fact to U.S. forces on April 11. One would have thought that his bonafides were established.

I expressed an interest in tracking down "Chemical" Ali, but he was protected by some twelve Syrian mercenaries and evidently moving from house to house in outlying villages. Even in Samarra there were many deeply indebted to the old regime and willing to hide the fugitive. Like all the fleeing Revolutionary Command Council members, Ali was rumored to be carrying hundreds of millions of dollars in cash, and even where tribal and blood ties run deeper than religion or politics, this buys you a lot of protection.

The stories I'd heard from "embedded" journalists were far better than the reports they sent their editors. I encouraged a few to write about their experiences for this magazine, but their reluctance proved the case against "embedding." The Pentagon's psych-warfare boys must feel truly vindicated: It's jailhouse psychology—the innocent man imprisoned with several hardened felons will inevitably bond with them. As Jimi Hendrix observed, "Loneliness is such a drag."

So I became "embedded." Dressed like an Arab I was more comfortable, for a start, and I was so inconspicuous that, with my rudimentary Arabic, most people assumed I was Omar's idiot nephew.

And Samarra proved an Aladdin's cave of intrigue. I'd interviewed Captain Abdullah Mohammed, who assured me Chemical Ali had come to him on April 9—nearly two weeks after his "death"—to have a stack of fake identity cards properly stamped, so I had little reason to doubt the veracity of Omar's intelligence sources in that area. Like Chemical Ali, Ahmed Hussein—Saddam's personal secretary—was also in town, hiding. So was "Comical" Ali—Information Minister Mohammed Saeed Sahhaf—reported earlier by the Iraqi press to have blown his brains out ("this is not a gun"). I'd heard the confession of one Mahi Atta, who, along with Ibrahim Alawi and two others, had allegedly buried alive some seventy-eight Kuwaiti civilians, mainly women and children, captured from a bus in 1990. Furthermore, Omar assured me that something very secret was located beneath

Samarra's Shaheen Hotel. Exactly what it was he couldn't say. It turned out to be an Iraqi military communications facility. On top of this I had an interview with Tariq Aziz set up. By now my laptop had been stolen and I had $300 to my name in a land where credit cards are the subject of jokes.

Omar claimed to have planned, in 1995, an elaborate coup attempt against Saddam, which was nixed at the last minute by his wife's brother, the preeminent Iraqi dissident Wafiq al-Samarrai, who had been based in London since 1994. Before that, starting in 1980, he had been Saddam's director of army intelligence.

Wafiq was due in town the next day, to begin his leadership campaign under the National Salvation Movement banner, and I persuaded Omar that Wafiq would be the ideal person from whom to receive help in managing our information overload. It would surely boost his political clout to be involved in the capture of so many criminals and the discovery of so many atrocities.

The Americans

The visit with Wafiq was a bust: Omar's brother-in-law, as it turned out, was less than enthusiastic about the P.R. opportunity. So we made the egregious mistake of approaching the U.S. Army 3rd Brigade Combat Team, which had finally arrived to intimidate a city already prepared to fete their presence and victory.

I don't know what it is about coiled razor-wire barriers with tanks behind them, or about men and women not so much dressed as bedecked for extreme danger and laden down with the stuff of killing, or about those wraparound sunglasses that all grunts seem to wear, but the overall effect is both alien and ludicrous. Packed into the old Baath Party headquarters in Samarra, the U.S. Army looked very much like a bunch of poorly educated, very scared post-teens from a distant planet, beamed down into what they believed to be very hostile terrain and absurdly overarmed.

"Hey!" shouted one of these creatures as I approached. "Stop right there!"

The dishdasha and turban had obviously thrown him, so I reached for my *Harper's* press card saying, "It's okay, I'm a Brit journalist."

"I said, 'Stop,' fucker!" he growled, pointing his machine gun at me. "You understand 'stop'?"

I nodded.

Another soldier appeared and asked me in an Arabic worse than my own what I wanted.

"I do speak English," I pointed out, in my best Oxonian accent.

"Get this motherfucker!" the first soldier shouted to no one in particular.

After the grace and courtesy of the Arabs, this jolt of American culture unnerved me. I removed the turban in an attempt to convince them I was friend and not foe, but the combination of tightly wound cloth and heat left my hair looking like a toupee basted in Vitalis or motor oil.

The second soldier patted me down roughly, then scrutinized my *Harper's* press card minutely. I had just got myself ready to defend its authenticity when he said, "What the fuck is *Harper's*?"

For the first time in my life I wished I was on assignment for *National Review*, to which I hastily compared *Harper's*—inasmuch as they were both magazines with a political focus.

"It have naked chicks in it?" he asked next.

"Not as many as we'd like . . ."

"Am I gonna see my name in it?"

"If you tell me what it is, I guarantee it."

I noticed that many soldiers, deliberately or otherwise, concealed the name patches on their helmets under sand goggles. Flak jackets hid the breast patch. He now turned the press card over and examined the two dense paragraphs on its back. I realized I'd never read them myself.

"Who the fuck is Ben Metcalf?" he asked, after two minutes.

"Editor. Senior Editor."

The expression on his face made me wonder if I'd said "pimp" or "crack dealer."

"You report to him?"

"Yeah. He's like the general. And I'm like . . . you guys. The ground troops."

I thought this inspired.

"I never talk to no fucking generals," he said, bitterly.

I quickly demoted Ben Metcalf to sergeant.

"Sergeant he'd fucking be here. Like me."

I wondered how he even knew about Ben, soon discovering the tiny point on the press card's back declared that all questions regarding the I.D. should be directed to Ben. I hoped Ben knew about this.

"What the fuck is this?" the soldier demanded, thrusting the card under my nose and prodding the second paragraph angrily, as if it contained something terrible. Maybe it did . . .

Mercifully, it proved to be a French translation of the former paragraph.

"Why the fuck is that there?"

"Good question," I said. "Maybe it's because I live in Canada."

"Let me get this straight," he said. "You got a British passport, you live in Canada, and you write for an American magazine . . ."

"Right."

"You gotta admit it sounds weird."

I admitted it did.

"So why you dressed like this fucking scum?" He indicated the growing crowd of locals, some of them clearly concerned for the welfare of Omar's idiot nephew. I told him I found his remark deeply offensive.

"Thatta fact?"

"Yep."

"Fuck you."

The Colonel

I was about to walk away, back to the "scum" whom I'd come—over thirteen years of documenting their joys and sorrows—to respect more deeply than any other people on earth, when brigade commander

Colonel Frederick Rudesheim showed up. Tall, humorless, with a face so dry and blotchy it looked camouflaged like the rest of him, the colonel at least asked, in English, what I wanted.

As I rattled off the embarrassment of intelligence riches, and mentioned the POWs freed by Omar, I could see more than a flicker of interest in his ungenerous eyes. He sent me to fetch Omar, who had been waiting patiently in his car outside.

We were then taken into the Baath Party H.Q. and interrogated by Rudesheim. Also present was a Kurdish translator wearing a U.S. Army uniform and a frightening pair of those wraparound shades.

"Why you concern yourself with Kuwaiti civilians dead when so many Kurdish peoples also dead?" he demanded at one point.

I wasn't sure what the right answer to this might be. Kuwaitis, it must be said, are not the most beloved of Arab peoples. Kurds, of course, are not Arabs but rank high among the most oppressed of peoples.

The Kurdish translator then flashed a smile his face appeared incapable of seconds earlier, and I gathered that he was joking. Kurdish humor is probably worth a doctoral thesis.

Half an hour into the grilling, Colonel Rudesheim announced, somewhat surprisingly, that he had a lunch appointment. Omar and I said we'd go back to Omar's house for lunch, but that didn't suit Rudesheim.

"You're the best intelligence assets I've come across," he informed us. "I'd rather not let you out of my sight."

What did that mean? Were we being detained?

"I'm just concerned for your safety," the colonel assured us, unconvincingly. "I'd prefer you just wait here. Then we're gonna fly you up to Tikrit so the C.I. guys can talk with you. Okay?"

I made another futile attempt at persuading him that we'd be fine driving back and forth to Omar's, but I could tell we were "detained."

"We'll make sure you're fed," the colonel added. And with that he was gone.

Lunch

A "Meal, Ready-to-Eat," or MRE, is more loot bag than meal; the fat khaki plastic pouch announces its main course but contains many surprise items, though the only unannounced item anyone wanted to find was the "dairy shake," a satchel of flavored coffee-creamer-like powder to which one added water and shook vigorously. They were unusually good—even the chewy sludge invariably left at the bottom. But "dairy shake" appeared in only one out of twenty MREs, and there was no chance of divining which pouch contained it.

The MRE menu is eclectic and daring: Country Captain Chicken, Beef Enchiladas, Beefsteak in Gravy, Spaghetti with Meat Sauce, Seafood Jambalaya, Chicken Tetrazzini, etc. But the in-flight meal supplied by Aeroflot at the height of the Cold War was a gourmet tour de force by comparison. The pouch pointed out, for those who may not have noticed, that active combat duty was more demanding than hanging around the base back home, thus a soldier required more nourishment. Then, curiously, it conceded that soldiers might not want to eat the actual M in the MRE, and if so should be sure to consume its high-carbohydrate side dishes, which were largely crackers and long-life bread products.

I require little from food—steak and potatoes is fine seven nights a week—but the main courses in MRE pouches plumbed culinary depths undreamed of even by the Brits. Among the paraphernalia designed to enliven the general tedium of a soldier's day—a fruit-punch mix, jam, two squares of chewing gum, four sheets of toilet paper, a miniature bottle of Tabasco sauce, a green book of matches designed to function in damp conditions (but, the blurb admitted, not in very damp conditions), cocoa mix, a plastic spoon, a "moist towelette" sachet—was a large, clear plastic envelope containing a thin slab of brittle foam.

The instructions explained each stage of the heating process in terms that made it sound like the assembly of a cyclotron. There were numerous diagrams, too—one of an amphibious blob labeled rock, illustrating the instruction to place the heated meal in its pouch against a "rock or something." There were several warnings about not eating the slab of brittle foam in the bag, which apparently played a crucial role in heating the meal. Evidently, every year a few soldiers did try eating it. No one seemed to know whether these soldiers were counted as "friendly fire" casualties.

My MRE was not in fact ready to eat for more than twenty minutes, at which point I extracted the pouch, tore off a notched strip near the top, dug in my plastic spoon, and ate.

One mouthful of Country Captain Chicken was enough to convince me not to attempt another. Omar, however, approached his Chicken with Salsa like a man offered $10,000 to eat a bag of earthworms. He was startled and perhaps disappointed to find the scarlet sludge had no taste at all.

Return of the Colonel

By the time Colonel Rudesheim returned from lunch, Omar and the Kurdish translator behaved like old friends—something the colonel clearly did not like. Rudesheim told us a Black Hawk helicopter would soon be arriving to take us up to Tikrit, and then he resumed his questions.

At the point where I stated that Wafiq al-Samarrai had little support for his National Salvation Movement in Samarra, the colonel bristled.

"I've just attended a big lunch hosted by him," he said, "and all the local Sheikhs were there. Looked to me like he had a ton of support."

I told him the two most prominent local sheiks—Adnan and Fadhel Hassan—had assured me the previous day that Wafiq would be lucky to get 10 percent of the vote in any election. He had three strikes against him, the sheikhs had pointed out: he was a military figure, and no one wanted the military involved in a new regime; he was a close associate of Saddam from 1980 to 1992; and lastly, he had been living in exile, which meant he had avoided the suffering in Iraq yet now expected to return as a leader.

"Looked like a popular guy to me," Rudesheim repeated, making me realize how ignorant he was of the customs and social norms in the land he occupied.

"The sheikhs are there out of courtesy," I told him. "And no one would show disrespect to their host. But they will also support the candidate they think will win."

"They're two-faced?"

"If you like, yes. But in different ways than we are two-faced . . ."

"We?" Rudesheim narrowed his eyes.

"Like when Bush says this war is to liberate Iraqis . . ."

"S'right." He was daring me to go further.

"We all know he's lying, don't we?"

"I don't believe the president of the United States is a liar," Rudesheim said in an eerily quiet voice.

"Wafiq is trying to impress you."

"And he succeeded."

I told him that Omar's wife was Wafiq al-Samarrai's sister and that she was willing to testify in court that her brother was guilty of mass murder.

Rudesheim was now edgy but determined not to show it.

I explained that Omar had arranged an elaborate coup against Saddam in 1995 involving two jet fighters and a thousand troops. It was carefully thought out and might have succeeded. But Wafiq, from his exile, had nixed the plan and undermined support for it, mainly because, in Omar's opinion, it did not involve Wafiq.

"Put it this way," I said. "If this war had been fought in '91, Wafiq would have been on your top-ten most wanted list."

"I'm sure C.I. will be fascinated," said Rudesheim.

Soon enough our Black Hawk was waiting. The colonel told us we were to be flown to Saddam's palace complex in Tikrit, where the CIA were eager to hear all we'd told him.

"They'll probably put you up in Saddam's bedroom," he shouted, over the din of revving Humvees.

Editor's Note:
Here the manuscript, handwritten by Mr. Roberts, and faxed from Le Hotel Royal Amman by a friend, trails off.

My Two Wars

by James Harris

James Harris, M.D., is a lieutenant commander in the Navy. This article ran on the Op-Ed page of The New York Times (April 20, 2003).

ALI AL SALEM AIR BASE, KUWAIT—A few hundred feet over Nasariya, through smoke rising from a city ablaze, a small shoulder-launched surface-to-air missile went hurtling past the aging CH-46 Sea Knight helicopter in which I was riding to deliver emergency medical care to Marines injured in a firefight. About then it occurred to me: I am too old for war.

My last war was different. In 1991, I was 30, flying an F/A-18 Hornet attack jet off the aircraft carrier *America*, and my views of Iraq were mostly from several thousand feet. Usually my targets were buildings or armor without visible troops, but even when my fellow pilots and I did see people killed we took comfort in knowing that they were soldiers who, given the chance, would have killed us, too.

Back then, I was flying an aircraft that could climb 40,000 feet in a minute. We ran in at high speed, picked the time and place of combat and then left. "Getting out of Dodge," we called it. The missions were long, but when they were over we always came back to the boat and hot showers and clean uniforms. When the war ended, there was just a little sense of disappointment. Many pilots, myself included, secretly wished that the fight had lasted a few weeks longer. It was a guilty thought and one we did not share outside the ready room, and certainly not with our wives.

This time, at 42, I spent the war flying into combat at 100 feet and 100 knots airspeed. There was not a day when I didn't want to go home.

I was a surgeon in the Marines' Casualty Evacuation Program, which was expanded and enhanced for this war. A more agile, fast-moving and flexible ground force, it was believed, needed more agile medical care. And so for this war, Navy doctors with surgical training like me were placed in Marine helicopters flying evacuation missions. The logic was that on a rapidly advancing battlefield, field medical facilities would not be able to keep up. Airborne doctors would fill the gap. They could perform life-saving procedures—inserting chest tubes, opening abdomens, clamping blood vessels—during the journey back from the front.

Casualty evacuation by air has historically not been a primary mission for the Marines. They would do it as a "lift of opportunity"—meaning that if a helicopter happened to be available while performing another mission it could be used for evacuation. In contrast, the Army has established medevac squadrons with specially equipped Black Hawk helicopters carrying medical aviation personnel. This is their sole mission and they are quite good at it.

At the war's outset, putting doctors on Marine evacuation teams seemed an excellent idea. But like some other new ideas in this war, it was revealed in practice to have some flaws, especially in the opening days of battle.

I arrived in the gulf four days before the war began. Home base was a previously unused section of the Ali Al Salem Air Base in Kuwait that the Marines call "Camp Snakepit." The Air Force part of the base—off limits to Marine and Navy personnel—has air-conditioning, a hospital and a gym. The Marine compound has dark tents, a garbage dump and several old unexploded bombs. What looks at first glance like the camp's one appealing feature, a lush oasis along the eastern border, turns out on second glance to be something else—a lagoon where the base's raw sewage is dumped.

This is where I spent the opening hours of the conflict—in Camp Snakepit's hastily constructed bunkers, sweating in full chemical protective gear. We were attacked 10 times in the first 12 hours. None of the notoriously inaccurate missiles did any damage, but some came close enough for Patriot batteries to engage them. It was therefore something of a relief when we left Snakepit's squalor for the combat zone on Saturday, March 22, the fourth day of the war.

Forward base was in an empty field in southern Iraq near the Rumaila oil fields—and just outside the security perimeter surrounding the Marine headquarters. We hadn't been there long before we had our first mission. A British soldier had been shot in the head, we were told. We flew a short distance to the pickup point. Corpsmen on the ground were frantically trying to get a breathing tube into an unconscious patient with a five-inch "gutter wound" on the left side of his head. I stopped their efforts and got him aboard our helicopter. His pupils were dilated and fixed. His breathing was labored. All signs pointed to a fatal brain injury.

I tried to get a tube in him, but found his tongue too swollen from previous attempts. I briefly considered cutting open a surgical airway, mostly for my own training. The next time it might actually keep a patient alive. But the conditions on board were too difficult: too much vibration, too little space, too little light. It was not until several minutes into this increasingly futile situation that I got a good look at the patient. He was wearing an Iraqi uniform. It seems he had been shot by a British soldier, and was not a British soldier himself. This type of miscommunication plagued us throughout the first week of combat.

Later, we were asked to pick up two Iraqi prisoners with gunshot wounds to the leg. Both were calm, polite and grateful for their care, which consisted only of pressure dressings and morphine to dull the pain. At the time, Kuwait would not allow prisoners to enter the country. Since there was nowhere in Iraq to take them, our air controllers told us to transport the two Iraqis to a Navy hospital ship in the gulf. Unfortunately, the helicopter had no rafts and the pilots weren't cleared for shipboard landings at night, so we couldn't go there. After three hours in the air and heated exchanges with our controllers, we finally dropped the patients off at the same place we had picked them up.

During the battle of Nasariya in the first week of the war, we received a frantic message that marines advancing through the city had been ambushed, leaving 16 dead and at least 25 wounded. We took off and promptly flew into what looked like a scene from *Black Hawk Down*. Enemy tanks were burning alongside the road. A small oil refinery was in flames—so were buildings across the city. Looking down, we could see marines fighting house-to-house, kicking in doors. Occasionally, dark-clothed men would run into the open, fire from their automatic weapons, and then dart out of view. Thousands of Iraqis lined the streets and balconies to watch. And in the middle of it all was the civilian fire department, trying to douse the flames that had broken out.

We had been given bad coordinates for the pickup location. And we did not have any radio communication with the ground forces. Our pilots circled and tried to contact the troops. Unwisely, in my opinion, they did this over the populated areas of the city. The ground fire that had been sporadic rapidly increased in intensity. Only after a small shoulder-launched surface-to-air missile was fired in our direction did the pilots take us south to open fields. Eventually, we landed along a road and ran over to some marines to ask for directions to the casualties and a good radio frequency.

We were told that the killed and wounded were from an ambush on the north side of town. We took off and instead of circling around the city flew down the main road, taking heavy but inaccurate ground fire the whole way. On the north side of town we found the site of the ambush. It was hard to miss: three destroyed amphibious personnel carriers—also known as Amtracks—were burning. The ground troops popped a smoke flare just in case there was any doubt. We landed next to an Amtrack. Something powerful must have hit it. The top and back were blown off. Only after landing did we notice the dozens of live grenade launcher rounds scattered in the road by the blast. Eight or 10 of them were under our helicopter.

As we were getting ready to go to work, a white pickup truck came racing over a nearby bridge. The aircrew deployed with M-16's, and when the truck came within 500 yards they fired warning shots. The truck turned around. We soon discovered that the number of casualties had been overstated. There were several dead, luckily not as many as we had been led to believe. And there wasn't much for us to do. We wound up evacuating a soldier with a broken jaw.

The night after Nasariya presented another challenge. Trying to land in the desert and pick up an Iraqi prisoner of war with a leg wound, we experienced a "brownout," which is what happens when the propellers kick up so much sand that you can't see. When the air cleared, we found ourselves tilting seriously to the left. If we had touched down I am certain we would have rolled the helicopter. (That's exactly what happened to a UH-1 Huey a few nights later, taking the lives of three Marine aviators.)

After the aborted landing, the pilots wisely asked that the patient be moved to a paved road less than a mile away for the second landing. After touching down, I ran out to get the patient and was promptly met by flashes of what I took to be gunfire. I raced back to the helicopter, grabbed a rifle and finally mustered the courage to sneak back out. Several more flashes came my way. This time, I realized their source. Multiple jackasses, most of them probably half my age, in nearby Marine vehicles were taking pictures of the scene.

The situation didn't improve. When I reached the prisoner, he yelled at me, in fluent English, to remove his handcuffs. After I refused, he tried to bite my corpsman. I calmed him with a large dose of pain reliever. In retrospect, given the atrocities Iraqis committed against civilians and American and British soldiers, I regret that I did not sedate him instead with a hard elbow to the jaw.

After four days at the front, I felt a palpable sense of relief when we were ordered back into Kuwait. Part of my concern was that like many laudable ideas, this one—taking surgical personnel and equipment to marines at the front—had serious problems. The cabin of a CH-46 is too open and noisy and filled with wind to even check for heart sounds, much less perform advanced surgical procedures. What's more, every patient I saw was either too wounded to be saved or not wounded enough to warrant the risks of airborne evacuation and medical treatment. We evacuated marines with fractures, infections, even one with undefined lower back pain.

When a fellow Marine evacuation doctor and I spoke to commanders about the wisdom of the mission, we were met with resistance. "It's just marines trying to help marines," came the response to our suggestion that the helicopter pilots were making bad tactical decisions. But my aviation background and my colleague's time as an officer in the Special Forces eventually helped our case. So, too, did common sense. The novelty of being fired on gradually wore off for many of the Marine pilots; the wisdom of not risking lives and equipment for minor injuries became self-evident. By the end of the conflict, communication between field and base over when to launch had improved, as had basic decision-making.

Despite its flaws, I imagine the Marines will keep the Combat Evacuation Program. The corps likes the idea of not relying on other services for help. (There's a gnawing suspicion among marines that Army medevac units, faced with mounting casualties, would take care of their own wounded first.) Moreover, for the Marine helicopter squadrons the program offers a direct combat mission in a service that values combat above all else. And the ground commanders seem to enjoy having their own assets parked right outside their tents. Of course, everyone likes the idea of saving lives.

But the inconvenient truth is that not that many lives were saved. In emergency medicine, there's the concept of a "golden hour"—the brief period after a traumatic injury when medical intervention can save a life. The golden hour exists, but you can take advantage of it only in wars that are fought from established fire bases and with fixed surgical facilities nearby. Today's battlefield is now too wide and fast-moving for such facilities to be of much use. They can't keep pace. In this conflict, and in the short, intense ones to follow, there may be no time for a golden hour.

That's not to say this war wasn't a huge and rapid triumph, a display of unprecedented power. It was. But both my tours in Iraq have shown the enduring gap between novel ideas and the chaotic realities of battle that deserve to be remembered amid the deserved glow of victory. As for myself, I've spent time wondering why I was so much more frightened this time around. Certainly, it's more dangerous to fly low and slow in an old CH-46 than it is in a new F/A-18. As a pilot, my destiny was in my own hands, as much as it could be.

But there was more to it than loss of control and frail equipment. In 1991, I had been married three years. My wife and I had one young son and another on the way. Death on a battlefield would have been sad, but my family would have gotten over it. Now we've been married 15 years and we have four boys. The loss would be impossible to fathom. There is a reason, it seems, wars are fought by younger men.

Survivor: Iraq

by Lawrence F. Kaplan

Lawrence F. Kaplan's story ran in the **The New Republic**
(October 13–20, 2003).

Visiting the Walter Reed Army Medical Center, a sprawling hospital complex in Northwest Washington, the first thing one notices are the young faces. Soldiers in their teens and early twenties sit in the waiting area, baseball caps on their heads, mothers at their sides. The second thing one notices about these young men evacuated from Iraq is that many of them are not whole. Where there should be arms and legs, there are too often only stumps. For all of its contemporary architecture, high-tech wards, and superb physicians, the place has the feel of a Civil War hospital.

Walter Reed is located only a few miles north of the think tanks, government offices, and, yes, magazines that pressed for war in Iraq. But it is a different country altogether. Different because, with the exception of two visits by the president, few of the war's architects have come to see the mangled 19-, 20-, and 21-year-olds on whom they rely to accomplish America's aims abroad. Neither, for that matter, have many news organizations. *The New York Times* has yet to devote a full article to the subject, unless you count a fictional story by Jayson Blair. Nor have any of the three major newsweeklies. This despite the fact that, nearly every evening, huge C-17 and C-141 transport planes land at Andrews Air Force Base, on the outskirts of Washington, ferrying wounded Americans from military hospitals in Europe. Unlike at Baltimore-Washington International Airport—where soldiers returning on leave navigate their way through crowds of news crews and cameras—flights at Andrews land under cover of darkness, with no TV lights to guide the wounded to waiting ambulances. Instead, their stories have been left to local newspapers in Texas, Georgia, upstate New York, and elsewhere, which convey news of the maimed to hometown readers.

The near-invisibility of the wounded has several sources. The media has always treated combat deaths as the most reliable measure of battlefield progress, while for its part the administration has been reluctant to divulge the full number of wounded. (Pentagon officials have rebuked public affairs officers who release casualty figures, and, until recently, U.S. Central Command did not regularly publicize the injured tally either.) Indeed, with so many injured from so many services being treated in so many places, the Pentagon itself does not possess an exact count. (The Army surgeon general's office has dispatched a team to come up with its own figure.) But even the rough estimates tell a sobering story. According to Central Command, in addition to the nearly 200 Americans killed in action in Iraq since the war began in March, as of last week more than 1,600 Americans have been wounded, more than 1,300 of them in combat.

The numbers tell a truth about the situation on the ground in Iraq—or at least about the Sunni triangle where most of them originate. Every day, Iraqi guerrillas wound an average of nearly ten Americans, many of them grievously. And these are just the ambushes that find their mark. Soldiers back from Iraq tell of coming under fire routinely, and, in recent weeks, about 20 separate attacks on American forces have been reported every day. As a result, the sheer number of wounded soldiers exceeds anything Americans have seen since Vietnam.

Horrifying as it is, the number contains a silver lining as well. The wounded have been maimed. But they have also been saved. During the Second World War, one in every three casualties died. During the Korean, Vietnam and Gulf wars, the figure declined to one in four. In the present conflict, that number has nearly halved, to one in eight. This, as much as the types of munitions directed against them, accounts for the large number of injured coming back from Iraq. Put another way, were it not for the advances of the past decade, half the wounded in Walter Reed today would probably be dead.

Specialist Brandon Erickson, a cheerful, round-faced 22-year-old from Grand Forks, North Dakota, offers living proof of how far battle-field medicine has progressed. Sitting in the physical therapy ward's "apartment," a mock living room and kitchen where amputees relearn the basics of daily life, Erickson recounts his journey to Walter Reed. In February, his National Guard unit, the 957th Multi-Role Bridge Company, was activated, and, in April, just as the assault on Baghdad was winding down, the unit followed the 4th Infantry Division into Iraq. Although Erickson was trained to build bridges, when he arrived at his base camp in Ramadi, west of Baghdad, there weren't any left to build. Instead, he found himself assigned to an MK-2 patrol boat, scouting riverbanks for suspicious vehicles.

Then, on July 22, as he was en route in a truck convoy from Ramadi to Camp Anaconda, north of Baghdad near Balad, Iraqi guerrillas set off a rigged artillery shell in front of Erickson's vehicle. Within seconds, three rocket-propelled grenades slammed into the truck, one exploding on the passenger side of the cab where Erickson sat, his elbow leaning out the open window. As the other vehicles in the convoy sped to a "safe zone," Erickson's first sergeant leapt out of his Humvee and tried to pry the wounded soldier from the wreckage. But the blast had sealed the door, and the truck was still under heavy fire. "Then, I crawled through the driver's side," Erickson says, "got out of his door, and dragged [the driver] behind the tire. When the Humvee drove by again, it stopped, and I jumped in. . . . Then they brought me to another Humvee, where a medic did first aid." The truck's driver, another guardsman from North Dakota, died on the spot.

"I was bleeding so bad," Erickson recalls, "they used a wrench to tighten the tourniquet." Within 25 minutes, however, he was being treated at a forward aid station and from there was rushed by helicopter to a larger combat support hospital at Camp Dogwood. "I remember a surgeon asking me if I could feel my fingers, and I tried so hard, but I couldn't feel a thing. My arm was hanging on by muscle tissue. . . . When I came out of anesthesia, I looked down, and it was gone." Despite losing his right arm—and half of his blood—Erickson was alive. Later that day, a medevac took him to Baghdad Airport, where he was put on a plane full of wounded soldiers headed for Europe's largest U.S. military hospital, Landstuhl Regional Medical Center in Germany. Doctors operated on Erickson soon after he arrived, cleaning his wound and inserting beads filled with antibiotics. He spent five days at Landstuhl, where "all the rooms were full with wounded." From Germany, Erickson and other injured soldiers were flown on a C-141 to Andrews and then bused to Walter Reed—where, nine weeks, three operations, and one prosthesis later, he remains today.

There was nothing improvised about Erickson's journey. From his first contact with a medic to his arrival at Walter Reed, every level of medical care he passed through had been elaborately choreographed months earlier. In a war where nothing else has proceeded according to plan, the medical-evacuation system has worked exactly as intended.

As throughout modern history, the most important variable in determining a wounded soldier's chances of survival remains the time that elapses between injury and hospitalization. Among those who die on the battlefield, roughly half die within 30 minutes of being wounded. By contrast, if an injured soldier makes it to even a field hospital, the likelihood he or she will survive improves exponentially. From the Civil War through the First World War, wounded soldiers were typically seen by a physician within twelve hours of being injured. During the Second World War, the interval shrunk to six hours. By Vietnam, where medical evacuation by helicopter became the norm, the delay was reduced to as little as 30 minutes.

The standard set by Vietnam has yet to be improved upon. Owing to simple geography and the fact that the Vietnam War lasted a decade—during which American forces erected military hospitals from one end of South Vietnam to the other—the distances between a gunshot wound and an operating room were shorter than before or since. "During Desert Storm," explains Dale Smith, a professor of medical history at the Uniformed Services University of Health Sciences, "the size of the battlefield and the forward movement of American forces made it a much longer trip than in Vietnam." This prompted the Army to rethink the medevac process and eventually yielded a system, on display in Iraq today, which brings surgeons to the wounded rather than vice-versa. Instead of being confined to hospitals in the rear, doctors now operate on the very edges of the battlefield (ideally within ten miles) in Forward Surgical Teams—mobile units consisting of between ten and 20 surgeons, anesthesiologists, and nurses, who provide sophisticated care to soldiers like Erickson before they arrive at support hospitals. Moreover, military doctors in Iraq have brought with them equipment that was until recently the exclusive property of major trauma centers here in the United States. Diagnostic imaging machines, traction devices, mobile operating rooms—in Iraq today, this equipment follows closely behind the tanks and armored personnel carriers that Americans ride into battle.

The time that passes before the wounded reach a sophisticated trauma center—that is, a military hospital in Europe or the United States—has been dramatically reduced as well. Hence, a soldier can be passed from a Forward Surgical Team near the point of injury to a Combat Support Hospital behind the lines and then on to Landstuhl all within 24 hours, as Erickson was. After being stabilized in Germany the wounded are then flown to Andrews Air Force Base and taken by bus or ambulance to Walter Reed or the National Naval Medical Center in Bethesda, Maryland. During the Vietnam War, the journey often took months. Erickson arrived at Walter Reed a week after being injured.

After rapid evacuation, doctors and patients alike credit body armor—the new Kevlar helmets and ceramic-plated flak jackets—with saving the most American lives in Iraq. Erickson, for example, whose shrapnel wounds track exactly above the neckline of his protective vest, probably wouldn't have survived had the grenade blast penetrated the large blood vessels in his chest. "We've got a tremendous increase in soldiers saying that body armor saved their lives," says Robert Kinney, chief of the individual protection division of the U.S. Army Soldiers Systems Center in Natick, Massachusetts. "Just look at the wound patterns." Surgeons at Walter Reed and Brooke Army Medical Center in Texas make the same point, noting that about 80 percent of the wounds they have seen from Iraq have been leg and arm injuries.

Leg and arm injuries, of course, kill soldiers, too. Indeed, about half of the battlefield injured who die before reaching a surgeon's table bleed to death, most within minutes of being wounded. Because even helicopters can't fly quickly enough to prevent hemorrhages and blood loss, military physicians in recent years began exploring new methods to stanch bleeding at the point of injury. "For a century, we've just had gauze bandages," says Army Colonel John Holcombe, commander of the U.S. Army Institute of Surgical Research in San Antonio, Texas. "But, in Iraq today, we have improved tourniquets, quick-clot powders, and hemostatic bandages." These bandages, which contain clotting agents and dissolve directly into wounds, arrived on the eve of the Iraq war, and, even now, only the Marines have made full use of them. Erickson, for one, had to make do with a tourniquet.

Still, he survived an attack that, but for his body armor and rapid medical care, would have placed him in a different column—a fact Erickson seems to comprehend better than anyone. Comparing the wounded with the healthy yields a tragic statistic. Comparing them with the dead reveals lives saved by angels on the battlefield. Combat took Erickson's arm. But combat medicine gave him his life.

Memories Don't Die So Easily
by Geoffrey Mohan

Geoffrey Mohan's piece appeared in The Los Angeles Times *(April 18, 2003).*

BAGHDAD—A man staggers from his exploding car after running a checkpoint but returns for the limp body of a woman.

A mother and 6-year-old child lie curled up in the cab of a civilian truck, riddled with bullets.

A major trudges toward the body of what appears to be a fallen Iraqi soldier, only to find a U.S. captain cut down by fire the senior officer commanded.

These are the enduring images of war. They're what remains after all the tales of sophisticated machinery and well-wrought plans are told, after combat patches fade. They're what soldiers of Cyclone Company, and those who led them, will carry home from the war in Iraq.

Cyclone Company, part of the U.S. Army's 4th Battalion, 64th Armor Regiment, came into Iraq with 77 soldiers. Some were barely out of boot camp. Others had more than a decade of service. Some joined because there weren't any other jobs. Others joined because it was a family tradition.

They weathered a brutal 48-hour convoy through untracked desert and were greeted in the small Euphrates River city of Najaf, in central Iraq, by a withering mortar attack and snipers. They fought their way out of an ambush south of Baghdad and fended off rocket-propelled grenades, or RPGs, to take the entrance to one of Saddam Hussein's palaces.

The 14 tanks of Cyclone Company logged an average of 800 miles and moved farther in two days than most tank units did in months during World War II. They blew up 40 tanks, 59 armored personnel carriers, 21 artillery pieces and more than 40 trucks, and took 32 prisoners, according to tentative tallies.

Everyone from Cyclone's mechanics to its tank commanders will get a combat patch when they get back to Ft. Stewart, Ga., home to the 3rd Infantry Division. Three Cyclone soldiers are under consideration for bronze stars with a "V" for valor, an uncommon medal in any war. The company's commander is up for a silver star.

The Cyclone Company that is settling into routine policing work in Baghdad's restive streets is not the same Cyclone Company that Capt. Steven T. Barry inherited in October and commanded through drill after drill in the deserts of Kuwait before leading it into Iraq.

"You definitely see some changes," said Barry, 29, a former high school athlete from central New Jersey who graduated from West Point as the top-ranking history major. "I think for some, it hasn't sunk in yet," he added. "Now, we'll have time to think about it."

Spc. Jarrid Lott, a 28-year-old tank driver, has been doing some thinking already. "I've seen a car blow up and then a guy run back and grab his wife from the seat and we couldn't do anything about it," Lott said. "I saw people taking pictures of dead people. I thought: That's disgusting. I asked my tank commander, 'Why are you doing that?' He said, 'If my son says he wants to join the Army, I'll show him this [photograph] and tell him this is what the Army does.' "

Lott, a native of Redding, Calif., who joined the Army to pay off

$32,000 in student loans for his bachelor's degrees in psychology and social science, sat on a tank nicknamed "Cycho" and declared that his killing days are over. He won't reenlist after serving three more years. His wife, Sheri, a graduate student in Portland, Ore., is expecting their first child this summer. While he was gone, Sheri found out she's having a girl. The baby is kicking. They'll name her Kara Lyn.

Sgt. 1st Class Jeff Lujan, a hard-laughing and hard-driving platoon sergeant, will take home a Republican Guard uniform, some Iraqi dinars and two indelible memories. One is the arduous trek across the desert into battle. The other: "Some of the people I killed who I didn't know if they were innocent or not. That won't leave me," he said.

Last week, on a dark bridge across the Tigris River, Lujan gave the order to shoot the cab of a truck that looked like a military vehicle and whose driver was not heeding warning shots at the checkpoint. When first light came, Lujan, a father of two girls, found a woman and child dead in the cab. Everyone else who had been in the truck—mostly men—had fled.

Lujan doesn't know what happened to the victims' bodies. "Who picked them up? Who buried them?" he wonders.

"I've reconciled myself," Lujan said. "We did the right thing, even though it was wrong."

Lujan, 36, is under consideration for a bronze star for destroying three Iraqi armored vehicles that were tearing into his platoon two weeks ago at an ambush on Highway 1 south of Baghdad. Barry said intelligence later showed that the rout of the ambushers prevented the Republican Guard's Medina Division from following orders to move up to Baghdad to protect the capital, which was taken by U.S. troops several days later.

Maj. Kent Rideout, 39, executive officer for the 4th Battalion, worked on the documentation for Cyclone Company's awards Wednesday. But his mind was on the worst day of his career.

Rideout gave the orders that killed Capt. Ed Korn, 31, of Savannah, Ga., who had strayed across enemy lines without Rideout's knowledge.

"I've replayed it over in my mind a hundred times, and I still would do it the same way," Rideout said.

The incident occurred April 4 as Rideout's unit and others were attacking Iraqi positions on a two-lane road about 15 miles southeast of Baghdad. The convoy of American tanks and armored vehicles was stopped on the road when Rideout and others spotted an Iraqi tank, a Russian-made T-72, apparently missed by other U.S. units that had driven through. They fired and blew it up.

While the vehicle was exploding and burning, Korn and a sergeant apparently dismounted and walked to the tree line near the tank, searching for Iraqi positions, Rideout said.

At some point, Korn spotted a second tank and sent the sergeant back for an antitank rocket before going on alone. Korn had on a brown T-shirt, a flak vest that was left open, and no helmet, according to Rideout, who was scanning the tree line for more Iraqi positions.

"Out of the corner of my eyes I saw behind the tank what looked to be an old campfire," Rideout said. "I could see tea or coffee steaming, sleeping bags, chickens. It had all the hallmarks of a place where people were living. I put two and two together that this was a place a tank crew was living. All of a sudden we saw movement. Someone dropped down, like he was going to fire, and then stood up and got behind another T-72."

A Bradley fighting vehicle commander spotted the same movement and signaled it to Rideout. "I looked that way, and he nods like he sees it too," Rideout said. Rideout's driver, Spc. John Durst, 24, of Grantsville, Md., poked his head out of the tank's hatch and leveled his M-16, telling his commander he saw an enemy.

"I said, 'Yeah, I see it too, engage,' " Rideout recalled. "He fired one shot. I'll never get over it. It was 200 to 250 yards away. He dropped him. I slapped him on the head and said, 'That's the greatest shot I've ever seen.' "

The greatest shot Rideout had ever seen hit Korn, a Desert Storm veteran who left Ft. Knox, Ky., to volunteer for war duty in March and had impressed Rideout with his battlefield knowledge.

A Bradley from Korn's unit then opened fire on the second Iraqi tank. Some of those 25-millimeter rounds apparently hit Korn directly or ricocheted off the tank, Rideout said. They cut the young captain in half.

When someone came to Rideout to say Korn was in the tree line, Rideout ordered a cease-fire and led a search party. He headed toward what he assumed was the body of an Iraqi soldier. He told himself that Korn was fine and had made it back.

"As we got closer, we realized it was Ed Korn," Rideout said. "It was gruesome. You look at that and you say, I don't know if I could've done anything different. He had no appearance to us that he was an American soldier.

"This was the worst day of my Army career. No doubt, the worst day. I get to go home with that. I get to live with that the rest of my life."

For some of the younger men of Cyclone Company, it is hard to piece together war memories into a coherent story. "Did this look like a war to you?" asked Spc. Royce Arcay, 26. "I've never been to a war, but it sure didn't seem like what they put on TV. . . . It's just kind of weird looking at dead bodies. They don't look real. I never thought I'd see dead bodies like that, or body parts."

Bodies killed by the powerful 120-millimeter main guns of an Abrams M-1A1 tank, or its mounted machine guns, don't lie in quiet repose with neat red circles for wounds. They are mangled, blown apart and burned beyond recognition.

Tank crews often could not escape their handiwork. Some of the Iraqis they killed lay pinned in blasted vehicles that the Americans used as roadblocks. Day and night, tank crews stood guard just yards away. On one bridge in Baghdad, a dead Iraqi soldier pinned in a jeep became known as "Mr. Bubble-Guts," a macabre nickname that seemed to help some get by the horror of his daily decay.

It didn't work for Lott. "I'm going to have nightmares," he said. "Last night I kept dreaming that I wanted to wake up, but I went from dream to dream to dream. When we're getting on that plane, do you know how that's going to feel? Just getting on the plane, going home?"

Cyclone Company will be in Iraq for weeks before Lott's question can be answered.

In the meantime, the soldiers take a measure of war and plan for their future as combat veterans.

Staff Sgt. Charles Wooten, 36, of Meridian, Miss., who is up for a Purple Heart, will leave the Army after 15 years and two wars in the Persian Gulf. He'll hunt raccoons with his hounds and show pictures of the fist-size dents and confetti punctures left in his tank and point to the eye that took shrapnel but is now healed.

"I thought there were going to be more casualties," Wooten said. "I was scared of RPGs, but I didn't think it would be this bad."

Barry will get command of a headquarters company, then he has a full-ride graduate scholarship to either Harvard, Yale, Duke or the University of Pennsylvania. He'll probably choose Pennsylvania because it's closer to his hometown and his girlfriend. After that, he'll finish a dissertation at West Point, where he'll teach military history.

Lujan will go to the National Training Center at Ft. Irwin, Calif., where he'll critique training exercises. He said he'll put in seven more years to reach retirement, then settle down anywhere but his hometown of Albuquerque.

Arcay, who joined the Army when he became depressed over a broken romance, has had enough of war. He'll leave the military after his hitch is up.

Rideout will take a job as a ground liaison officer to the Navy in San Diego. When he gets back to Ft. Stewart, he'll look up Korn's mother and explain what happened, and hope she'll understand.

Like much of the rest of Cyclone Company, Sgt. Arnoldo Spangaro, 29, a native of Cape Coral, Fla., has a simpler short-term plan.

He'll start the process of moving his family to Ft. Stewart from Colorado. He'll watch his 8-year-old stepson, Taylor, play soccer. He'll push his 4-year-old daughter, Madison, on a swing.

"She doesn't like to stop on the swing," Spangaro said. "I'll probably be there for four hours."

The trick, he says, is to switch arms so you don't get tired. Even a gunner's arm needs to rest.

Where the Enemy Is Everywhere and Nowhere

by Daniel Bergner

Daniel Bergner reported on American soldiers hunting for al-Qaeda in southern Afghanistan during early 2003—long after the end of America's major military operations in that country. His article ran in The New York Times Magazine (July 20, 2003).

Stones and scrap metal are laid out on the sand. The officers gather for what they call the rock drill, a last session of planning. Strips of white cloth, along with the rocks and metal, form a map of Lowri Kariz, the village the troops will search, hunting Al Qaeda and the Taliban. Steel bars split the village into quadrants. Squads will cover each section, making sure no suspect can shift from one to another—making sure no suspect can edge away.

In a few hours, after nightfall, the soldiers will leave their Kandahar base. They have been warned to anticipate resistance. The search zone is tight to the border; the frontier is an enemy refuge. Ambushes might be sprung and mortars might be launched, and then there are the old, unmarked minefields and others that might be newly laid. After the rock drill, platoons meet between the tents. With a quiet, cursing indifference that mitigates fear, they talk through the responses to assaults, to mines. If someone in their units takes an unlucky step and gets his body blasted into fragments, the men will squat down and inch toward the victim, using their bayonet blades to stab delicately at the desert floor.

This is America's war on terror, in the southern and least stable part of Afghanistan, over a year and a half since that war began. "This mission," Charles Flynn, the Army lieutenant colonel in charge of tonight's operation, tells me, "I expect to apprehend enemy." Then the convoy of trucks and Humvees moves out, lurching and jouncing through cratered terrain, Afghanistan's powdery sand rising from the tires, coiling and unfurling like mist, radiant in the headlights. All is obscure behind it.

Resolute Strike, Valiant Strike, Carpathian Lightning: the names of recent United States military operations in Afghanistan. And beginning with the name that encompasses them all, Operation Enduring Freedom, there have been victories to go along with the grand, triumphal language. American missiles, in the fall of 2001, annihilated Al Qaeda training camps where men like Ramzi Yousef and Mohamed Atta had taught and learned. Afghan militias directed by Army Special Forces crews drove the Taliban from power and destroyed, in less than two months, the terrorist sanctuary Al Qaeda had found under the Taliban's extremist rule. It's a crucial word, sanctuary. It's one-third of the way the American military—with about 8,500 troops on the ground, aided by 3,000 coalition soldiers—defines its aims in the country. Kill. Capture. Deny sanctuary. These are the measures of the war's success as the 300 Americans ride out tonight on Vigilant Guardian, hoping that Flynn's prediction is more than a wish.

The troops doze, bodies packed crushingly into the open beds of the trucks. Turreted gunners peer out through night optics above each cab; for the rest, jolting at eight miles per hour through hostile territory on a scarcely marked track, closer and closer to the border, the tension of possible ambush is gradually overcome by the pain of entangled, contorted limbs and torsos. Sleep may be dangerous, but it is escape.

The best chance at killing or capture may have been deep in the past. Below the white peaks of the Spin Ghar near the Pakistani line, Osama bin Laden was spotted, in late November and early December 2001, along with at least 1,000 of his Qaeda fighters. The American high command believed this was it but didn't want to put its soldiers— even Delta Force, renowned for risk-taking—in severe danger; didn't want British special forces—who also had teams in the area, eager to move in—to claim the war's greatest prize; and couldn't compel Pakistan to close off the frontier. (Why the Americans didn't block the frontier themselves has never become clear, though the perils of landing helicopters at high altitudes in terrible weather probably played a part.) Without much support on the ground, with only the troops of Afghan warlords to rely on, a bombardment from American jets merely chased bin Laden between the ridges, most think, and across the border. He may well have bought the warlords off and been allowed to escape. He may well have had the help of the region's Pashtuns, the ethnic group most loyal to his Taliban collaborators. Months later, Canadian coalition soldiers dug up bodies from a cluster of graves that had become a local shrine, bodies from December's bombing. The hope was that one would be bin Laden's. None were.

The next time, the military chose to take more risks. In March 2002, farther southwest along the frontier, an unmanned surveillance plane, guided by C.I.A. technicians, sent back photographs of Al Qaeda fighters massing. About 200 enemy troops seemed to have gathered in the Shah-i-Kot Valley, with "H.V.T.'s" probably among them. High-Value Targets was now the military's preferred term; after bin Laden's December escape, it no longer liked to speak of him or other terrorist leaders by name. That put too much stress, and focused too much public judgment, on the killing or capturing of specific figures.

More than a thousand coalition soldiers, most of them American, surrounded the screes of Shah-i-Kot. When Al Qaeda fled, it would be cut off. But this time, Al Qaeda didn't flee right away. It crippled Special Forces helicopters with rocket-propelled grenades and tore men apart with heavy machine guns. And the C.I.A.'s high-tech intelligence had been far wrong. There weren't 200 enemy fighters waiting behind the crags; there were more like a thousand. When two weeks of fighting wound down, 8 American and 3 Afghan coalition soldiers had been killed, about 80 wounded. No H.V.T. bodies were found. American commanders claimed 800 enemy dead, but estimates quickly shrank to less than half that. And ever since, the military has been reluctant to talk of success in terms of body counts. "You mean for the bad guys?" Maj. Bob Hepner, a public affairs officer, asks when I request casualty figures going back to the start of the Afghanistan campaign. "We don't have them. Because a lot of times you can't match the parts. We just know we've got a lot of legs and hands." He smiles as he speaks, implying that the enemy has been blown to smithereens.

But according to terrorism experts at the International Institute for Strategic Studies, a London-based policy group devoted largely to world security, the estimates run something like this: about 20,000 jihadic soldiers had graduated from Al Qaeda's training camps in Afghanistan as of October 2001, when the American-led war began there. Up to 10,000 of those were inside Afghanistan at the time. Since then, the coalition campaign has killed or captured around 2,000. Ninety percent of bin Laden's forces, and more than half of his top commanders, remain free. And no one is quite sure where they are. Some of the Arabs among them have probably made their way back to the Middle East. Many of the rest seem to straddle the frontiers of Afghanistan, Pakistan and neighboring Iran. Al Qaeda is, the institute judges, "more insidious and just as dangerous" as before the 9/11 attacks.

Two weeks before the Vigilant Guardian convoy crosses the desert, a tape has surfaced, probably made recently, since it refers to the war in Iraq. "If you started suicide attacks, you will see the fear of Americans all over the world," the voice, which seems to be bin Laden's, preaches. The tape was given to The Associated Press by a source who said he had come from the Afghan borderlands, where many believe the tape was recorded.

When the soldiers reach the search zone at dawn, when they scour the village of Lowri Kariz for caches of rockets, for hidden grenade launchers, for signs of enemy safe houses, Capt. Kevin (Kit) Parker will be in charge of collecting intelligence. He will seek out village headmen, greet them and declare America's good intentions. He will try somehow to befriend them, gather whatever leads he can coax from them and whatever evidence his men turn up—possibly pointing to Al Qaeda or Taliban suspects who might prove the missing link to finding the highest-ranking terrorist figures. He has learned to expect little. He explains that we haven't managed in the least to understand the country, let alone transform it, to keep it from serving again as an easy terrorist sanctuary as soon as we leave. Afghanistan, he says, "has a level of complexity that is almost unfathomable."

Tall and lean but with a slightly cherubic, sun-pinked face, Parker was in the reserves before 9/11. His civilian life consisted—after a doctorate in physics from Vanderbilt and postdoctoral work in pathology and biomedical engineering at Harvard and Johns Hopkins—of research into treatments for cardiac arrhythmia. Right after 9/11, he got himself switched to a unit that he guessed would be leaving soon for Afghanistan. But intricate lab work can seem simple compared with the intricacies of this country. He talks of the vicious rivalries among the country's seemingly infinite subtribes, how often the tips the Army receives are the attempts of one clan to spur the Americans against an ancient enemy. He speaks of the way such ethnic anarchy brought the Taliban to power and gave Al Qaeda its haven. He talks about the landscape itself, with its countless outcroppings and caves and desiccated gulches, so hard to navigate, so easy to hide in. And he tells of spending Christmas day with a village leader he felt he could trust, a man whose information he relied on. "We were sipping tea and burning dung to keep warm," he recalls. The leader told him there was no suspicious activity in the area. Soon after, Parker learned that stockpiles of weapons were moving through the village.

Vigilant Guardian's trucks and Humvees come to a stop at Lowri Kariz. Dawn barely suggests itself at the horizon, a low line of faint blanching. A few miles away, Spinbaldak, a town on the border, shows a ragged spine of lights, thinly spread.

Here and across Afghanistan, the work of "humint," as the Army calls human intelligence, has been badly frustrated. Christopher Langton, a retired British colonel and military attaché in Central Asia, now with the International Institute for Strategic Studies, speaks of the attempts to befriend and the attempts to pay. The paying hasn't bought much in the way of trustworthy information, and a psychological operations officer on Vigilant Guardian tells me that the Army has mostly abandoned it. The befriending hasn't worked well either, because, Langton says, the Americans have failed "to capture the virtual territory, the territory of the mind of the population." The troops on missions like Parker's, operations that set out from American bases every two weeks or so, should pick up the kinds of details that form the foundation of military intelligence. But the troops are handicapped, Langton explains, because the people sense a shortsighted American involvement, a powerful wish to be gone.

The Afghans feel that the Taliban, with Al Qaeda behind it, could take hold again in the country as soon as the Americans go home. For the villagers, survival when that happens could depend on keeping their mouths shut now.

And without the help of the people, Langton adds, the beaming from all the satellites and unmanned planes in the sky can be futile. The jagged terrain creates blind spots, and what the high-tech systems can photograph they can't interpret. They can't calibrate for local sympathies or even, as happened in the Shah-i-Kot Valley, determine sheer numbers of bunkered, armed enemy soldiers.

"I'm not optimistic," Captain Parker says, thinking forward five years. "The smart terrorist in Afghanistan will simply wait us out, wait for us to lose interest, lose will." Mullah Muhammad Omar, the Taliban leader who has kept himself so mysterious and secreted that, the military's top officers acknowledge, he could drift through their bases without any chance of being recognized, sends out edicts against the invading infidels, demanding their deaths. Three weeks before Vigilant Guardian, a Special Forces convoy dipped through a gulley and found itself under ambush, taking machine-gun fire. Two soldiers were killed and one was critically wounded before the attackers disappeared.

American casualties in Afghanistan haven't been high, with about 60 dead and about 245 wounded since the beginning of the war. But the casualties—and the forces that want America gone—show no sign of letting up. Parker's sense of the future echoes what I've heard from another captain, Mike Gonzalez, who will be running security as the truckloads of men enter the alleys of Lowri Kariz to start searching. "As long as we're here," Gonzalez says, "it will be all right. But when we go. . . ." His voice drifts off, the implication clear: sanctuary will be waiting—ample freedom, as before, to train jihadic soldiers and to launch their missions.

Now squads of a dozen troops take up positions, lying prone on the night-chilled sand, the guns of the different groups pointing in different directions, all on guard, all waiting for orders to step across what may be a minefield. A hundred yards away, the mud village begins with a compound's wall, everything behind it concealed. Reports say the Taliban or Al Qaeda have either been coming through the area or made themselves at home. That's about as specific as the military's information is, going in. Just behind the village surge hills where, three months before, shots exchanged with suspects sparked a gun battle that was fought cave to cave and boulder to boulder. "It's a big cat-and-mouse game," the soldier lying next to me says, with a mixture of nervousness and exhausted resignation.

And everyone is aware of the border close by. Within 70 miles of Spinbaldak lies the Pakistani city of Quetta, where rumors have placed bin Laden and Omar in the past few months. Plenty of Taliban and Al Qaeda fighters have fled to Quetta and the surrounding mountains since October 2001. Whether or not the top leaders are there, the area around Spinbaldak is a frontier transit spot for weapons and instructions aimed at breaking American will in Afghanistan. Yet beyond small-scale, discreet operations—like the C.I.A.-aided arrest in Pakistan of one of bin Laden's lieutenants, Khalid Shaikh Mohammed—the Americans can't venture into that country to reach the elusive enemy. They fear stirring more anti-American hatred than already exists and jeopardizing Pakistan's president, Pervez Musharraf, who is at least somewhat compliant to American desires.

In Quetta, after 9/11, thousands chanted "Death to America." Musharraf's government has little control in the region. More than one American officer, asking to be nameless on this sensitive point, compares the situation to the war in Vietnam, to the way enemy bases in neighboring Cambodia and Laos compounded the immeasurable problems America faced. Lieutenant Colonel Flynn, leading Vigilant Guardian, says he worries about the Taliban or Al Qaeda emissary who meets his Afghan contact around Spinbaldak and tells him, "Deliver these guns in Afghanistan, lay these mines in Afghanistan, set these explosives in Afghanistan." Then Flynn imagines the attack on his troops that might follow. "You'll never see it coming," he says.

Northeast of Spinbaldak, near the Shah-i-Kot, a Special Forces commander, Chris Allen, lives in a fort made of sun-bleached mud, thickened and flecked by bits of straw. His fort sits in a Pashtun region that has been among the most hostile to the Americans, the most hospitable to the Taliban and Al Qaeda. Like so many of the structures of Afghanistan, its architecture seems to rise from the Dark Ages. Its low-ceilinged rooms look inward upon a square courtyard, not outward at all; to gaze outward, you have to tunnel up along a twisting set of mud stairs. Then, from the level of the parapets, you can duck into one of four guard towers to peer across the valley and keep watch for your enemy.

Allen takes boyish pleasure in the fort's storybook feel. But the enthusiasm that animates his round face goes beyond his headquarters, which include a second fort beside his home, both rented from a local owner. With unrelenting good cheer, he believes that in time, the United States military will "bring light to Afghanistan." He predicts that the Americans will be able to reduce their forces and eventually return home entirely without leaving behind a haven and cultivating ground for terrorists. Partly, he says, this will happen through the training of a national army, a program meant to instill not only new battlefield techniques but also new values—an allegiance to the moderate, American-backed government whose power now does not extend far outside the capital. The program's implementation has been painfully slow; after a year, there have been just 4,500 graduates toward a goal of 70,000. Yet his optimism depends, too, on small outposts like his own.

He speaks of himself as a "baby hugger," hoping to bring aid to civilians in order to win Langton's "virtual territory," to convince the people of America's long-term commitment, to draw them away from past allegiances. He wants to build schools and health clinics, to start the job of reconstruction, which foreign-aid workers still feel too unsafe to begin. But he has little budget for such things; the Pentagon has allotted just $12 million for Army-run reconstruction projects throughout the country. So his soldiers grind their Humvees and 4-by-4's around the valley, handing out crayons to children clambering over ruins to reach them (the ruins left by Russian shells from the era before the Russians were worn down and driven away, the ruins left by American bombs last year). They talk to village elders about building schools—projects, the soldiers have to emphasize, they may not be able to carry out.

And meanwhile, Afghanistan's children suck on bin Laden candies, sugary balls in wrappers showing the leader's face, his pointed finger and the tip of a rocket.

Rockets have been shot at Allen's base about 80 times since December. They have been poorly aimed—not the work of top Al Qaeda operatives but apparently of low-level members or sympathizers. The rockets have struck within a hundred yards of the fort walls, exploding at thunderous volume, spewing shrapnel. So far they have done no harm. Allen can't retaliate because he can't be sure exactly who has been launching the attacks. "The hard part about intelligence here," he says, "is for every report saying this guy's Al Qaeda, there's another saying this guy's a saint." A mine recently blew up a vehicle driven by a soldier from one of the forts. A foot was lost, a face ravaged.

Between explosions, the local police often take potshots at Afghans the Americans have hired to help guard Allen's base. On a pair of round hills, a tribal warlord, with a militia of a thousand at his call, has—or had, until lately—two mud forts overlooking Allen's. Because the warlord is an enemy of the American-backed provincial governor and because the Americans suspect he may be supported by Al Qaeda, the superior elevation of his hilltop stations made Allen uneasy. So Special Forces raided one of the forts, chasing off the warlord's troops or— depending on who is telling the story—choosing a time when the place was unmanned and blowing up its weaponry along with its walls. In Afghanistan, the Americans can seem lost within the world they are trying to transform and stabilize. They can seem as if they are just one more militia, staking and defending small claims. On poles atop the guard towers of Allen's fort, American flags ripple above his portion of the valley.

"So we ain't got no terps?" a soldier asks, after the troops of Vigilant Guardian, fingers poised on trigger guards, cross the sand and walk into the sprawling village of Lowri Kariz. The entire operation—with team after team disappearing into separate compounds, and with officers like Captain Parker trying to find local elders and glean intelligence—has just two "terps." There are mixed feelings about having many Afghan interpreters along. They can distort answers or aid ambushes. "We can't tell if they're loyal," Captain Gonzalez says, telling of one the Army recently arrested for running information and instructions back and forth over the border.

But even without a common language between them, the villagers seem to know what the Americans have come to do. Silently, turbaned men in long gray tunics open doors in compound walls for five- or six-man groups of helmeted men in desert camouflage. The wooden doors are cracked, withered. The courtyards behind them hold low mud homes and lush gardens of pink and white poppies. The troops don't bother with the opium-producing crop. There's too much else to worry about. They pat down the men. (The mission's few female soldiers mutely frisk the men's sisters and wives, who have been quartered in dark chambers.) They poke through cellars, peer for signs of trick walls and compartments full of grenade launchers. They find nothing. They smash with a gun stock into a mirrored cabinet when the owner can't find his key. The owner doesn't cry out as shards of glass hit the dirt floor. The cabinet is more or less his only piece of furniture, yet he seems to have gestured that the door should be smashed through. All seems accepted: in bitter helplessness against what the Americans are doing or—as the Americans hope—in gratitude for the American defeat of the repressive Taliban. It is impossible for the soldiers to know. Gonzalez speaks of trying to guess the sentiments of the locals not by their smiles but by the firmness of their handshakes. His soldiers say the compounds could be full of terrorists, and they might have no clue.

A report comes in over the radio: at Shkin, to the east along the frontier, the sighting of 20 men, armed with rifles and R.P.G.'s, draws an American platoon. In a gun battle, the Americans believe they kill three combatants. Two Americans die. The enemy vanishes over the border.

Parker stoops on plunging stairs, at the start of Vigilant Guardian's second day. He climbs down into a narrow cellar, dug beneath the desert floor of a compound on the outskirts of Lowri Kariz. Troops wait above. He sits in a cool underground chamber on a carpet of red and blue. A high portal gives a shaft of light. Beside it hangs a framed painting in the style of hotel art: white stallions prancing through a marsh of reeds. This is the meeting room of a figure Parker has been asking to see since yesterday, the village leader—or someone representing himself that way. Nothing is clear. All that's certain to Parker and Gonzalez, and to the three other officers who accompany them, is that they feel suspicious. The headman—features sharp as mountain ridges between beard and turban—has avoided them throughout their first day in the village. Only now has Parker been allowed a meeting. And the man lives well beyond the perimeter of the village, with armed guards posted on each corner of his roof, above the crypt the Americans now sit inside, surrounded by Pashtun faces they cannot read.

The rooftop guards in themselves aren't unusual. It's yesterday's avoidance and the position of the compound that unnerves, as though this figure and his guards don't really belong, as though they're Taliban or Al Qaeda who have just lately taken up residence and taken on local power.

"We've got a target on this place," Gonzalez assures the other Americans, all sitting on scarlet cushions. Gonzalez assumes no Afghan except the two "terps" can understand. "We'll level this place if anything happens."

He has radioed in his coordinates. An American helicopter and plane, he says, circle overhead. The Americans may not be able to comprehend the men they face, or the circumstance they're in, or the country that surrounds them, and they may not be able to prevent their own deaths, but if they are slaughtered, the aircraft will rocket and bomb the compound into oblivion, bodies to bone chips, headquarters to dust.

Parker starts his questioning. Everyone sips tea and nibbles biscuits. All is polite, but the headman's answers, about battling Al Qaeda in the hills to the east, strike Parker as attempts to distract. "There are no bad guys here," Parker's interpreter says repeatedly, translating the leader's replies. The man claims that his militia, most of it based in Spinbaldak, has chased all the nearby enemy fighters over the border. The reports of Taliban and Al Qaeda being in this village are lies. "Other tribes are fighting against us. They are giving you bad reports." They are using the Americans. Because of this, his own men have been arrested elsewhere in the area—even after they have fought Al Qaeda so well. They should be freed. Please, can their freedom be arranged? "There are no bad guys here."

All is polite; the headman's claims are plausible. But an hour later, by the time everyone emerges upstairs and outside, a helicopter gunship swoops 40 feet above the headman, joined by his guards who have come down off the roof and been replaced by American soldiers. The switch has occurred peacefully. The gunship, banking and diving, its missile launchers so close and the throb of its blades so loud, has guaranteed that.

Almost wordlessly, the headman points out and relinquishes a stock of weapons. It is kept covered in the back of a pickup truck parked in his yard: a few grenade launchers, a light machine gun. Without protest he surrenders himself and his guards. They are "pucked," a new verb used by the American soldiers, taken from the military phrase "persons under control." The Americans cuff their wrists and cover their heads in burlap sacks. Maybe because of my presence or because of their uncertainty about this arrest (could the weapons, as the man says, have been used to fight Al Qaeda?), the Americans lower the hoods with a measure of delicacy. They guide the captives toward a Chinook transport helicopter. Hoods quiver in the rotor gust. The men step into the bay with such thorough compliance, such calm, I wonder if they are thinking, as Parker does, that the smart terrorist will simply wait the Americans out.

The chopper lifts off, flying to a base the Russians built in another time. The Americans now run it. There, in a dingy Soviet-style concrete block where no reporter is allowed inside, the men will be held indefinitely and interrogated, plied for information that might somehow show the way to Al Qaeda or Taliban leaders, that might somehow point to bases or hint at terrorist plots, that might somehow change everything.

That afternoon, Parker moves on with his troops to another village. He finds no suspects, but he and another officer give away three bright yellow radios, powered by hand crank, in this abject settlement where batteries scarcely exist. The radios are gestures of outreach for Parker and, for the military, tokens that might bring leads later on. Then the vehicles head for a landing zone where some of the officers will be flown back to their Kandahar base. The zone's coordinates are clear. It's a 20-minute drive, at most. An amber dusk falls over the land. We drive and drive. The Afghan desert, sectioned off by ridges and ravines, can be a bewildering place. The sky blackens. The stars appear in all their extravagance. We can't find the landing zone. For hours we search, hunting the way out, circling and retracing our route in the sand.

Stretched Thin, Lied to
& Mistreated

by Christian Parenti

Christian Parenti's piece ran in The Nation (October 6, 2003).

A n M-16 rifle hangs by a cramped military cot. On the wall above is a message in thick black ink: "Ali Baba, you owe me a strawberry milk!"

It's a private joke but could just as easily summarize the worldview of American soldiers here in Baghdad, the fetid basement of Donald Rumsfeld's house of victory. Trapped in the polluted heat, poorly supplied and cut off from regular news, the GIs are fighting a guerrilla war that they neither wanted, expected nor trained for. On the urban battlefields of central Iraq, "shock and awe" and all the other "new way of war" buzzwords are drowned out by the din of diesel-powered generators, Islamic prayer calls and the occasional pop of small-arms fire.

Here, the high-tech weaponry that so emboldens Pentagon bureaucrats is largely useless, and the grinding work of counter-insurgency is done the old-fashioned way—by hand. Not surprisingly, most of the American GIs stuck with the job are weary, frustrated and ready to go home.

It is noon and the mercury is hanging steady at 115 Fahrenheit. The filmmaker Garrett Scott and I are "embedded" with Alpha Company of the Third Battalion of the 124th Infantry, a Florida National Guard unit about half of whom did time in the regular Army, often with elite groups like the Rangers. Like most frontline troops in Iraq, the majority are white but there is a sizable minority of African-American and Latino soldiers among them. Unlike most combat units, about 65 percent are college students—they've traded six years with the Guard for tuition at Florida State. Typically, that means occasional weekends in the Everglades or directing traffic during hurricanes. Instead, these guys got sent to Iraq, and as yet they have no sure departure date.

Mobilized in December, they crossed over from Kuwait on day one of the invasion and are now bivouacked in the looted remains of a Republican Guard officers' club, a modernist slab of polished marble and tinted glass that the GIs have fortified with plywood, sandbags and razor wire.

Behind "the club" is a three-story dormitory, a warren of small one-bedroom apartments, each holding a nine-man squad of soldiers and all their gear. Around 200 guys are packed in here. Their sweaty fatigues drape the banisters of the exterior stairway, while inside the cramped, dark rooms the floors are covered with cots, heaps of flak vests, guns and, where possible, big tin, water-based air-conditioners called swamp coolers. Surrounding the base is a chaotic working-class neighborhood of two- and three-story cement homes and apartment buildings. Not far away is the muddy Tigris River.

This company limits patrols to three or four hours a day. For the many hours in between, the guys pull guard duty, hang out in their cavelike rooms or work out in a makeshift weight room.

"We're getting just a little bit stir-crazy," explains the lanky Sergeant Sellers. His demeanor is typical of the nine-man squad we have been assigned to, friendly but serious, with a wry and angry sense of humor. On the side of his helmet Sellers has, in violation of regs, attached the unmistakable pin and ring of a hand grenade. Next to it is written, "Pull Here."

Leaning back on a cot, he's drawing a large, intricate pattern on a female mannequin leg. The wall above him displays a photo collage of pictures retrieved from a looted Iraqi women's college. Smiling young ladies wearing the *hijab* sip sodas and stroll past buses. They seem to be on some sort of field trip. Nearby are photos clipped from *Maxim*, of coy young American girls offering up their pert round bottoms. Dominating it all is a large hand-drawn dragon and a photo of Jessica Lynch with a bubble caption reading: "Hi, I am a war hero. And I think that weapons maintenance is totally unimportant."

The boys don't like Lynch and find the story of her rescue ridiculous. They'd been down the same road a day earlier and are unsympathetic. "We just feel that it's unfair and kind of distorted the way the whole Jessica, quote, 'rescue' thing got hyped," explains Staff Sgt. Kreed Howell. He is in charge of the squad, and at 31 a bit older than most of his men. Muscular and clean-cut, Howell is a relaxed and natural leader, with the gracious bearing of a proper Southern upbringing.

"In other words, you'd have to be really fucking dumb to get lost on the road," says another, less diplomatic soldier.

Specialist John Crawford sits in a tiny, windowless supply closet that is loaded with packs and gear. He is two credits short of a BA in anthropology and wants to go to graduate school. Howell, a Republican, amicably describes Crawford as the squad's house liberal.

There's just enough extra room in the closet for Crawford, a chair and a little shelf on which sits a laptop. Hanging by this makeshift desk is a handwritten sign from "the management" requesting that soldiers masturbating in the supply closet "remove their donations in a receptacle." Instead of watching pornography DVDs, Crawford is here to finish a short story. "Trying to start writing again," he says.

Crawford is a fan of Tim O'Brien, particularly *The Things They*

Carried. We chat, then he shows me his short story. It's about a vet who is back home in north Florida trying to deal with the memory of having accidentally blown away a child while serving in Iraq.

Later in the cramped main room, Sellers and Sergeant Brunelle, another one of the squad's more gregarious and dominant personalities, are matter-of-factly showing us digital photos of dead Iraqis.

"These guys shot at some of our guys, so we lit 'em up. Put two .50-cal rounds in their vehicle. One went through this dude's hip and into the other guy's head," explains Brunelle. The third man in the car lived. "His buddy was crying like a baby. Just sitting there bawling with his friend's brains and skull fragments all over his face. One of our guys came up to him and is like: 'Hey! No crying in baseball!' "

"I know that probably sounds sick," says Sellers, "but humor is the only way you can deal with this shit."

And just below the humor is volcanic rage. These guys are proud to be soldiers and don't want to come across as whiners, but they are furious about what they've been through. They hate having their lives disrupted and put at risk. They hate the military for its stupidity, its feckless lieutenants and blowhard brass living comfortably in Saddam palaces. They hate Iraqis—or, as they say, "hajis"—for trying to kill them. They hate the country for its dust, heat and sewage-clogged streets. They hate having killed people. Some even hate the politics of the war. And because most of them are, ultimately, just regular well-intentioned guys, one senses the distinct fear that someday a few may hate themselves for what they have been forced to do here.

Added to such injury is insult: The military treats these soldiers like unwanted stepchildren. This unit's rifles are retooled hand-me-downs from Vietnam. They have inadequate radio gear, so they buy their own unencrypted Motorola walkie-talkies. The same goes for flashlights, knives and some components for night-vision sights. The low-performance Iraqi air-conditioners and fans, as well as the one satellite phone and payment cards shared by the whole company for calling home, were also purchased out of pocket from civilian suppliers.

Bottled water rations are kept to two liters a day. After that the guys drink from "water buffaloes"—big hot chlorination tanks that turn the amoeba-infested dreck from the local taps into something like swimming-pool water. Mix this with powdered Gatorade and you can wash down a famously bad MRE (Meal Ready to Eat).

To top it all off they must endure the pathologically uptight culture of the Army hierarchy. The Third of the 124th is now attached to the newly arrived First Armored Division, and when it is time to raid suspected resistance cells it's the Guardsmen who have to kick in the doors and clear the apartments.

"The First AD wants us to catch bullets for them but won't give us enough water, doesn't let us wear do-rags and makes us roll down our shirt sleeves so we look proper! Can you believe that shit?" Sergeant Sellers is pissed off.

The soldiers' improvisation extends to food as well. After a month or so of occupying "the club," the company commander, Captain Sanchez, allowed two Iraqi entrepreneurs to open shop on his side of the wire—one runs a slow Internet cafe, the other a kebab stand where the "Joes" pay US dollars for grilled lamb on flat bread.

"The haji stand is one of the only things we have to look forward to, but the First AD keeps getting scared and shutting it down." Sellers is on a roll, but he's not alone.

Even the lighthearted Howell, who insists that the squad has it better than most troops, chimes in. "The one thing I will say is that we have been here entirely too long. If I am not home by Christmas my business will fail." Back "on earth" (in Panama City, Florida), Howell is a building contractor, with a wife, two small children, equipment, debts and employees.

Perhaps the most shocking bit of military incompetence is the unit's lack of formal training in what's called "close-quarter combat." The urbanized mayhem of Mogadishu may loom large in the discourse of the military's academic journals like *Parameters* and the *Naval War College Review*, but many US infantrymen are trained only in large-scale, open-country maneuvers—how to defend Germany from a wave of Russian tanks.

So, since "the end of the war" these guys have had to retrain themselves in the dark arts of urban combat. "The houses here are small, too," says Brunelle. "Once you're inside you can barely get your rifle up. You got women screaming, people, furniture everywhere. It's insane."

By now this company has conducted scores of raids, taken fire on the street, taken casualties, taken rocket-propelled grenade attacks to the club and are defiantly proud of the fact that they have essentially been abandoned, survived, retrained themselves and can keep a lid on their little piece of Baghdad. But it's not always the Joes who have the upper hand. Increasingly, Haji seems to set the agenda.

A thick black plume of smoke rises from Karrada Street, a popular electronics district where US patrols often buy air-conditioners and DVDs. An American Humvee, making just such a stop, has been blown to pieces by a remote-activated "improvised explosive device" or IED, buried in the median between two lanes of traffic. By chance two colleagues and I are the first press on the scene. The street is empty of traffic and quiet except for the local shopkeepers, who occasionally call out to us in Arabic and English: "Be careful."

Finally we get close enough to see clearly. About twenty feet away is a military transport truck and a Humvee, and beyond that are the flaming remains of a third Humvee. A handful of American soldiers are crouched behind the truck, totally still. There is no firing, no yelling, no talking, no radio traffic. No one is screaming, but two GIs are down. As yet there are no reinforcements or helicopters overhead. All one can hear is the burning of the Humvee.

Then it begins: The ammunition in the burning Humvee starts to explode and the troops in the street start firing. Armored personnel carriers arrive and disgorge dozens of soldiers from the 82nd Airborne to join the fight. The target is a three-story office building just across from the engulfed Humvee. Occasionally we hear a few rounds of return fire pass by like hot razors slashing straight lines through the air. The really close rounds just sound like loud cracks.

"That's Kalashnikov. I know the voice," says Ahmed, our friend and translator. There is a distinct note of national pride in his voice—his countrymen are fighting back—never mind the fact that we are now mixed in with the most forward US troops and getting shot at.

The firefight goes on for about two hours, moving slowly and methodically. It is in many ways an encapsulation of the whole war—confusing and labor-intensive. The GIs have more firepower than they can use, and they don't even know exactly where or who the enemy is. Civilians are hiding in every corner, the ground floor of the target building is full of merchants and shoppers, and undisciplined fire could mean scores of dead civilians.

There are two GIs on the ground, one with his legs gone and probably set to die. When a medevac helicopter arrives just overhead, it, too, like much other technology, is foiled. The street is crisscrossed with electrical wires and there is no way the chopper can land to extract the wounded. The soldiers around us look grave and tired.

Eventually some Bradley fighting vehicles start pounding the building with mean 250-millimeter cannon shells. Whoever might have been shooting from upstairs is either dead or gone.

The street is now littered with overturned air-conditioners, fans and refrigerators. A cooler of sodas sits forlorn on the sidewalk. Farther away two civilians lie dead, caught in the crossfire. A soldier peeks out from the hatch of a Bradley and calls over to a journalist, "Hey, can you grab me one of those Cokes?"

After the shootout we promised ourselves we'd stay out of Humvees and away from US soldiers. But that was yesterday. Now Crawford is helping us put on body armor and soon we'll be on patrol. As we move out with the nine soldiers the mood is somewhere between tense and bored. Crawford mockingly introduces himself to no one in particular: "John Crawford, I work in population reduction."

"Watch the garbage—if you see wires coming out of a pile it's an

IED," warns Howell. The patrol is uneventful. We walk fast through back streets and rubbish-strewn lots, pouring sweat in the late afternoon heat. Local residents watch the small squad with a mixture of civility, indifference and open hostility. An Iraqi man shouts, "When? When? When? Go!" The soldiers ignore him.

"Sometimes we sham," explains one of the guys. "We'll just go out and kick it behind some wall. Watch what's going on but skip the walking. And sometimes at night we get sneaky-deaky. Creep up on Haji, so he knows we're all around."

"I am just walking to be walking," says the laconic Fredrick Pearson, *aka* "Diddy," the only African-American in Howell's squad. Back home he works in the State Supreme Court bureaucracy and plans to go to law school. "I just keep an eye on the rooftops, look around and walk."

The patrols aren't always peaceful. One soldier mentions that he recently "kicked the shit out of a 12-year-old kid" who menaced him with a toy gun.

Later we roll with the squad on another patrol, this time at night and in two Humvees. Now there's more evident hostility from the young Iraqi men loitering in the dark. Most of these infantry soldiers don't like being stuck in vehicles. At a blacked-out corner where a particularly large group of youths are clustered, the Humvees stop and Howell bails out into the crowd. There is no interpreter along tonight.

"Hey, guys! What's up? How y'all doing? OK? Everything OK? All right?" asks Howell in his jaunty, laid-back north Florida accent. The sullen young men fade away into the dark, except for two, who shake the sergeant's hand. Howell's attempt to take the high road, winning hearts and minds, doesn't seem to be for show. He really believes in this war. But in the torrid gloom of the Baghdad night, his efforts seem tragically doomed.

Watching Howell I think about the civilian technocrats working with Paul Bremer at the Coalition Provisional Authority; the electricity is out half the time, and these folks hold meetings on how best to privatize state industries and end food rations. Meanwhile, the city seethes. The Pentagon, likewise, seems to have no clear plan; its troops are stretched thin, lied to and mistreated. The whole charade feels increasingly patched together, poorly improvised. Ultimately, there's very little that Howell and his squad can do about any of this. After all, it's not their war. They just work here.

Night Raid in Baghdad
by Jen Banbury

During the fall of 2003 Jen Banbury accompanied

American soldiers on the raid of an Iraqi home. Her

article ran on Salon.com.

ECEMBER 4, 2003, BAGHDAD, IRAQ—A few nights before Thanksgiving, I stood in a light but very cold rain on a dark residential street in Baghdad, loosely surrounded by two tanks, five Humvees, a prisoner transportation truck, 52 soldiers, three Iraqi translators, two armed canine handlers, and one bomb-sniffing dog named Elsa. The soldiers—representing both infantry and armor from the 1-36 Charlie Company of the 1st Armored Division—were preparing to raid a house where a member of the resistance supposedly lived. A dozen of the soldiers crouched, guns ready on either side of the house's front gate. Other soldiers cordoned off the block and pointed their weapons at nearby windows and roofs.

I had chosen to spend a day with these soldiers. Just moments before, I had been sitting in a convoy's lead Humvee as the whole operation sped from the soldiers' base to the target house. Iraqi cars and pedestrians scrambled to move aside as we rumbled through the nighttime city, often going the wrong way on one-way streets. Now I watched as they banged on the gate and demanded (through one of the interpreters) that the house's occupants come outside.

After a few minutes, the gate opened. Some of the soldiers marched an older man and a number of young women to the curb and sat them down on the wet cement. One of the girls spoke very good English. She said, "Why are you doing this? We've done nothing. We always defend the Americans. We love the Americans. Now we hate you." I hovered nearby feeling sad and a little ridiculous in a flak jacket that said "press" and a borrowed helmet that misidentified me as a Sgt. Maj. Hudgins. After about 15 minutes, the search ended, the family went back inside, and the soldiers redeployed down the block to another house—the correct house as it turned out. The first time, they had the wrong address.

Though I've been in Baghdad for a total of over three months since the end of the war, I've spent very little time with soldiers. I've mostly tried to understand what's going on here from an Iraqi perspective. And, because of that, I've tended to think about America's occupying force in fairly simplistic terms. Dumb guys with guns who have little interest in understanding Iraqis or seeing them as anything but the enemy. Of course, I should know by now that nothing in Iraq holds up to oversimplification. Out on the mission that night, I found myself feeling (not surprisingly) terrible for the Iraqi family mistakenly rousted from their home. But that feeling was tempered, even nudged aside (very surprisingly), by how sorry I felt for the soldiers themselves. I had hung out with them for several hours by then, talking, joshing. I liked these guys—respected them, even. It wasn't their fault that we went to the wrong house first. Intelligence here is notoriously bad. They go to the wrong house all the time, some soldiers later told me. And they hate it. It's a waste of time and adrenaline. It makes them feel lousy for the Iraqis, and dispirited about their missions.

I arrived at the soldiers' base early that afternoon. The base used to be a tourist spot called "Baghdad Island," though the soldiers have renamed it "Bandit Island," after the nickname of their regiment. At the front gate Iraqi guards, acting as the first line of defense, searched me and checked my I.D. While I waited for a nearby soldier to radio my presence to the base's headquarters and confirm that they were expecting me, I took a moment to scuff up my very white sneakers with mud. I bought those sneakers right before coming to Baghdad and hadn't worn them once. Given how dirty everything gets in the city from the dust, pollution and now (in the rainy season) mud, those sneakers made me look like I had just gotten off the plane from Jordan. The Iraqi guards watched me with wide-eyed disbelief. In Iraq, people are always trying to make old stuff seem new. And here I was instantly adding years to a perfectly pristine pair of sneakers. Crazy.

I got my clearance and followed a soldier to a nearby jeep for a ride to the Tactical Operations Center, or TOC. We walked past a line of tanks with their guns aimed at the gate. Soldiers poked halfway out the tanks' top hatches. They looked cold and bored. They also looked as though they were trying hard not to stare at me. With only about six women stationed on a base containing hundreds of men, I definitely stood out.

My escort drove me past temporarily sidelined Army vehicles, rows of large olive-drab tents, clutches of sickly looking palm trees, and a handful of guys in Army-issue sweat suits jogging. It took me a moment to figure out why that particular sight was so shocking—you just never see anyone jogging in Iraq.

We pulled in front of the prefab TOC building just as Sgt. Maj. Mark Schindler was gearing up to go in a four-jeep convoy to inspect a checkpoint in the Al Shaab neighborhood. He invited me to go along, so I did.

That was the first time I've ever worn body armor—bulletproof vests, flak jackets, helmets (Kevlars, the soldiers call them). My uniform in Baghdad tends to be a long skirt and sweater, and I travel around sitting in the back of a beat-up car with a broken windshield. When I mentioned this to some of the soldiers, they were incredulous.

How could I possibly feel safe in this city without body armor? I told them that, in all honesty, I felt safer not wearing it. That it made me feel like a target. Or, at the least, a potential object of derision among Iraqis. In short, it made me feel like one of them.

I sat in the back of Sgt. Maj. Schindler's jeep, next to the big, booted feet of the jeep's gunner who rode standing, his finger on the trigger of his very large gun. We left the base and went down a nearby highway where many IEDs (improvised explosive devices) have been killing soldiers. Resistance fighters disguise the IEDs in garbage bags or soda bottles or plaster made to look like rocks or even, occasionally, dead animals. They wait in the distance and use cobbled-together electronic triggers to detonate the explosives as the soldiers drive past. Sgt. Maj. Schindler had recently survived two such attacks. The first, on Nov. 8, missed all the vehicles in his convoy. The second, on Nov. 15, ripped through his jeep, piercing him with shrapnel and killing Sgt. Timothy Hazlit. "A day in this country," says the sergeant major, "is 23 hours, 59 minutes of boredom and one minute of hell."

We reached the crowded, poor Al Shaab neighborhood and drove through streets bordered by swells of garbage. Houses puzzled together from unmortared brick and scraps of wood and metal sat canted and sagging behind the garbage. Beat-up cars and donkey carts choked up the traffic, forcing us to slow down significantly. It was Eid—the end-of-Ramadan celebration—and tons of kids filled the streets in their finest shabbery. As we drove past, every single kid I saw waved or saluted or gave a thumbs-up to the soldiers. I found this utterly surprising. It seemed to me that, given all that's happened since the war's end, at least some of the kids would be staring the soldiers down or throwing rocks. But no, these kids acted downright ecstatic. Many of the boys ran alongside the jeeps waving and yelling "Hello, mister!" The soldiers waved back.

"It does them good to see the kids like that," said the sergeant major. The way he sees it, 90 percent of Iraqis like the Americans and 10 percent hate them. Of those 10 percent, 5 percent actually do something about it. I didn't say anything, but those statistics seemed very wrong to me. Most Iraqis I meet, even moderate Iraqis, feel pretty pissed off at the U.S. these days.

At the checkpoint, tanks and Humvees lined the road. Soldiers waved over cars, directed drivers to pull into a dirt lot. They shooed the passengers out of the cars so that a bomb-sniffing dog could hop into the vehicle and snuffle around. In some cases, impossible numbers of people unfolded themselves from the cars. I watched as a family of 14 got out of a pickup truck. They stood in a line, with their backs to the truck (at the soldiers' instructions). The men looked furtively over their shoulders, angry and dismayed at the sight of the dog inside the truck's cab. Iraqis think of dogs as inherently unclean. A dog in your home or car makes those spaces unclean as well. It's very disrespectful. One man started to argue with the soldiers about the dog. They shouted him down, finished the inspection, and sent him on his way.

It's disturbing to watch a scene like that. Undoubtedly, the use of dogs alienates Iraqis, fertilizes their resentment. On the other hand, Iraqis want security more than anything right now. These checkpoints do make a difference, and the dogs significantly speed the process, alleviating long traffic snarls. It's one of the million or so conundrums here.

Sgt. Maj. Schindler favors using the dogs. We stood on the roadside, watching the checkpoint at work. The sergeant major towered over me. A tall, lean guy who looked disconcertingly like Sam Shepard, he spoke with the slight pseudo-Texan drawl that most soldiers seem to have, regardless of their place of origin. But I found him smart and thoughtful, and from what I could see, his men liked him very much. He told me that working in Iraq demanded constant adjustment, that at the beginning the military didn't understand how to deal with Iraqis, and they were still playing catchup. They try harder to recognize the Iraqis' enormous sense of pride now, he said. Because to insult one Iraqi means you hurt the pride of their whole family. I asked how the use of the dogs fit in with that. He said that the Iraqis respect a strong show of authority. "It's not just what the dogs can do," he said, "but the message they send."

Later, back at the base, I asked him his opinions about the situation in

Fallujah, the town west of Baghdad that is considered the center of the anti-American resistance. The 82nd Airborne controls that town. I've heard from a number of journalists that they act with unnecessarily extreme force, and treat every Iraqi like the enemy. Sgt. Maj. Schindler thought for a moment before replying. "The 82nd tends to go at it up there like they're picking a fight," he said. "In addition, you've got a lot of new people up there who have the mistaken impression it's a war zone. You're asking these young soldiers to do some very hard things. Make fast, complicated assessments. Maybe they're a little trigger-happy."

I wandered around the checkpoint and talked to soldiers. None of the guys I spoke to demonstrated the blind dismissal of Iraqis that I had expected. Sure, Iraqis confused the hell out of them. Frustrated them. But they were just people. Rules of engagement have been changing, the soldiers said. No one's supposed to fire his weapon unless an Iraqi is pointing a gun right at him. (A few months ago, soldiers were told to shoot any car approaching a checkpoint too fast. A lot of innocent Iraqis—sometimes whole families—got killed that way.) Another change: The soldiers go on fewer dismounted patrols now. This isn't good, they told me. It means losing personal relationships with the Iraqi people. Mostly the soldiers do drive-around patrolling or traffic stops. "It's all gonna get worse if we have no working relationship with the people—talking with them," one soldier said.

I made notes, leaning against a jeep. Fifty feet away, a small mob of children capered around and chanted, "Good good MISTER!" A soldier asked me who I wrote for. "Salon magazine," I replied. He paused for a second. "Boy," he said, "I can't believe they would send you to a place like this." It took me a moment to realize that he thought I must be employed by a hairdressing journal.

Later that evening, I ate in the base mess hall with some other men (they call the mess hall "the KBR" after the name of Kellogg, Brown and Root, the private subcontracted company that runs it and all other military mess halls in Iraq) where I had the chance to reiterate, a few times, that, no, I didn't work for a hairdressing magazine. I explained that Salon covered news, politics and culture, but not hair.

"You're not one of those reporters that said that they named Iron Hammer [the name given to the new U.S. policy of using massive military force against attackers] after the Nazis, are you?" asked one guy.

I said, "Well, it wasn't named after the Nazis, but it had the same name that the Nazis used." I didn't mention that I had, indeed, written about the topic in my last piece.

I sat with soldiers at a long table punctuated by clusters of condiments. They had steak that night. "You have to understand," said one soldier. "We, like, never get steak." The soldiers sawed away with flimsy plastic knives and forks; they broke so easily that each man went through from two to five of them in the course of dinner. We talked about what they perceived to be too many negative stories in the media. The news just wants the stories about death, they said. Not the good stories. I tried to explain that journalists do want to cover good stories. There just aren't that many of them these days.

For many of the soldiers, President Bush's surprise Thanksgiving trip probably seemed like a positive story. I happened to be in the TOC when word came that seven soldiers from Bandit Island would be going to a special Thanksgiving event with a surprise guest, unknown even to the base commanders. The officers inside the TOC groaned and told me how much the soldiers hate that meet-and-greet shit. They'd rather stay on base. One of the officers said, "This isn't about handing out more soccer balls, is it?" They reluctantly picked out seven of the best and brightest for this mission. "The magnificent 7," they joked.

A photographer who lives in my house happened to be covering the event for *Time* magazine. Like all the soldiers there, she had no idea that Bush would show up. The soldiers, gathered from bases all over Baghdad, were grumpy, bored and very hungry. They had been around for hours. And then, enter Mr. Bush. The soldiers went nuts. If the guys I spoke to are any indication, it's probable that many soldiers there that day don't even like President Bush. But he is their commander in chief. It must have been quite a morale booster to see him in the flesh.

From what I gather, it made much less of an impression on Iraqis.

The brevity of the trip left many Iraqis I've spoken to feeling that Bush acted a bit cowardly.

That night, on the mission, I followed the soldiers down the block to raid a second house. The intelligence they had told them that a young man living in the house might be working with al-Qaeda. None of the soldiers felt particularly optimistic about this mission, though. On 90 percent of the house raids, the soldiers find nothing more than confused families and a couple of guns used for home protection. (They used to confiscate all guns; now a family gets to keep one.) The soldiers followed the same procedures as before—taking positions, banging on the gate, and demanding the family come out. An elderly couple and six young men emerged from the house and, following orders, squatted, mid-street, in the glare of one tank's headlights. The man in question was not among them.

A dozen soldiers entered the house and began searching. After a moment, I asked whether I could go inside. A soldier barked, "Friendly on the way!" and I followed him into a dark courtyard, through a front door, and into the family's home. By the door, piles of sandals indicated where the family de-shoed so as not to track up their carpets. For a brief moment, I considered pulling off my artificially filthy sneakers, just as I would if I was visiting Iraqi friends. Soldiers in muddy boots entered the house behind me and walked across the rug without a thought. And I knew that removing my sneakers would, most likely, bug them. This was no visit. It was a raid.

I went upstairs where soldiers were rifling through drawers, cabinets, boxes. They piled dinars and a few discovered guns on a flowery quilt covering the bed. Word came up from below that they had found something, and I descended to see. In a mostly empty room sat an unearthed box containing an assortment of electronics—switches, circuit boards, antennae, batteries, soldered bits and pieces. Nearby, a bag containing half a dozen electric garage door opener kits. The kind used to make detonation devices for IEDs. The colonel in charge stood by while I knelt by the box. "Take a good look," he said. "We got some bad guys tonight."

Making Enemies
by Nir Rosen

Nir Rosen, a freelance writer living in Iraq, filed this report for The Progressive. *It ran in the magazine's December 2003 issue.*

'm in Al Qaim, in the Anbar province of western Iraq, by the Syrian border. The men of the 1st Squadron, 3rd Armored Cavalry Regiment, occupy what they have named the Wild West. Lieutenant Colonel Gregg Reilly is the SCO, or squadron commander, of Tiger Base. A relaxed Californian, he is comfortable answering tough questions but gets tense for the first time when asked why the United States is in Iraq. He removes his legs from the desk and places an elbow on the table as he leans his forehead in his palm. "We're here for the right reasons, to enable this region of the world to progress," he says. "And America has always had to be there to stand up for the basic human rights of people. The reputation of the United States is on the line."

Most of Reilly's troops echo his sentiments, but not all the men are thrilled to be in Iraq. When asked how long he had been there, one enlisted twenty-one-year-old snaps, "Way too long. When we first got here it felt like we were doing something good. Now it feels like a waste."

"If we find weapons of mass destruction it was worth it," says another twenty-one-year-old. "But if we don't and we're just here because Bush wanted to finish what his daddy started, then a lot of boys died for nothing, and that's fucked up."

Staff Sergeant Joseph Alfeiri expresses sympathy for the Iraqis. "I wonder how I would feel if someone was breaking down my door," he says. "Or if it was my grandfather who didn't understand instructions at a checkpoint and panicked and was shot by the foreign force."

Sergeant Scott Blow, a twenty-seven-year-old from Denver, worries about security. "Nobody knows who the enemy is here until they shoot at you," he says. "Any time you kick down a door, you don't know what to expect."

On June 7, one of Reilly's soldiers, Sergeant Michael Dooley, was standing at a checkpoint when a car approached containing three men. Two of them called out that their friend was injured and needed attention. When Dooley approached the vehicle to assist, the men shot him in the face, killing him immediately.

In early October, Reilly decides he has enough "actionable intelligence" to pursue those who are attacking his soldiers every day. "We have the most concrete set of targetable data in Iraq," Reilly says of the operation code-named Tiger Strike. "We have built this over many months with multiple sources." He has two organizational charts on his wall. One chart is for Al Qaeda cells, including safe houses, financiers, and fighters. The other chart is for the resistance led by three former generals from the elite Republican Guard who coordinated cells of suppliers, trainers, financiers, and trigger pullers. Altogether, there are sixty-two names on the wanted list.

On the wall beside the charts are large satellite images of the towns with the targeted houses marked and numbered. Reilly plans to raid a minimum of twenty-nine locations, taking out the "nervous system of the area and the guys who actually do the shooting," he says, slapping the satellite images on the wall. "Everything I have here will be there:

two cavalry troops, fourteen tanks, twenty-three Bradleys, fifteen gun trucks, 100 dismounts, a total of 300 soldiers." He also plans to use all his human resources, including a long range surveillance team which would leave early and observe the targets in hiding; a paramilitary officer from the OGA, or "Other Government Agency," as the CIA is euphemistically known in Iraq; and a team of special forces. In case he needs to, he can call upon an Orion spy plane and an unmanned aerial vehicle, as well as the listening capacities of several different intelligence agencies. The plan is to target the leaders, homes, and the Al Qaeda safe houses first. This would be a "dynamic operation," he says, meaning they would not be knocking on doors.

By 0100 on October 5, soldiers move M1 A2 tanks, Bradley Armored Personnel Carriers, large trucks with mounted guns, and unarmored Humvees into position. The mood among the several hundred men is like that of athletes before a big game. They joke, psyche themselves up, and receive final reminders by their team leaders, like coaches, to focus, to keep their eyes on the ball.

One after another, the vehicles in the convoy rumble out the gate of Tiger X-Ray, as the base is called, round the bend, and pass the electrical station, stopping at the test-fire range. "The hardest part of the mission is going in there and pulling some father away from his kids," says Captain Justin Brown, commander of Apache Troop, whose half of Tiger Strike is called Operation Decapitation. "Yeah, it sucks," his driver, Sergeant Bentley, avers. "But," continues Brown, "if it's going to let my men get home safe to see their kids, I'll do it." They resume discussing football. Brown, a Texan, is a Cowboys fan.

Apache's teams drive in black light, guided by the night-vision goggles worn by the driver. After half an hour of navigating in the dark, the convoy approaches the first house and the vehicles go into white light, illuminating the target area as a tank breaks the stone wall. "Fuck, yeah!" cheers Bentley. "Hi, honey, I'm home!" The team charges over the rubble, breaks through the door with a sledgehammer, and drags several men out. The team marches the barefoot detainees, dazed from their slumber, over rocks and hard ground. A soldier shoves forward one short, middle-aged man limping with painful difficulty. The soldier says, "You'll fucking learn how to walk." In response to questions, each male gives his name. None match the names on the list.

The soldiers ask a prisoner where the military officer lives. "Down the road," he points. "Show us!" say the soldiers, pushing the prisoner ahead so he stumbles across the rocky street. He is terrified that he would be seen as an informer in the neighborhood. He stops at the house, but the soldiers run ahead. "No, no, it's here," yells a sergeant, and they run back, breaking through the gate and bursting into the house. It is a large villa, with grapevines covering the driveway. Soldiers order the women and children to sit in the garden and give them a card that explains in Arabic what is going on. Squadron members shove the men to the ground on the driveway and ask their names. It is the first high-value target. A son of one man begs the soldiers, "Take me for ten years but leave my father!" The soldiers take both father and son, as the other children scream, "Daddy, Daddy!"

House after house meets the same fate. Some homes have only women in them. The 3rd Armored Cavalry ransacks the houses, breaks into closets, overturns mattresses, and throws clothes out of drawers. In one house, the CIA commando and soldiers seem to miss the smiling face in the large picture pasted to the suspect's bedroom dresser. It is Uday, Saddam's notorious son, dressed in tribal clothes.

In a big compound of several houses, the soldiers take all the men, even the ones not on the list. A sergeant explains that the others will be held for questioning to see if they have any useful information. The men cry out that they have children still inside. In several houses, soldiers tenderly carry out babies that had been left sleeping in their cribs. When a house search is complete, or at the "Home Run" stage (the different stages are divided into 1st, 2nd, 3rd, Home Run, and Grand Slam, meaning ready to move on), soldiers relax and joke, breaking their own tension and seeming to ignore the trembling and shocked women and children crouched together on the lawns behind them.

Prisoners with duct tape on their eyes and hands cuffed behind them with plastic "zip ties" sit in the back of the truck for hours without water. They move their heads toward sounds, disoriented and frightened, trying to understand what is happening around them. Any time a prisoner moves or twitches a soldier bellows at him. By daylight the whole town could see a large truck full of prisoners.

From the list of thirty-four names, Apache Troop brings in sixteen positively identified men, along with another fifty-four men who are neighbors, relatives, or just happened to be around. By 0830, Apache is done and starts driving back to base. As the main element departs, the psychological operations vehicle blasts AC/DC rock music through neighborhood streets. Neighbors awakened by the noise huddle outside and watch the convoy. One little girl stands before her father with her arms outstretched and legs wide, guarding him from the soldiers.

The prisoners spend the night on a large dirt field in a square of concertina wire, beneath immense spotlights and next to loud generators. They sleep on the ground, guarded by soldiers. One noncommissioned officer expresses surprise. "Did they just arrest every man they found?" he asks, wondering if "we just made another 300 people hate us."

Three days after the operation, a dozen prisoners march in a circle outside the detention center, surrounded by barbed wire. They are shouting "USA, USA!" over and over again. "They were talking when we told them not to, so we made them talk something we liked to hear," says one of the soldiers with a grin. Another gestures with his hands, letting the prisoners know they have to raise their voices. A first sergeant quips that the ones who are not guilty "will be guilty next time."

American forces have detained 7,000 Iraqis, according to a major from the judge advocate general's office. Many stay in prisons indefinitely. The military holds some "security detainees" for six months pending a review to determine if they are still a security risk. A lieutenant colonel involved in the process adds that there is no judicial procedure for the thousands of detainees.

One person the Apache Troop picks up a few days before the big raid is named Ayoub. Soldiers break through his door early in the morning, and when Ayoub does not immediately respond to their orders, they shoot him with a non-lethal ordnance, little pellets exploding like gunshot from the weapon's grenade launcher. Ayoub's blood covers the floor of the house. The soldiers drag him into a room and interrogate him forcefully while others push his family back against a garden's fence. Ayoub's frail mother, covered in a shawl, with traditional tribal tattoos marking her face, pleads with the immense soldier to spare her son's life, protesting his innocence. She takes the soldier's hand and kisses it repeatedly while on her knees. He pushes her to the grass, along with Ayoub's four girls and two boys, all small, and his wife. They squat barefoot, screaming, their eyes wide open.

Apache Troop brings Ayoub out and pushes him onto the truck. He gestures to his family to remain still. He sits frozen, staring numbly ahead as the soldiers ignore him. The medic looks at Ayoub's injured hand and chuckles to his friends, "It ain't my hand." The truck blasts country music on the way back to the base. Ayoub goes to the detainment center.

Several hours later, Apache Troop intercepts a call from Ayoub. "Oh, shit," says the captain. "It was the wrong Ayoub." However, in order to avoid the risk that the other Ayoub would learn Apache is after him, they do not release the father of six who has the misfortune of sharing a name with the suspect. The night after his arrest, soldiers escort Ayoub to call his family to tell them he is fine, but that he would not be home for a while.

Apache sends the tapes of the other Ayoub's conversations for analysis. In them, he speaks of proceeding to the "next level" and obtaining land mines and other weapons. This alarms the army's intelligence officers. The meaning of the intercepted conversation confounds them until somebody realizes Ayoub is not a terrorist intent on obtaining weapons. This Ayoub is a kid, who had been on the phone with a friend, discussing a video game he was playing.

Dispatch from Iraq
by John Hendren

This article ran in The Los Angeles Times *(July 25, 2003).*

F ALLOUJA, IRAQ—Three men careen toward a checkpoint in a car with no plates. A soldier—it's midnight and too dark to tell which one—gives the heads-up: "Here we go." The sedan spurts to a staggering stop before a dozen tense soldiers on alert for attacks.

Wearing a broad grin, the driver stumbles out, red-eyed and reeking of liquor. His two passengers smile and wave at the Rhode Island National Guardsmen leveling M-16s at their heads. As the car pulls away, a guardsman shouts in a thick New England accent, "Don't drink and drive—you might spill yuh drink!"

Meet the soldiers of the 115th Military Police Company of the Rhode Island National Guard. They are the only guardsmen in Fallouja, the Wild West of the Middle East. The part-time soldiers who patrol the meanest streets in Iraq don't enforce the 11 p.m. curfew. And they don't bother with drunk-driving statutes.

There is no Iraqi code of justice to guide them, just military law. And enforcing it is often more an art than a science, with potentially lethal consequences. With the Army straining to meet demands in Iraq, the Pentagon announced Wednesday that two National Guard brigades will be deployed next year after six months of training.

As the New England MPs acknowledge, many guardsmen bring a less-than-gung-ho attitude to their duty.

Unlike their active-duty colleagues from the Army's 3rd Infantry Division, who grouse about being stuck in Fallouja but remain largely supportive of the Army, the boys from Rhode Island freely acknowledge that they had planned on wearing their uniforms only on weekends and would rather be back at their jobs selling advertising, policing colleges and detailing cars.

"There's some lying recruiters out there," Spc. Patrick Camp says.

"They told me it was one weekend a month," Spc. Christopher Oldham adds.

This night, the guardsmen are looking for cars full of men and guns. They have been told that military intelligence sources—often Iraqi detainees and snitches—say that 30 men plan an attack to mark the anniversary of the 1958 coup that toppled the Iraqi monarchy. But they are skeptical.

"The intel is rarely good. It's only been right once—when it said they were gonna hit us at the police station," says Staff Sgt. Matthew Hayden, 34, who normally works as a campus cop at Johnson & Wales University.

A rocket-propelled grenade soared across the wall of the police station compound that night, and a second missed the patrol by 40 feet after it left. The third RPG hit, and the boys from Rhode Island returned fire.

"The next day, the police came out and said, 'We're gonna quit if you don't get out of there,' " Hayden recalls with disgust.

This night's patrol gets off to a tense start. A former Iraqi military compound housing the 2nd Brigade of the 3rd Infantry has been hit by seven mortar rounds, which struck without injury, by the time the guardsmen begin their 10 p.m. patrol, a guardsman reports.

The Americans insist that they are liberators, not occupiers, but the nuance is rejected by the guerrillas the MPs face nearly nightly.

In the moonlit sky around the base, one can see sporadic flares, a well-known method the guerrillas use to communicate the whereabouts of troops. Red flares are for armored vehicles, green for light vehicles. White flares track American troops from one spot to the next, and a series of red flares designates a kill zone, where guerrillas have drawn blood.

Attackers also use whistles and enlist confederates at local power stations, soldiers say. As the guardsmen slow down to set up a checkpoint a few miles east of Fallouja, a neighborhood just off the highway suddenly goes dark, then lights up again.

"See how fast that grid went down?" Hayden asks. "That's pretty common. As soon as they see coalition forces in the area, they shut the grid down."

Keen-eyed drivers, accustomed to running into new checkpoints, rarely get stopped. "Usually they'll just turn around if they see us," Hayden says.

The guardsmen have had just one casualty, a battalion commander whose finger was severely injured when an RPG hit his Humvee. They don't count the time Cpl. Scott Keegan took shrapnel from an RPG that struck the asphalt near him—a flesh wound. But they have taken repeated fire from AK-47 assault rifles as well as RPGs.

As four guardsmen speed off for the night's rounds, over the squeaking transmission of a 20-year-old Humvee, all say they'd rather be back in Rhode Island than drawing bullets in Fallouja.

"Rabbits, that's what we are," Sgt. Frank Newton says. "They send that rabbit out, and when they shoot at us, we come back and the next day they go looking for who shot at us."

As the guardsmen establish the second of three checkpoints for the night, a driver pulls up and carefully lifts his white dishdasha robe to reveal a weapon, then a permit from the mayor's office. The guardsmen shrug, search his trunk and wave him on.

"That guy had a freakin' Beretta SMG 9-millimeter," one guardsman says, referring to an automatic pistol.

"Somebody should shout, 'Gun!' when you see that," another says.

A third examines the bullet he's pocketed from an ammunition clip in the trunk.

"You take that bullet?" a colleague asks.

"Why not?" the other says. "He's not gonna miss it."

War Wounds

by Yaroslav Trofimov

The Wall Street Journal *ran this piece on October 29,* *2003.*

BALAD, IRAQ—Shortly after 11 a.m. last Thursday, the crackle of the radio brought the first of the day's bad news to the U.S. Army's 21st Combat Support Hospital.

"Two U.S. soldiers injured," a helicopter pilot said on the radio. "Six minutes to landing." An armored ambulance Humvee rushed to the nearby landing pad.

As the chopper's blades churned up sand and dust near the field hospital, the ambulance driver and the pilots unloaded a stretcher carrying the more severely injured soldier and ran back to the Humvee. Sgt. Chuck Bartels, a reservist, was still clear-headed despite his injuries. His face was bloody and swollen, one of his arms was a mess of torn flab.

"We drove on that road a hundred times—and nothing happened before," he said in the ambulance. "I don't know how they got us."

With Sgt. Bartels during the bumpy ride was Maj. Beverly Beavers, the hospital's operations officer, who tried to comfort him. "Chuck, I'm glad you're still talking," she said.

The emergency room was an air-conditioned tent decorated with Halloween skeletons and drawings mailed by children from the U.S. Doctors and nurses quickly converged on Sgt. Bartels, 25 years old, and his injured buddy, Sgt. Jared Myers, 23.

In this part of Iraq, deep in the so-called Sunni Triangle north and west of Baghdad, the attacks on American soldiers have become so frequent that emergency medical procedures are now almost routine. Medical personnel here—one of four such U.S. facilities to Iraq—have to deal with the biggest influx of military casualties since the Vietnam War. The Iraqi campaign has been producing far more fatalities and nonlethal casualties than the Persian Gulf War in 1991, the Balkans action in 1999 and the war in Afghanistan since 2001.

While attention focuses on the number of American soldiers killed in Iraq—115 by enemy fire since President Bush announced the end of major combat on May 1—the military doesn't generally publicize the more-frequent incidents in which soldiers are wounded. According to a tally kept by the U.S. Central Command, as of 7 p.m. on Oct. 27, the U.S. military had sustained a total of 1,737 nonlethal casualties from hostile action in Iraq, including 1,186 since May 1.

The toll includes American casualties in the rocket attack on Baghdad's Al Rasheed hotel on Sunday, and U.S. military police killed and wounded in suicide bombings that devastated four Iraqi police stations across Baghdad the following day. October has been the bloodiest month for U.S. troops in Iraq since the occupation began.

Advances in medical care and bulletproof vests allow more soldiers to survive the kind of injuries that would have killed them in past conflicts. But the recent switch by Iraqi insurgents to powerful roadside bombs as their main offensive weapon has raised the number and severity of wounds even for those with high-tech protection. These bombs are usually rigged artillery shells that, hidden in vegetable crates, bicycle baskets or simple debris, can be detonated close to their target and shower it with shrapnel.

"Since May, the number and the rate of casualties has increased," says Col. Doug Liening, commander of the 21st Combat Support Hospital, which also operates a facility in the northern city of Mosul. "People in the United States do not appreciate what's going on here." In peacetime, the 21st Combat Support Hospital is based at Fort Hood, Texas, as are many of its personnel currently in Balad.

For many doctors and nurses, the daily gore makes it hard to sleep at night. "It's like a horror movie," says Capt. Nancy Emma, 49, a nurse for 16 years who worked on Sgt. Bartels in the emergency room. "I served in a trauma unit, I saw death in the face—but nothing like here. And those who live, you've got to wonder how they are going to make it back in the States."

After the emergency room, Sgt. Bartels was wheeled into the operating room. His buddy Sgt. Myers, who received shrapnel wounds in his right arm and face, called his family back in Kansas as he waited to be treated. The two sergeants, reservists attached to the Fourth Infantry Division, were driving from a meeting at the town of Baqouba's agriculture ministry office. They accompanied a civil-affairs officer, Capt. John Teal, who was filling in for their usual captain, on leave in the U.S.

Sgt. Myers asked nurses what happened to Capt. Teal. No one could muster the courage to tell the sergeant the captain was dead, instantly killed by the roadside bomb that went through their unarmored Humvee.

After Sgt, Bartels' surgery was over, he was wheeled into an intensive-care tent and put on a cot next to an 8-year-old Iraqi girl being treated for massive burns. A large, muscular man, the sergeant was called up just as he was finishing his work for a master's degree in Russian studies at the University of Kansas. The operation had left his right arm just a short bandaged stump. Pieces of flesh were missing from his face.

The orthopedic surgeon, Lt. Col. Kim Keslung, sat down after the surgery and sipped Kool-Aid. Her desert-tan uniform was stained with blood. "His nerves and blood vessels were just shredded. There wasn't anything to fix in his arm," she said. "He'll have to adjust to his new life."

Like most doctors and nurses here, Col. Keslung preferred not to venture outside the confines of the Sustainer Air Field, the sprawling base where the hospital is located. "I don't volunteer to leave because I've seen what happens outside," she said.

Many doctors and nurses, deployed to Kuwait and then Iraq, have been overseas for more than 400 days in the past two years, which is considered the upper limit on such deployments. Few expected to deal with such a steady stream of casualties more than six months after the fall of Baghdad.

It was a mistake to discount the Iraqi resistance, Col. Keslung said, adding, "If someone invaded Texas, we'd do the same thing."

As she spoke, new patients arrived at the hospital. Another remote-controlled roadside bomb had exploded near a Humvee that was leading a convoy 10 miles outside the Sustainer base. The blast made the windshield cave in, but it went off too early to inflict serious injuries on the three military policemen from Rhode Island inside the car. They had ringing in their ears, which a doctor said would go away in a week or two.

Specialist Kindre Marines, the gunner who stood in the Humvee, says he saw the blast's flash and instinctively ducked inside before he was hit by the shrapnel. This may have saved his life. After being examined, the soldiers went back on the road.

In the intensive-care tent, Sgt. Bartels woke up. He had known right after the bomb attack that the captain was dead, and he praised Sgt. Myers for driving on to the safety of the nearest U.S. base with a piece of shrapnel the size of a pocket watch lodged in his arm.

Sgt. Bartels spoke in a clear voice, without betraying emotions. "We never had a close call before," he said. "You just drive around—and next there's a boom, and your life changes." Just before going to war, Sgt. Bartels had a job interview with the State Department, and was expecting a posting with diplomatic security in Moscow. That's not a job he could do without an arm, he said matter-of-factly.

Sgt. Myers, a phlebotomist in civilian life, learned that Capt. Teal, 31, was dead. A few tears fell from his eyes. Sgt. Myers was the driver, while the captain sat in the passenger seat. The agriculture official whom they were to see in Baqouba wasn't there when they arrived; a rich businessman, he was traveling to Canada. On the way back to the base, just before the blast, Capt. Teal complained about the trip.

"Then there was a big puff of dust, smoke and a sharp pain in my arm," Sgt. Myers said. The radio was fried by shrapnel, he said. The captain, who sat between the bomb and Sgt. Myers, took the brunt of the explosion. "If Capt. Teal wasn't there, I would probably have died," the sergeant said.

The civil-affairs team has been lobbying for months to get armored vehicles—equipment they lack because, in conventional war, civil-affairs teams are supposed to be operating far behind the front lines.

It was dark outside as Lt. Col. Trip Buckenmaier, an anesthesiologist from the Walter Reed Army Medical Center in Washington, walked into Sgt. Bartels's tent and offered him a new procedure that would take away the pain. Col. Buckenmaier pierced the skin atop Sgt. Bartels's shoulder and then tried to locate with an electric stimulator the nerves responsible for the hand and the arm.

As the sergeant's body convulsed, the surgeon kept talking: "Chuck, I know you don't have a hand, but can you feel your fingers moving? Now? And now?"

After finding the nerve, Col. Buckenmaier inserted a catheter linked to a painkiller dispenser that Sgt. Bartels could control with the other hand. This procedure—tried on battlefields for the first time during the Iraqi campaign—allows patients to stay conscious and in control while disabling only the nerves that produce pain from injuries.

"We're kind of pushing the science right now," Col. Buckenmaier said. "War tends to do that." He hadn't finished the procedure when an assistant walked in to say that choppers were bringing in a new load of casualties.

Around the stretcher bearers in the emergency room, doctors and nurses huddled again, both those on duty and those, in gray army

T-shirts and black shorts, who were supposed to be resting for the next shift. A Fourth Infantry Division base had just been shelled with mortars in Baqouba. This shelling, like the mortars that rain almost every night in the Sustainer Air Field, is usually inaccurate. But when the attackers manage to hit the base camp, they can cause serious damage because soldiers inside the perimeter don't usually wear helmets or body armor.

Almost 20 soldiers were injured in the Baqouba attack tonight, but only three seriously enough to be brought to Balad by helicopter. A piece of shrapnel had carved out part of one soldier's face and lodged behind the eye; he had also received severe shrapnel wounds in the back. A nurse picked up his blood-soaked ID card to fill in a report. Two other soldiers, a male and a female, had sustained less-serious wounds.

In the morning, Sgt. Bartels and Sgt. Myers prepared for their flight to the Landstuhl Army Medical Center in Germany, the first stop for wounded American troops evacuated from Iraq. Air Force flights to Landstuhl leave Iraq almost every day. Sgt. Myers's parents were already on the way there. Sgt. Bartels, given his injuries, was likely to be transferred quickly to Walter Reed. Col. Buckenmaier told the sergeant he could call the colonel's wife in Washington if he needed any help while at Walter Reed.

That morning, two soldiers were killed and several wounded in a mortar attack on a base in Samarra, less than 20 miles north of here. "This has been a typical workload," said Col. Carol McNeill, the Balad hospital's chief nurse. "We're getting smarter, but the bad guys are getting smarter too."

A Soldier's Life

by Nancy Gibbs
with Mark Thompson

This story ran in Time *(July 21, 2003).*

First Sergeant Christopher Coffin knew how to stay close to his wife Betsy even when he was far away. Before he left in February, bound for the Persian Gulf, he took her outside on a cold, clear Maine night, pointed to an especially bright star and told her he would be able to see it from Iraq. They could both look at it, and find each other. "Every night when I walked the dog," Betsy says, "I would stop and talk to the star. The dog was so confused; she could tell I was talking to Chris, but she couldn't see him."

After he had left, Betsy began finding notes hidden all around their Kennebunk condo. He had tucked them in the pocket of her jacket, between the cans of dog food, on the bathroom mirror, under her pillow. She has no idea whether she has found them all, in the months since he has been gone.

"I miss doing the laundry with you and helping you hang it up," one said.

"When you take [the dog] to the beach, remember us taking her and how much fun we had," said another.

"Dearest Bets—Right this minute, I'm thinking of you, and smiling." They were signed "Trobs," short for Trouble, her nickname for him since they started dating in college 25 years ago, when she would spot him and say, "Here comes Trouble."

He tried to call from Iraq nearly every day, even just for two seconds, especially if there had been some incident—one more dead soldier in the news. Chris' Army reserve unit was a civil-affairs team, the ones who hand out medicine and rebuild schools and are supposed to stay a safe distance from actual combat. But somehow Chris had wound up leading convoys back and forth between Kuwait and Baghdad, and Betsy knew that was a much more dangerous mission than normal. On June 30, he phoned Betsy from Iraq to tell her he was heading back to Kuwait. "I'll be there for a little while, so you'll be able to breathe a little easier and relax—I'm going to be there for my birthday," he said. "I love you, and I'll call you tomorrow when I get back to Kuwait."

But that night Betsy was still restless. It was nearly midnight, and she found herself wandering through the living room when her eyes fell on their wedding albums. "I hadn't taken them out in ages." She started paging through the pictures of their ceremony on Swan Mountain in Colorado, where they loved to ski and where she had married her soul mate. It was not until the next evening that she learned what Chris was doing at that very moment.

Betsy always kept the TV on at home, checked the Internet at work. The next afternoon she heard there had been another attack. "He hasn't called," she told a colleague at the hospital where she is a social worker. When she got home, Betsy found a pair of Army officers waiting in their car. They had been there most of the day.

Chris had not made it back to Kuwait. His vehicle had apparently swerved into a ditch trying to avoid a civilian vehicle outside Baghdad; he died shortly after being airlifted to a hospital south of Baghdad.

But by the next day, Betsy had learned there might be more to her husband's death than a highway accident. And even weeks later, the

Army cannot tell Betsy exactly what actually happened to Chris on the morning of July 1.

First Sergeant Coffin was the first American soldier to die in Iraq this month, and before the week was out, six more would be killed. On July 2, Marine Corporal Travis Bradach-Nall died clearing mines near Karbala. He was eligible to return to Camp Pendleton, Calif., soon after the war officially ended, but he volunteered to sign on for an extra three months because he wanted to earn more money for college, and because he felt there was still work to do. The next day Private Corey Small died from a gunshot wound "in a noncombat incident," and Private First Class Jim Herrgott was killed by a sniper as he guarded the Iraqi National Museum. Three days later, Sergeant David Parson was shot in Baghdad while raiding a house, and Specialist Jeffrey Wershow was shot in the back of the head while guarding a U.S. delegation at Baghdad University. The next day gunner Chad Keith died when a bomb blew up his convoy on a Baghdad street.

Seven deaths in seven days, each one different, each in its own way a warning. This is a twilight war, the kind America is loath to fight, is reluctant even to train for, as though we can make our enemies agree to our terms of combat, meet us at noon on the field of battle and be crushed by our overwhelming force into absolute surrender. Not since 1945 has a major war wrapped up so clearly or cleanly. Korea ended in a truce, Vietnam in a loss; the Gulf War required a replay. Winning fast but not completely, as in Afghanistan or Iraq, may save lives in the course of the war but transfers an advantage to the enemy when it's over. Once Saddam Hussein's statue fell, Americans hoped to cease fire, store the tanks and bombers and drones, and start rebuilding. For the enemy, the fight had just started—let the sabotage and sniping begin. "The war's not over," declared Lieut. General Ricardo Sanchez, the commander of coalition ground forces in Iraq, at a press briefing last week. "I keep saying that every time I get up here: the war's not over."

More than 70 soldiers have died in the past three months. At this rate it will not be long before more people will have perished since the end of combat than during it. The Iraqi army may have melted away in battle, but its shadow legions of Saddam loyalists and foreign jihadists seem to be growing more organized and more lethal: twice as many U.S. soldiers died in June as in May, and July's rate so far is worse. Soldiers have died in accidents—some caused, no doubt, by the stresses of life under fire and the fear of attack. And they have died after being kidnapped and tortured, died by gun and grenade and mortar. The mortar attacks are especially troubling, since they require a team of insurgents, a leader and a plan.

Casualties have now reached a level such that the Senate passed a resolution on Thursday, 97 to 0, calling on the White House to get over whatever arguments it is having with NATO, the U.N. and the rest of the world and get our soldiers more help on the ground. "We will get a lot more support from the Iraqis, who will be a lot less suspect of us, if we are not the only game in town," said Delaware Democrat Joseph Biden. But the reverse holds as well: if security and stability are not restored quickly, the insurgents may find more allies within the rest of the Iraqi population. There's a race under way, to wipe out the resistance and get the country moving before the frustration boils over. And the U.S. military has only a limited amount of time to prevail.

Chris Coffin loved being a soldier. "In Chris' family, that was what you did," Betsy explains. "His father expected it, and he just grew up believing in serving your country." Chris joined the Army in 1971, served as a tank crewman for 3½ years, then moved to the reserves, where he was a tank commander. About 10 years ago, he joined a civil-affairs unit and worked for the rest of the time as a policeman or a summer ranger in national parks like the one in Gettysburg, Pa. He would have loved to work at Gettysburg full-time, says his ranger colleague Tim Sorber. But a National Park Service rule sets the maximum age for law-enforcement rangers at 35. Chris was already 45 when he started part-time, though he regularly passed the Army's physical-training tests in the 18-to-20-year-old range. "It was a running joke between us," Sorber says. "Chris was too old to get a job in the park service, but never too old to go to war."

But he was getting older, and the separations were getting harder.

He and Betsy, 42, had found a piece of land in Maine and were planning to build a new home, maybe even finally start the family they had
never had—unless you counted Samantha, their 18-year-old golden
retriever–German shepherd mix. After nine months in Kosovo in 2001,
where he turned 50, Chris was ready to come home and stay there. But
as it happened, when he went to talk to his supervisor about retiring
from the reserves, he learned that the Pentagon had recently
announced a "stop loss" order in the wake of 9/11, halting retirements
for people with his specialty.

Civil-affairs reservists hand out food and supplies, just the people
who would be needed to get Iraq back on its feet once the fighting
stopped. In February Chris was called to Fort Bragg, N.C., for training,
and by the time the bombs began to fall, he was in Kuwait. "This
deployment felt different to both of us," Betsy says. When Chris went
to Kosovo, they knew the separation would be hard and that there was
still some risk. "But we both knew Iraq was a more hostile environ-
ment," she says. It was some comfort to know that a unit like his
would be more sheltered: not since Vietnam had a civil-affairs reservist
been killed in combat. "We thought he wouldn't be going into
Baghdad until things pretty much had been resolved there," says
Betsy's sister Candy Barr Heimbach.

Yet Coffin was tapped to lead truck convoys ferrying troops and
materiel across the 400 miles from Kuwait to Baghdad, which
involved a dangerous passage, and then spend days or weeks in
Baghdad between trips. "He told me his biggest concern was, 'I want
to make sure I get all my guys home,'" Betsy says. "'I want to make sure
I don't have to look a wife or mother in the face and tell her I didn't
bring their son or daughter home.'"

By and large, when the soldiers of Operation Iraqi Freedom complain, it is not about the scorpions and tarantulas they must evict
from their boots as they dress in the morning; not about 110° heat
that requires extra changes of T-shirts so their sweat does not poach
their skin; and not about purified water that tastes like boiled
Windex. It is about the new challenges of their mission for which

they were not prepared. Like knowing how to contend with a 12-year-old girl with a rifle. How to check whether the soft-drink stand has been booby-trapped. How to capture the hearts and minds of a population that seems to be riddled with people who are trying to kill them. "It's really hard to know who your enemy is," the soldiers say, especially when bystanders clap as soldiers are killed.

Chris didn't like the traffic. His job was to protect convoys, but he was sharply aware of the risks of an ambush, and he didn't like the way the traffic snarled, trapping you in a web while the spiders descended. "He said there were big traffic jams in the larger towns and cities that made him nervous," says Sorber. "There would be blown-up vehicles on the side of the road and all these locals crowding around them. He said it was very, very scary." And yet he would always end his e-mails to Sorber in the same way: "Be careful." "I found that astonishing," says Sorber, "considering where he was. But he cared a lot about those around him."

June 3 was the birthday of Chris' twin nephews Jon and Nick, 16. He had mailed off a pair of Army Ranger hats with their names embroidered in English and Arabic. And he sent them a message. "I got back into Kuwait from Baghdad yesterday," he e-mailed. "The convoy was long, hot and dusty, and just a wee bit scary in a couple of spots. Thankfully we made it through the three trouble spots without being ambushed. Possibly because we had all our weapons 'locked and cocked' and in plain sight so they knew we were ready for trouble. It looks like I will be going back up north in a few days. Probably for a couple of weeks. Rumor has it we might get out of here in early fall. I really hope so."

So what actually happened on that last run? Did Chris swerve off the road—or was his vehicle blown off the road by a bomb? The Pentagon can't say whether he was in a truck or a humvee or even whether he was driving or not. And the official statements that were released do not begin to tell the whole story.

According to Coffin family members and U.S. government officials looking into the case, Coffin's vehicle ran off Route 8 at about 8 a.m.

Iraqi time on July 1—perhaps to avoid an Iraqi vehicle barreling directly toward it. "We understood it might have been a kamikaze-type thing," Candy says. Once the vehicle was in a ditch, it was swarmed by an angry Iraqi crowd. A humvee traveling behind pulled over to try to help Chris and his comrade, 19, who were both badly hurt, but all four soldiers were quickly surrounded by the crowd and the humvee was set on fire. It took a third American team rushing in, firing rifles into the air, to scatter the crowd and rescue the four trapped soldiers. A helicopter was able to get in to try to rush Chris and his injured truck mate to a medical facility. But Chris died from what the military described as "massive head trauma."

The officers who broke the news to Betsy, and a press release from his unit, said he died in a road accident. But the next day Betsy came across a statement from U.S. Central Command: "A U.S. Army 352nd Civil Affairs Command soldier died of wounds received July 1, when his convoy was hit by an improvised explosive device in Baghdad." It didn't mention Chris by name, but Betsy knew he was the only one in his unit to die that day. "I was shaken—I wanted to know what happened because I wanted to know what my husband went through," Betsy says. "Was he alone? Was someone he knew with him? Did he suffer in any way?"

Pressed about the mystery by Maine Senator Olympia Snowe, who was alerted by his family to the inconsistencies surrounding Coffin's case, the Army launched a board of inquiry into Coffin's death. "I'm horrified by what she's going through," Snowe told TIME. "She not only lost him, but she doesn't even have the peace of mind in knowing what happened." The Army has said it could be four months before she knows more. Betsy has faith in the process. "I have talked to people high up in the Army, and they have given me a promise that this review board will take a serious look at all of the conflicting information," she says. "I need to give them an opportunity to do that."

Two days after Coffin died, more than 100 of his comrades and two generals crowded into a room in his unit's Baghdad headquarters, spilling out into the hallway. All had their weapons in hand, as required in Iraq; Coffin's combat boots, his rifle and helmet were on a table at the front of the room, next to two framed pictures of him. The soldiers remembered his professionalism, his kindness and his humor. They sang "Amazing Grace". And finally they were called to attention, told to "Present arms!" by the officer in charge. Coffin's full name was called out loud and clear, three times. "First Sergeant Coffin," the officer intoned, "has met his last formation."

Five days later, Coffin's body was back in Bethlehem, Pa., where Betsy was staying with her family. The funeral was held in the church where he and Betsy had renewed their wedding vows two years earlier. Two-thirds of the choir rearranged their schedules so they could come to sing, and the organist took the day off in order to be there to play. A college professor, a drama teacher and a fund manager helped the rector trim hedges; an elderly parishioner spent the night before the funeral freezing lemonade and ice rings because the day of the funeral was to be sweltering. "Betsy and Chris would do anything for other people, and it was mutual," observed Rev. Nick Knisely. "That's where the outpouring came from, and that's what makes it so painful."

Betsy was presented with Chris' Bronze Star for meritorious service, which had been approved before his death. He never learned about the honor. Candy read aloud the eulogy Betsy had written about "the love of my life, my best friend, my soul mate, my hero." Friends who had known the couple for years found themselves learning about sides of Chris they had not known: "When you left to go overseas, you gave me a prayer to hold on to . . . and now I pass it back to you . . .

> "May the Lord hold me and thee in his care
> While we are apart from one another
> Until we are together once more.
> So rest easy, my love, until we are together again."

Betsy placed two red roses on her husband's coffin before it was loaded into the hearse, led by a police car and trailed by a lone bagpiper. The wind was blowing, the sidewalks were full, and the air was silent, except for the pipes. It would have been Chris Coffin's 52nd birthday.

a c k n o w l e d g m e n t s

Many people made this anthology.

At Thunder's Mouth Press and Avalon Publishing Group:
Thanks to Will Balliett, Maria Fernandez, Linda Kosarin, Dan O'Connor, Neil Ortenberg, Paul Paddock, Susan Reich, David Reidy, Michelle Rosenfield, Simon Sullivan, Mike Walters and Don Weise for their support, dedication and hard work.

I'm especially grateful to Taylor Smith. He did most of the research for this collection, finding and nominating selections, tracking down copyright holders and negotiating rights.

Finally, I thank the writers whose work appears in this book.

permissions

We gratefully acknowledge everyone who gave permission for written material to appear in this book. We have made every effort to trace and contact copyright holders. If an error or omission is brought to our notice we will be pleased to correct the situation in future editions of this book. For further information, please contact the publisher.

bibliography

The selections used in this anthology were taken from the editions listed below. In some cases, other editions may be easier to find. Hard-to-find or out-of-print titles often are available through inter-library loan services or through Internet booksellers.

Banbury, Jen. "Night Raid in Baghdad." This article first appeared in Salon.com (http://www.Salon.com), December 4, 2003. An online version remains in the Salon archives.

Bergner, Daniel. "Where the Enemy Is Everywhere and Nowhere." Originally appeared in *The New York Times Magazine*, July 20, 2003.

Gibbs, Nancy with Mark Thompson. Originally appeared in *Time*, July 21, 2003.

Harris, James. "My Two Wars." Originally appeared in *The New York Times*, April 20, 2003.

Hendren, John. "Dispatch from Iraq." Originally appeared in *The Los Angeles Times*, July 25, 2003.

Hendren, John and Maura Reynolds. "The U.S. Bomb That Nearly Killed Karzai." Originally appeared in *The Los Angeles Times*, March 27, 2002.

Hendren, John and Richard T. Cooper. "Fragile Alliances in a Hostile Land." Originally appeared in *The Los Angeles Times*, May 5, 2002.

Kaplan, Lawrence F. "Survivor: Iraq." Originally appeared in *The New Republic*, October 2003.

Koopman, John. "McCoy's Marines: Darkside Toward Baghdad." Originally appeared in *The San Francisco Chronicle*, November 13–15, 2003.

Lorch, Donatella. "Green Berets Up Close." Originally appeared in *Newsweek*, January 14, 2002.

Meek, James. "With the Invaders." Originally appeared in *Granta 83: This Overheating World*, October 2003.

Mohan, Geoffrey. "Memories Don't Die So Easily." Originally appeared in *The Los Angeles Times*, April 18, 2003.

Parenti, Christian. "Stretched Thin, Lied to & Mistreated." Originally appeared in *The Nation*, October 6, 2003. Portions of each week's *The Nation* magazine can be accessed at http://www.thenation.com.

Pelton, Robert Young. "The Legend of Heavy D and the Boys." Originally appeared in *National Geographic Adventurer*, March 2002.

Roberts, Paul William. "Beyond Baghdad." Originally appeared in *Harper's Magazine*, July 2003.

Robertson, Phillip. "All Kinds of Metal Was Flying Through the Air." This article first appeared in Salon.com (http://www.Salon.com), April 4, 2003. An online version remains in the Salon archives.

Rosen, Nir. "Making Enemies." Originally appeared in *The Progressive*, December 2003.

Sack, John. "Anaconda." Originally appeared in *Esquire*, August 2002.

Sager, Mike. "The Marine." Originally appeared in *Esquire*, December 2001.

Trofimov, Yaroslav. "War Wounds." Originally appeared in *The Wall Street Journal*, October 29, 2003.

Wright, Evan. "The Make-Believe War." Originally appeared in *Rolling Stone*, August 8, 2002.

Wright, Evan. "Not Much War, But Plenty of Hell." Originally appeared in *Rolling Stone*, July 25, 2002.